Thinking through the Mothers

THINKING THROUGH THE MOTHERS

Reimagining Women's Biographies

JANET BEIZER

CORNELL UNIVERSITY PRESS
ITHACA AND LONDON

The epigraph on the dedication page is taken from "The Pomegranate," from *In a Time of Violence* by Eavan Boland. Copyright © 1994 by Eavan Boland. Used by permission of W. W. Norton & Company, Inc. and Carcanet Press Limited.

Chapter 2 appeared in an earlier French version as "Dévoiler la momie: A La Recherche de Kuchuk Hanem" in *Lieux littéraires / La Revue* no. 7–8 (2005), ed. Christine Planté. Reprinted by permission of the editor.

Parts of Chapter 3 appeared in two different versions as "The Mother, the Bird, and the Letter" in *George Sand Studies* 17, nos. 1 and 2 (1998), and as "Writing Origins: George Sand as The Story of Our Life" in *Women Seeking Expression: France 1789–1914*, Monash Romance Studies 6 (2000), ed. Rosemary Lloyd and Brian Nelson. Both reprinted by permission of the editors.

Chapter 5 originally appeared in *Tulsa Studies in Women's Literature* 21, no. 2 (Fall 2002). Reprinted by permission of the editor.

First published 2009 by Cornell University Press

Printed in the United States of America

Library of Congress Cataloging-in-Publication Data

Beizer, Janet L., 1952–
   Thinking through the mothers : reimagining women's biographies / Janet Beizer
       p. cm.
   Includes bibliographical references and index.
   ISBN 978-0-8014-3851-6 (cloth : alk. paper)
   1. Women—Biography—History and criticism.   2. Women—Biography—Authorship.   3. Biography as a literary form.   I. Title.
   CT3203.B37 2008
   920.72—dc22

   [B]   2008031950

Cornell University Press strives to use environmentally responsible suppliers and materials to the fullest extent possible in the publishing of its books. Such materials include vegetable-based, low-VOC inks and acid-free papers that are recycled, totally chlorine-free, or partly composed of nonwood fibers. For further information, visit our website at www.cornellpress.cornell.edu.

Cloth printing   10 9 8 7 6 5 4 3 2 1

FOR JENNY

It is another world. But what else
can a mother give her daughter but such
beautiful rifts in time?

CONTENTS

ACKNOWLEDGMENTS

This book first saw the light—as it poured from the brilliant Santa Barbara sun—as a paper at a Nineteenth-Century French Studies Colloquium. It is a pleasure now to remember and to give thanks to the ears and voices that responded then, and that over the years nurtured the project and helped me to hone so many of the pages that followed. My good friend and colleague Evelyne Ender, frequent interlocutor on work and life and all that lies between, walked the beach with me and talked for hours about just those subjects. My debt to her and to all those other colleagues and friends who come together annually at the NCFS colloquium is enormous. Special thanks go to Ross Chambers, Nelly Furman, Melanie Hawthorne, Rosemary Lloyd, Isabelle Naginski, Marina van Zuylen, Peggy Waller, and Cathy Nesci (organizer as well of that particularly magical colloquium), who have listened and read and given precious counsel through the years I have been working on the book. I am grateful as well to Peter Brooks, Ruth Weeks, and the late Charles Bernheimer for their enduring conversation and support.

In Charlottesville and beyond, Farzaneh Milani has been a peerless reader and friend, challenging me by her example. Paul Barolsky, Jessica Feldman, and Deborah McDowell all read and commented on early drafts of the first rough sketches; Claire Lyu, Mary McKinley, and Susan McKinnon helped out with references and more. Suzanne Raitt and the late Janet Hiddleston generously gave me access to unpublished materials. In the Boston area, my debts to colleagues and friends are many. Diana Sorensen found time in an impossible schedule to read some pages at a critical point; Alice Jardine has been a sustaining force in the intellectual and real world; Ginger Chappell, Beth Cooley, Esther Gross, Carol Oja, Kathy Richman, Nancy Salzer, and Arlene Stevens offered vital friendship and conversation; Tom Conley, Christie McDonald, and Susan Suleiman were ready sources for references; and Mary Beth Clack unwound a never-ending Ariadne's thread to guide me through Widener Library and its mine of resources. In the wider world, I am tremendously lucky to have been hosted by Anne-Marie Baron in Paris; Claude and Roland Lazard in Paris and London; Lynne Carlin in Canberra; Peter and Christine Tremewan in Christchurch; and Raylene Ramsay in Auckland.

Holly Laird was instrumental in changing the course of this book when she asked me, by way of an invitation to contribute to her volume on adoption and academia, to think about how my ostensibly watertight personae of academic scholar and adoptive mother might intersect. I thank her for provoking and persisting. Raylene Ramsay generously helped to arrange a pivotal interview with Huguette Bouchardeau. To Bouchardeau, in turn, I am immensely grateful for finding the time to come up to Paris from her home in the Doubs to be interviewed, and for having the kindness to do so. Rosemary Lloyd, my no longer anonymous reader for Cornell University Press, lent her keen eye to these pages, which are the better for the revisions she suggested. She is not responsible for the few modifications I stubbornly resisted.

I was able to carry out the research for this book on time afforded by fellowships at the Australian National University in Canberra, the National Humanities Center in North Carolina, and the University of Canterbury in Christchurch. My thanks to these institutions, which offered scholarly communities for interchange as well as the luxury of time in which to enjoy it. I am grateful as well for the support of a research grant from the National Endowment for the Humanities, for summer research grants from the University of Virginia, for support from the Murray Anthony Potter Fund, Department of Romance Languages and Literatures, Harvard University, and for sabbatical leaves from Harvard that allowed me to continue writing.

I am indebted to Brian Nelson, Peter Tremewan, Raylene Ramsay, Rosemary Lloyd, Christopher Miller, Christie McDonald, Lawrence

Kritzman, Sonya Stephens, and Jacqueline Carroy for invitations to present earlier stages of this book at the University of Melbourne, University of Canterbury, Christchurch; University of Auckland, Indiana University, Yale, Harvard, Dartmouth, Cambridge, and the European Science Foundation in Paris, respectively. I owe many thanks as well to the audiences whose perceptive questions and provocative dialogue helped me to expand and refine my thinking, and also to my dissertation and seminar students, from whom I continue to learn.

This book would not have come together without the incredible dedication and skills of my research assistants: most recently and intensively, Liz Carter and Kathryn Rose, and in earlier years, Lauren Fortner, Dana Lindaman, and Mehdi El Hajoui. Sara Kippur formatted the manuscript and the bibliography with precision and aplomb. I owe them all a huge debt. I would like to thank Peter J. Potter, my editor at Cornell University Press, as well as Ange Romeo-Hall, Kay Banning, and Amanda Heller for expertly shepherding the book from manuscript into print, and Bernhard Kendler, who believed in the project in its earlier incarnation.

A faithful corps of former babysitters become family friends and colleagues gave me the remarkable gift of being a writer and a mother. My gratitude to Margaret McColley, Nathalie Charron Marcus, and Caitlin Sullivan-Thompson is boundless. Thanks too to Mary Malgodi and the Driscoll Extended Day Program for the safe and joyful afterschool days, and to Lia Brozgal for stepping in (and out) in Paris in the rain. The French-Keaches and the Milanis have my undying gratitude for extending our nuclear family in Charlottesville, as do the Wagner-Goodmans, the Stevenses, and the Kantrowitz-Scheindlins in Boston. Special thanks to the White-Freemans and the rest of the Charlottesville adoptive families' community for their abiding friendship. To my friends in the larger Driscoll community, a heartfelt thanks for creating an urban village.

Finally, a word of appreciation to my family, whose presence behind the scenes of this book has never faltered. My father did not live to see the book in print, but the knowledge that it would be on his bookshelf—with the pages cut, as it were—if he had, has encouraged me to finish. My mother always remembered to ask how the book is going—even when it wasn't—and I have been touched by her unquestioning faith in its existence. My sister Laura talked me through the substance of some of these pages (though she may not know it) in conversations as stimulating as they were free associative. My daughter Jenny was born with the book. She has lived with it, and it with her, on and off for her whole life; I think sometimes that they are siblings. To Jenny, my deepest thanks and love for learning to live with a writing mother, and for teaching me how to think ahead—and on all sides—through the daughters.

Brookline, Massachusetts
June 2008

A Note on Translations

All translations from the French are mine unless otherwise indicated. For the sake of readability original French citations appear in the text only in chapters where close textual readings of dense prose are at stake (chapters 3 and 6), and they follow the English translations. In the other chapters, original French citations appear in the footnotes whenever the original language has seemed important. Original sources are provided throughout. Emphasis, unless otherwise noted, is in the original text.

THINKING THROUGH THE MOTHERS

PROLOGUE

Few authors relish the prospect of introducing their book. The task of moving from a work in process to a work as product means discarding a mode of writing experienced as thinking through and reworking in order to write with detachment and finality. After years of living with a baggy monster, the author as prefacer or introducer must begin to nip and tuck, reshaping the monster into fixed, describable form, and must finally, with one fatal stroke, change Proteus into stone. And so (to switch monsters and metaphors) she fixes the work to the ground, puts a stake through its heart, and kills the living, growing, metamorphosing matter into circulation with the classic introductory statement—be it explicit or implicit—"*this is a book about....*" And it is only a small exaggeration to say that now, at this penultimate moment, the author needs to sit down and figure out—that is, *determine* (literally, "set a boundary"), *decide* (etymologically, "cut off")—exactly what the book is, in fact, *about.*

The dictionary tells us that *about* derives from the Old English *abútan, onbútan,* "on the outside of."[1] Its nautical definition, "onto a new tack," "onto a new course," usefully emphasizes the position of externality and remoteness from which the author necessarily speaks in order to describe her book, having moved on to a place that is both outside and beyond its writing. Yet even as I speak from this newly

---

[1]   *OED, Random House College Dictionary.*

outsider-ed position, I'm convinced that it is crucial, in order to convey with any fidelity the shape of the pages to follow, to indicate not only what they are *about*, which is to say, where and how they have ended, but also what they once were, what they might have been, what they are not: to preserve a trace of their becoming. For this book perhaps more than for some others, it seems essential to simulate, though in an infinitesimal trace sense, the process I consign to death by writing these opening words.

This book was twelve years in the making. It existed as process for a longer period than do many books, and, perhaps accordingly, ends like an Ouroboros manqué, with its tail several coils away from its mouth. *Thinking through the Mothers* began as an exploration of the intersection of women's biography and autobiography, under the original title *Vicarious Lives*. It initially took off from the New Historicist–feminist quest for lost stories of women's lives, the feminist version of a post-1960s roots quest variously represented as the recuperation of a lost matriarchal tradition, a search for literary "foremothers," a retracing of feminine authorial lineage. At play in resurrections of illustrious maternal precursors is a revision of Harold Bloom's now classic male paradigm of strong precursor fathers whose textual precedents instill an anxiety of influence in a line of literary sons.[2] What happens, I asked, when there is no lineage of powerful precursor texts with which to do battle? What kind of recuperative efforts—what Alison Booth has called "scenes of autobiographical dispossession"—play out on empty fields of combat?[3] Might nostalgic reconstructions of an irretrievable feminine heritage not reflect a particularly postmodern anxiety about not having an anxiety of influence? Looking mostly at France and the United States, I was particularly struck by the ways in which the quest for foremothers, for many feminist biographers, New Historians, and literary critics, is personally motivated, becomes a search for the self and its biological

---

[2] Harold Bloom, *The Anxiety of Influence: A Theory of Poetry* (New York: Oxford University Press, 1973).

[3] Such scenes act out the question "Where were the eminent models when I needed them?" according to Booth. Alison Booth, *How to Make It as a Woman: Collective Biographical History from Victoria to the Present* (Chicago: University of Chicago Press, 2004), xi.

maternal origins, and itself becomes part of the story. Biography and autobiography then fuse, often flirting with the fictional, blurring generic boundaries, and creating an intergenre I named "bio-autography": the writing of a self through the representation of another's life.[4] This hybrid genre, I thought, might provide a privileged perspective on the intersubjective foundations of biography in general.[5]

The project began to shift, however, when I began to look more closely at the maternal rhetoric that dominates the expression of desire for a feminine literary lineage. I noticed a tendency for contemporary feminist discourse to slide unthinkingly from mothers to female precursors, as if the metaphor in Virginia Woolf's observation that "we think back through our mothers if we are women" had become perfectly transparent.[6] I saw, too, that efforts to revive the buried lives of women in the hope of finding spiritual foremothers tend to wake maternal phantoms who are alternately wrestled to the ground and embraced. And I recognized that quests for the lives of metaphorical mothers and hunts for the lives of real-life mothers are often not only congruent but also significantly intertwined. I realized that any exploration of women's biographies of women begged to begin with women writing about their mothers. But it could not rest there, because narratives of literal and figurative mothers are locked in an eternal two-step, caught in a cultural dance with no exit or break.

If it is true, in the biological-genealogical tradition and in the psychoanalytic teachings that derive from it, that the mother is known and the father most uncertain, it is paradoxically also true, according to *biographical*-genealogical conventions, that the (lives of the) fathers are known and largely accounted for, while the (lives of the) mothers are unknown, unrecorded, and, until relatively recently, little explored. I came to believe, in the course of the journey

---

[4] Despite recent American trends toward personal narratives, bio-autographical writing has dual roots in French intellectual soil. It has been fed by the modern autobiographical tradition of the decentered subject (from Rousseau through poststructuralism), and by the unbounded voices embodied by French feminist writing practices of "écriture féminine."

[5] See especially chapter 1. For a review of the "extraordinary elasticity of autobiographical experimentation," see Nancy K. Miller, "The Entangled Self: Genre Bondage in the Age of the Memoir," *PMLA* 122, no. 2 (March 2007): 537–48, 545.

[6] Virginia Woolf, *A Room of One's Own* (London: Harcourt Brace Jovanovich, 1929), 79.

that this book inscribes, that the reasons for the unknown-ness of our mothers' lives, and the difficulties of knowing and making them known today, are not exhausted by the economic, sociological, and historical variables that begin to account for a lack of information.

As I unpacked the maternal metaphor, I was led to wonder if, as women, we have any greater access to our mothers' lives than to the lives of other women whose stories have been swept away like dust in the debris of the past. I came to understand that each of the two salvation projects reflects the other's impossibility in a ricocheting display of loss. That is, a sense of the mother's story as insufficient creates the need to recuperate a foremother whose life might redeem the maternal lack. But the sought-after foremother can't help but be recuperated in the image of the mother's lack. As Lynn Davidson has remarked in her study of women whose mothers died prematurely: "Even people who felt that their mothers were generally good and available...expressed disappointment over the mothering they received: it never met the standards of our society's idealized constructions of mothering and motherhood....Mothers cannot be replaced when they are gone [because] there is a confluence and confusion as to who is missed—the ideal mother or the real one."[7] What is lost is idealized, and what is idealized is loss itself. In much the same way, feminist biography as a genre, in its attempts to retrieve foremothers made in the mother's image and mothers made in the foremother's image, might be said to mourn not only each individual missed target but also the (missing) place of the feminine in culture. In other words, the peculiarly postmodern phenomenon of women's bio-autography, by its interminable identification with the lost object, may approach that chronic state of mourning we have come to know as melancholia.[8]

As the project evolved to foreground the parallel quests for the lives of foremothers and mothers, it became grounded in a reflection on the conjoined impossibility of both projects and a critique of the maternal metaphor in biography. Yet this metaphor takes

---

[7] Lynn Davidson, *Motherloss* (Berkeley: University of California Press, 2000), 33.

[8] See chapter 1. I allude to Judith Butler's reinterpretation of Freud's work on mourning and melancholia as related to gender formation in *Gender Trouble* (New York: Routledge, 1999), 73–84.

its place not only within a rhetorical framework but within dominant epistemological and discursive structures as well, all bound to what we might call the culture of genealogy. I'm referring, first, to the fascination with tracing family ancestry and its contemporary biological-genetic crystallization, but also, and more significantly, to its ideological underpinnings. These include the primacy of lineage, inheritance, property; the form of thought structured by these, which emphasizes the line, the path (origins and ends and the teleology that connects them), hierarchy, unity, resemblance, and reflection; and the aesthetic that depends on these ideas: mimesis. Any evaluation of the maternal salvation project—the effectiveness of its means, the fate of its ends, the nature of its ethos—must eventually be integrated within this larger genealogical context. Similarly, any critique of this project must take the measure of its reliance on genealogical thinking and begin to suggest alternatives to these ways of thinking, saying, and knowing. For now it will suffice to map the genealogical model along with its critique onto the evolutionary chart of this book. I will have more to say about it later on (particularly in chapters 5 and 6 and the epilogue) because it is one of the late-breaking preoccupations of this book, and as such, I hope, the opening of a discussion.

Implicit in the various permutations of this book and present every step of the way, at least latently, was a burgeoning reflection on my own responsibility as a critic and a musing on the source of the authority from which I speak. Though I was not aware of this underlying current when I began the project, I often remembered, once I was embarked on it, the words with which Paul de Man had responded to my term paper outline when I was a first-year graduate student: "Well, that's fine, but you know, funny things happen when you start to write." Indeed.

One of the funny things that happened in the course of my writing was a turning inward of the questions I was asking externally about the writer's relationship to her biographical subject and text, and the ethics of the project. (Or to put it more accurately, perhaps, the questions I was projecting outward returned home to roost.) Questions of intellectual and literary lineage led into questions of aesthetic and discursive authority, and to corresponding formal concerns about my own critical voice and stance, about structure of address, and about responsibility: not only that of literature to life but also that of criticism to literature. My concerns were at once aesthetic and ethical, having to do with both the accountability and the violence of a mimesis that is as much critical as literary, whose reflective aims inevitably rely on reduction, approximation, and appropriation.

I chose not to begin here by talking *about* or *from* the last stages of thought this book involved but rather to talk *through* them, from *within* their coiling arc: to retrace my path through these chapters as process. All books evolve in the course of their writing. I suspect that the series of revolutions I lived (historically, professionally, personally) as this book slowly emerged has played a significant role in choreographing its wide spirals of change. I began to write this book in the twentieth century and finish in the twenty-first. By what I suppose to be chance, the midpoint of my writing sits squarely at the turn of the century. I began writing as an associate professor and end as a full professor, with all the freedoms and constraints that implies. I moved from a French Department in a state university to a Department of Romance Languages and Literatures in a private institution, which is to say, to a department that is by definition more inclusive, and by position more exclusive. Geographically, I left the pastoral for the urban.

A move, by nature, means at least a relative upheaval of one's world. Mine took place in late August 2001, two short weeks before September 11 (though in retrospect the two dates seem to coincide). I had written roughly half of these chapters before, and wrote the rest following. The events and aftershocks of 9/11 were a strong presence in my thinking and my writing after that date, as becomes explicit in chapter 5. Before I began this book, I had not mixed academic and personal writing, in fact had held them vigorously apart. For a variety of reasons, which are, as in most cases, overdetermined, this book catalyzed or at least recorded a radical change in that sphere. And finally, perhaps most significantly, I began this book not yet a mother and end it with a daughter moving steadily into adolescence.

I have little doubt that the personal and global transformations I experienced in the course of writing had epistemological and narrative repercussions in my writing life, changed the nature of knowledge for me, and, more fundamentally, changed my perceptions about the possibilities and imperatives of knowing and telling. This book, made in the image of its subject, contains bio-autographical elements, performs, to a certain extent, the subject of its discourse, playing out elements of my own story through the stories of my others. I hope, though, to have avoided doing this confessionally, and in any case have borrowed some of Colette's ruses. I've learned from Colette that autobiographical flashes serve well to hide deeper truths when carefully dosed and thoroughly dissolved in a murky soup containing "what I know about myself, what I've tried to hide, what I've invented and what I've guessed."[9]

At this latter-day stage in its evolution, *Thinking through the Mothers* has become a collection of essays written around a slowly unfolding nexus of motifs. In the wide turns the different chapters take there are also returns, and in this spiraling play of departure and repetition the central preoccupations of the book emerge: processes of identification at work in biography; the relational underpinnings of biography; feminist biography as a work of exhumation, resuscitation, veneration, denigration, and mourning for the missing place of women in culture; the shifting metaphorical foundations of biography; the course of the maternal metaphor in the wake of Virginia Woolf; the all-encompassing nature of genealogical thinking; the discovery or invention of new, nongenealogical metaphoric bases for women's auto/biographical recovery. The first two chapters set out the problem in different ways: the first identifies and exemplifies, and the second allegorizes. The last four chapters work through possibilities for developing new metaphors and models for writing women's lives by focusing on particular cases and adopting different perspectives and forms, including literary works, critical readings of these works, biography and memoir, interview and interchange, personal experience, self-interrogation, and dialogue.

Chapter 1, "Cat's Cradle: Transfiguring Women's Lives," lays out the problems of retrieving women's lives and the challenges that arise for biographers, and theorizes potentially dynamic, collaborative, and metamorphosing forms of biography. When few traces of a

---

[9] Colette, *Break of Day*, trans. Enid McLeod (New York: Farrar, Straus and Giroux, 1961), 62; Colette, *La Naissance du jour*, in *Œuvres*, vol. 3, ed. Claude Pichois (Paris: Gallimard [Pléiade], 1991), 315.

woman's life are available, the biographer must decide how much recuperation is possible, and to what extent the processes and motives
for the search should be included in the account. I explore women's
recent experiments with bio-autography (notably Eunice Lipton and
Christa Wolf), and survey the work of precursors and fellow travelers
(including Vladimir Nabokov, Richard Holmes, Julian Barnes), arguing that the biographer's imaginative and emotional identification
with the biographee is not proper to women, but is intensified by the
self-consciously autobiographical perspectives of new women biographers. Through a reading of a series of self-consciously reflexive
late-twentieth-century women's biographies (published under the
series title "Elle était une fois" [Once Upon Her Time]), I define and
develop the concept of "salvation biography" or "resurrection biography," and consider its inevitable failings.

Chapter 2, "Unwrapping the Mummy: In Search of Kuchuk
Hanem," is an allegorical critique of contemporary women's literary
excursions to an irretrievable past. Using as a lens contemporary reconstructions of Louise Colet as intellectual and authorial precursor,
I track her unsuccessful search (recounted in her 1875 travelogue, *Les
Pays lumineux*) for the Egyptian courtesan celebrated by her lover,
Flaubert. I rely on the elusive narrative(s) of Colet's failed quest to
posit a chain of gazes that represents a common (negative) paradigm
for contemporary feminist biography. Colet's quest stands as a paradigm for a certain kind of feminist life narrative which, in the guise
of a retrieval mission, takes on a fetishistic aspect, interprets difference as absence, gets stuck in mirror thinking.

Chapter 3, "Writing Origins: George Sand as the Story of Our Life,"
reads Sand's maternal memoir (dispersed in her 1854 autobiography)
through the lenses of two works by the writer-politician Huguette
Bouchardeau, who in 1990 published both a biography of Sand and
a memoir of her own mother. I suggest that if Sand as biographer-
daughter is foremother to Bouchardeau, then Bouchardeau is doubly
invested as daughter in her two-pronged biographical venture. Her
dual project exemplifies the slide from childhood nurturer to intellectual precursor common to many feminist biographers, crystallizing
links between literal and figurative mothers. Bouchardeau's reading
of Sand elicits my rereading, which resists reconstruction and defers
to silence.

Chapter 4, "A Different Story: In Dialogue with Huguette Bouchardeau," is a transcription and analysis of my interview of Bouchardeau, incorporating her voice into my prior construction of her double biographical project. Writing self-reflexively, I explore the problematic of mirroring, projection, and reconstruction that is central to the concerns of this book, through my own unwitting performance, as interviewer, of the literary critic–biographer's quest for foremothers. The dialogic structure of this chapter modifies what I came to understand as my earlier monologic reading of Bouchardeau in chapter 3.

Chapter 5, "One's Own: Reflections on Motherhood, Owning, and Adoption," is a theoretical and empirical consideration of the concept of owning posed from the intersection of adoptive motherhood, storytelling, and life writing. I weave through anthropological and journalistic adoption literature, literary theory, biography theory, and personal experience to propose a mode of writing lives that would unweave wholes, commemorate gaps, and abandon a genealogical rhetoric and logic to find its metaphor in un-owning.

Chapter 6, "Mothers and Lovers, or the Great Banalities of Existence," focuses on Colette's *La Naissance du jour* with forays into *La Maison de Claudine* and *Sido,* which together form a trilogy of anachronistically modern writings about her mother (1922–1930). Colette's mother-texts help me to begin to articulate alternatives to more recent reconstructive tendencies of maternal "mirror biography." I argue that the originality of Colette's mother-writing lies in a certain "transformational aesthetic" (Christopher Bollas's term), by which her writing, analogous to maternal handling of an infant, works to punctuate, reformulate, and metamorphose textual experience. I suggest that in privileging change, she is moving into a radically experimental writing, breaking with an aesthetic of presence and absence, mirroring and mimesis.

In the epilogue, "Books and Children: New Mythologies," I return to Roland Barthes's astute analysis of the cultural mythologies promulgated by an *Elle* magazine article of 1954 equating women's books and children. I read Barthes here as not only descriptive of the mid-1950s climate in which he was writing but also pre-scriptive, ironically prescient in his comments that unwittingly anticipate persisting ideological biases. Weaving among Barthes's mid-century writing about perceptions of mothering (both children and books), the genealogical ideology that permeates the article he is discussing, and the theorization of and by mothers writing since then, I work, with recourse to peripheral models (including fostering, as proposed by Ross Chambers; rhizomes as opposed to roots, as proposed by Félix Guattari and Gilles Deleuze; and recognition, as opposed to mirroring and mimesis, which I borrow from a patchwork of readings and misreadings of Terence Cave, Jessica Benjamin, Kaja Silverman, and Kelly Oliver), to open a critical and aesthetic discourse I would like to think of as post-genealogical and post-mimetic.

It is probably clear by now that this book makes no claims to comprehensiveness or historical completeness. It is problem- rather than coverage-oriented, devoted less to specific women's lives than to the problematic writing of these lives, and is not *about* any single author or group of authors. Rather, it uses what and whom it needs (literature high and low, current events, experience, Colet, Sand, Colette, Bouchardeau, Oprah Winfrey, Julian Barnes, Alex Haley, Henry Louis Gates Jr., Flaubert, and so on) to think with and to think through a series of problems that are simultaneously generic (in the double sense of gender- and genre-related), narrative, literary-critical, epistemological, empirical, and ethical. My choice of texts and authors is unabashedly "loaded." That is, there are certainly biographies of women by women that do not fall under my rubric of "salvation narratives." I did not choose to include them because they are not illustrative of the tendencies and problematics that interest me here. I have, however, included some voices that may initially surprise by their frequency or apparent marginality to a book about women writing women's lives: notably, Flaubert's. Intimately related—by passion or friendship, respectively, and in both cases by intellectual exchange—to two of the writers who hold center stage in these pages, Flaubert takes his place as a background player, crucial interlocutor, and primary example of the methodology of lateral reading and collaborative construction that develops as the chapters unfold.

Neither is this a linear narrative leading toward resolution, but instead, to expand on my earlier description, a grouping of *essays*, a term I use first, of course, in the etymological sense of attempts or experiments: attempts to experience and to relate experience.

Montaigne, one of the founding fathers of the genre, explained the usefulness of the form to his purpose of recording what is provisional and speculative:

> I do not portray being: I portray passing. Not the passing from one age to another...but from day to day, from minute to minute. My history needs to be adapted to the moment....This is a record of various and changeable occurrences, and of irresolute and, when it so befalls, contradictory ideas: whether I am different myself, or whether I take hold of my subjects in different circumstances and aspects....If my mind could gain a firm footing, I would not make essays, I would make decisions; but it is always in apprenticeship and on trial.[10]

More recently, feminists have found in the essay's openness, nonlinearity, and potential dialogism possibilities something like that of *écriture feminine*. For Ruth Behar, the essay is the genre "through which to *attempt*...the dialectic between connection and otherness that is at the center of all forms of historical and cultural representation."[11] Behar's highlighting of both relating and tentativeness in the life of the intellect suits my own purposes well, as does Elizabeth Mittmann and Ruth-Ellen Boetcher Joeres's summary of the genre as "marked by a tendency to wander around a subject, to investigate various paths towards a point, to enjoy the possibility of digression, of playfulness...[to invite] dialogue and connection...[to assume] a personal presence...[to] stress process rather than product."[12]

In the same spirit I have respected the organic unfolding of this book, resisting the temptation to rewrite or to reorganize its chapters from the standpoint of my thinking today. They appear in their original chronological order of writing, with the exception of a few chapters that were written as patchworks in time, which appear in

---

[10] Michel de Montaigne, "Of Repentance," in *The Complete Essays of Montaigne*, trans. Donald M. Frame (Stanford: Stanford University Press, 1957), 611.
[11] Ruth Behar, *The Vulnerable Observer: Anthropology That Breaks Your Heart* (Boston: Beacon Press, 1996), 20.
[12] Ruth-Ellen Boetcher Joeres and Elizabeth Mittman, eds., *The Politics of the Essay: Feminist Perspectives* (Bloomington: Indiana University Press, 1993), 17–20.

the sequence at the point of their most substantial development (chapters 1 and 4 and the epilogue). Although any of the chapters may be read individually, out of order, there is a development and a process that is part of the story, and that emerges in the course of a chronological reading. For much the same reasons I haven't made the chapters "know more" than I knew at the time of writing. Rather than belatedly adding footnotes to account for relevant sources that hadn't yet appeared when I was writing, or with which I was unfamiliar then, or that were related but not necessary to my discussion, I've integrated such references here in the prologue, in the epilogue, and in the bibliography.

As I bring this project to a close, my very deliberate guiding intent has been to preserve the essay mode with which I somewhat inadvertently began, understanding now that its ways of working—by meandering freely through associations and relationships, and in so doing, to borrow Adorno's useful rhetoric, "abandon[ing] the main road to the origins"[13]—are of special significance to this project. For I began precisely with the question of nostalgia for maternal lineage, looking at the problem of retrieving origins and reconstructing lines, and went on to suggest alternatives to a linear genealogical model of precursor biography that leans on established lines of origins, inheritance, and property. My travels through women's biography and beyond led me to new biographical modes and processes relying on nonproprietary, alinear, relational metaphors such as fostering, adopting, and un-owning. I discovered the working of lateral collaborative processes through which we might not simply confront gaps and blanks in the lost stories of women's lives but cultivate them, turning hollows and holes into richly unfilled textual sources, dignifying absence and silence as vital modes of signification. My hope is that these metaphors, these modes, these processes might help to reorient our reading and writing of lives lived and lost, and to reinvent the means to represent them.

---

[13]   Theodor Adorno, "The Essay as Form," trans. Bob Hullot-Kentor and Frederic Will, in *New German Critique*, no. 32 (Spring–Summer 1984): 159.

1

CAT'S CRADLE

Transfiguring Women's Lives

Alias Biography

1968: The author is pronounced dead in a short essay published by
Roland Barthes in an obscure French journal.[1] Barthes's grammar os-
cillates between the indicative and the subjunctive, his tone between
description and prescription. His rhetoric is alternately appropriate
to cultural commentary and to quasi-religious *fatwa.* The author is
"buried," reports Barthes, yet he also relates that "his empire remains powerful."[2] How dead is the author?

1973: Barthes announces the unmaking of the author in the text, using
the analogy of a spider dissolving in the constructed secretions of its
own web. He proposes a neologism—*hyphology,* literally the discourse
of the tissue or the web—to define a theory of textual production.[3]

1977: Stephen Heath's English translation of Barthes's ambiguous
death notice (record or warrant?) gives currency to "The Death of the
Author," and arguably performs it as well.[4] The author is returned

---

[1] Roland Barthes, "La Mort de l'auteur," *Mantéia* 5 (1968): 12–17.
[2] Ibid., 15, 13.
[3] Roland Barthes, *Le Plaisir du texte* (Paris: Seuil, 1973), 100–101.
[4] See the widely disseminated translation: Roland Barthes, "The Death of the
Author," in *Image-Music-Text,* trans. Stephen Heath (London: Fontana/Collins,
1977), 142–48.

to the grave, a stake driven through her heart by a widening circle of readers. I use the feminine possessive advisedly here, to reflect the historical coincidence of the author's proclaimed death and the feminist revival—also highly popularized in the late seventies—of literary foremothers.

1986: Nancy Miller shifts the terms of Barthes's theory of text production, countering his "hyphology" with her own "arachnology." Literally the study of spiders as embodied by the spider-artist Arachne, ex-woman weaver of texts, arachnology for Miller describes a practice of reading against the weave of indifferentiation—"overreading," as she puts it—to discover the signature of a gendered subjectivity, to interpret and reappropriate a missing story.[5] Moving from hyphology to arachnology, we focus on the spider instead of the web, the lacemaker instead of the threads of lace. Barthes and Miller, 1968 and 1986, can serve as emblematic markers. They frame a period that began by deconstructing notions of unified selfhood, reliable memory, and authentic life narrative and that ended with a gesture toward reconstruction: a gender-identified self possessing a past awaits its teller. I don't mean to have Miller speak in the name of feminism or Barthes in that of patriarchy; neither do I want to suppress all other theoretical plots from this twenty-year period. I want rather to place signposts over a course of time during which biography, steadily flourishing in the marketplace but banished from the academy, came to be admitted there by the side door that feminism opened. If by the mid-eighties biography was an admissible genre, it was still an obscure object of literary desire. It is only in the intervening years of declining optimism about the feasibility of retrieving women's life stories that such stories—and, correlatively, biographies in general—have become possible and even alluring objects of theoretical inquiry.[6]

---

[5] Nancy K. Miller, "Arachnologies: The Woman, the Text, and the Critic," in *The Poetics of Gender,* ed. Nancy K. Miller (New York: Columbia University Press, 1986), 270–95.

[6] Two examples are indicative. Shoshana Felman's *What Does a Woman Want? Reading and Sexual Difference* (Baltimore: Johns Hopkins University Press, 1993) revises the early optimism emblematized by Carolyn Heilbrun's pioneering *Writing a Woman's Life* (New York: Columbia University Press, 1988). The essays in the collection *The Seductions of Biography* are shot through with skepticism about the biographical project. Such a collection would have been neither possible

November 11, 1993: In the amphitheater the audience is waiting. The art historian Eunice Lipton, author of the intriguingly titled *Alias Olympia*, is about to be introduced. In the back of the hall a table is stacked with books, the covers replicating ad infinitum the reclining woman Manet displayed as the courtesan Olympia. The air is charged. The talk has been well publicized, and we are expecting to rediscover Manet's model as the artist Victorine Meurent, perhaps even to identify with a gaze regendered and redirected through her own. Lipton tries on the microphone. "Now, how do I do this? Will it go over my head? I have a big head, it turns out." It does go over her head. "Do I still look good?"[7] She laughs a long, belting Joan Rivers laugh. The infusion of a New York Jewish discourse in this conservative southern academic setting is incongruous. Lipton drops her *r*'s, dentalizes, and flattens her *a*'s—everything my third grade teacher drilled out of our speech so that we would not betray our origins.

Lipton is telling about her research trip to Paris in search of Victorine, her days in the archives, her nights with her husband, the verbal legacy of her father, Louis, the paralyzing dreams of her witchy mother, Trudy. Tracked through Paris by maternal phantoms, Eunice works through her relationship with the unmaternal Trudy. She loses Victorine's trail but finds her own way. There are many questions at the end of the talk. Lipton diverts all inquiries about Meurent to the book, which is manifestly displayed at the exit.

November 12, 1993: Curious about whether *Alias Olympia* might deliver the biography Lipton withheld in her talk, I stop at the library. The book is no different from the talk, only longer. To my New-York-Jewish-expatriate-in-Charlottesville ears, Lipton's stylized delivery (apparent on the printed page as well) is both daring and embarrassing. Scattered bits echo the text of the talk with a jarring familiarity: "Anyway, we got there and I got my usual depressed for a couple of

---

nor seductive in the earlier phase discussed. See Mary Rhiel and David Suchoff, eds., *The Seductions of Biography* (New York: Routledge, 1996).

[7] Eunice Lipton, "Tracking Manet's Olympia: An Art Historian's Trip Out of Art History," lecture delivered at the University of Virginia, Charlottesville, November 11, 1993.

weeks....I also like [her]...*chutzpah.*"[8] "'Interesting.' What a nerve
to just say it like that....'[Y]ou're smart, *maydeleh.*'"[9]

Late into the night I page through *Alias Olympia,* subtitled *A Woman's Search for Manet's Notorious Model and Her Own Desire,* reading it as a belated product of a certain feminist narrative project that is beginning to sound dated. Lipton's quest for Manet's model, more specifically a craving for evidence that the woman painted was painter as well, impresses me as a textbook example of a tradition of plot deprivation in women's lives and a revisionist insistence on remedial readings of our lives. "**WHAT IF BIOGRAPHY WERE A TALE OF DESIRE?**" Lipton's book asks on the flyleaf. If we heed typography, we must take this question to be both capital and bold. It takes Eunice Lipton's narrator to the point of identification with Victorine: "I had no idea what the ramifications of the search [for Victorine] would be," she says. "I didn't even realize that our names were the same: 'Eunice' is a translation from the Greek of 'Evnike'; it means 'Happy Victory.' And I certainly didn't *intend* to end up a redhead" (16). This is not quite autobiography. Blocked by a recalcitrant subject, biography flows back to the self.

But I'm not convinced that Lipton's archaeology of personal desire restores to woman a narrative of her own. Nor am I sure that her attempted excavation of an ancestral heroine serves to innovate biography—even though Meurent turns out to be a postmodernistically correct elusive antiheroine. It isn't simply that I feel cheated by having Manet's model disintegrate like a mummy exposed to the air of our time. Biography manqué has a long heritage, and Lipton some worthy literary predecessors. Nabokov's narrator reneges on his title's promised biography in *The Real Life of Sebastian Knight* and records instead "the echo of some possible truth, a timely reminder: don't be too certain of learning the past from the lips of the present."[10] In more graphic terms, the biographer-narrator of *Flaubert's Parrot* compares the past to a greased pig. Julian Barnes's alinear life of Flaubert goes

---

[8]   Ibid.
[9]   Eunice Lipton, *Alias Olympia: A Woman's Search for Manet's Notorious Model and Her Own Desire* (New York: Scribners, 1992), 10, 25; subsequent references are provided in the text.
[10]   Vladimir Nabokov, *The Real Life of Sebastian Knight* (New York: Vintage, 1992), 50; subsequent references are provided in the text.

on to refigure biography through the metaphor of a redefined net: "You can define a net in one of two ways, depending on your point of view. Normally, you would say that it is a meshed instrument designed to catch fish. But you could...reverse the image and define a net as...a collection of holes tied together with string. You can do the same with a biography."[11] Bypassing a theory that would hold biography in an ichthyological or otherwise zoological snare, Barnes gives up the fish with the pig, choosing instead what we could call an "aerology" of the text. Neither a hyphology nor an arachnology, Barnes's image of biography's text displaces our attention from the web and its maker, privileging instead all that escapes containment. Here is a life story with room to breathe.

Lipton's mapping of desire onto biography creates a more rarefied textual space. Victorine Meurent is arguably smothered by the narrator's embrace of recognition. Her fate poses broader questions about the conjugation of feminism and biography. When history is no longer confined to the (largely public) lives of great men, yet women have left sparse personal records, what story can be written, and how? When ostensibly objective discursive modes are abandoned for a more intimate engagement with biographical subjects whose lifelines are too dim or blurred to read, how do biographers avoid speaking for their missing subjects? Does the entry of identity politics in the text inevitably produce an identification aesthetics—an uncritical, sentimental (and perhaps deadly) mirror writing? Must the force of a biographer's identification with the subject necessarily disable textual pleasure? Writes Nabokov, "I am Sebastian, or Sebastian is I, or perhaps we both are someone whom neither of us knows" (203). In place of the withered life story, Nabokov's narrator delivers an aesthetic supplement that I take as antidote and challenge to Lipton.

---

[11] Julian Barnes, *Flaubert's Parrot* (New York: Knopf, 1985), 38; subsequent references are provided in the text. As my examples suggest, I am using the term "biography manqué" to cover not only biography that cannot "net" its subject but also biography that slides into fiction, even when it is not quite in the realm of what we clearly recognize as "biographical fiction." Although a detailed discussion of the increasingly fine line that separates biography and fiction is outside the scope of this essay, I should state that I will—taking the cue from my texts—be playing on and around the border.

May 1994: Chance has provided a vacant apartment in New York and a summer respite from pastoral life. The apartment is on the Upper West Side, a long subway ride from childhood. The East River cleaves Manhattan and Queens like an ocean.

Browsing in a bookstore before leaving for New York, I come upon *Alias Olympia.* I flip through it once again and impulsively buy it. When I board the plane, Meurent's aborted life is in my bag.

July 1994: Over half the works of nonfiction reviewed in each Sunday's *New York Times* are biographical. The subjects vary: a sculptor, an actress, a poet, a shop clerk, a traveler to the desert, the woman whose body underwrote *Roe v. Wade,* Barbie, God, somebody's great-aunt. Each passing week carries advertising for a new chronicle of O. J. Simpson's life. On television Nicole Brown Simpson's jogging partner recounts her friend's story to Barbara Walters. On public radio prostitutes narrate their daily lives and retrace paths from the past. On talk shows rape victims relive their violation in the telling. I watch biography Oprahfied. It has been feminized as it has been popularized—and perhaps revolutionized in the process. In 1988 Carolyn Heilbrun mentions having added 150 new biographies of women to her collection since 1970, the year that for Heilbrun emblematically ushered in a new period in women's biography because that was when Nancy Milford published *Zelda,* retrieving the narrative Fitzgerald had "usurped" from his wife.[12] The explosion of women's biographies has been accompanied by a generic evolution characterized by a relational aesthetic that the gender differential work pioneered by Carol Gilligan, Nancy Chodorow, and others prompts me to name "feminization."

The apartment turns out to be two blocks from a building where I spent many weekends with my grandparents. Yet time has made childhood sites foreign to me. Once I catch myself starting to speak French in a café. I come home with odd finds, *pleurotes* or shoes I may never wear. And books that narrate lives I have sometimes never heard of.

Biography collections in bookstores spill into piles scattered on the floor. "Writers' lives," notes Erica Jong, "tend to have more

[12]   Heilbrun, *Writing a Woman's Life,* 12.

commercial viability than their own books."[13] Janet Malcolm's excursus into the nether parts of biography around the Sylvia Plath family tracks no fewer than ten biographies of the poet.[14] And I find myself—with some horror—reading biography with the voracity I used to reserve for novels.

I renounced biography after an adolescent flirtation with it because of an impatience with the predictable pattern of a body of information laid out with the certainty of death. Most biographies were "faking it with the truth," to borrow Anne Sexton's description of her colorful mode of self-disclosure.[15] Less exhibitionistically but with equal inauthenticity, most biographers were using facts to feign life. In college I read Sartre's *La Nausée* and found confirmation for my intuitions in Roquentin's decision to stop organizing the life of the Marquis de Rollebon and listen to jazz. What has changed? Is media bombardment now blasting wide my horizons? Or am I a victim of postmodern contingency, seeking between biography's narrative lines a coherence depreciated by our electronic age? If the novel is a dying form, is biography a sign of bereavement? Do we turn to biography as consolation for the order that the novel can no longer provide?[16] Such a cultural critique is tempting, but its assumption that biography takes as model the linear design of the traditional novel overlooks the novel's own deviations from this form.[17]

In fact scant guidelines remain; no Ariadne's thread leads through to the end. Gone are the ties mooring biography to history, and to the lives of great men. Scrapping her original plan to write the "biography of a prominent woman," Susan Cheever writes *A Woman's Life:*

---

[13]   Erica Jong, *The Devil at Large: Erica Jong on Henry Miller* (New York: Turtle Bay Books, 1993), 50.

[14]   Janet Malcolm, *The Silent Woman: Sylvia Plath and Ted Hughes* (New York: Knopf, 1994).

[15]   Quoted by Gail Hornstein in "The Ethics of Ambiguity: Feminists Writing Women's Lives," in *Women Creating Lives: Identities, Resilience, and Resistance,* ed. Carol E. Franz and Abigail J. Stewart (Boulder: Westview Press, 1994), 65.

[16]   See, for example, Sven Birkerts, "Biography and the Dissolving Self," in *Harper's Magazine* (March 1995): 24–26, and Jong on Henry Miller in *The Devil at Large.*

[17]   On the nineteenth-century novel as implicit model for biography, see Sharon O'Brien, "Feminist Theory and Literary Biography," in *Contesting the Subject: Essays in the Postmodern Theory and Practice of Biography and Biographical Criticism,* ed. William H. Epstein (West Lafayette, Ind.: Purdue University Press, 1991), 125.

The Story of an Ordinary American and Her Extraordinary Genera-tion, changing her subject's name to protect her identity.[18] Biography comes to coincide with anonymity.

All the rules have changed. Disrespecting death, Nicholson Baker tells John Updike's story live in *U and I.*[19] One of the cardinal pre-cepts of traditional life writing is violated. For despite etymology, biography is authorized by death.[20] Biography strives asymptotically toward a death that both sanctions and eludes it. Although autobi-ography can't include its subject's death (unless the autobiographer is a vampire, a near-death survivor, or a diva), death narration is the-oretically possible for biography, whose author and subject are not identical.[21] But an important obstacle remains: no biographer can be privy to the death knowledge of the biographee. The inner conscious-ness of death's victims is simply not accessible to the biographer. Although dates and other factual information may be conveyed, and simulations of death consciousness forged by artifices such as free indirect discourse, experienced death is simply beyond the limit of what biography can represent. Looming but invisible, death is the vampire in the mirror of biography. It leaves its trace as blank or gap when it is not covered over or bridged.

---

[18]   Susan Cheever, *A Woman's Life: The Story of an Ordinary American and Her Extraordinary Generation* (New York: Morrow, 1994), 9.

[19]   Nicholson Baker, *U and I: A True Story* (New York: Vintage, 1992).

[20]   On the relationship between life writing and death, see Walter Benjamin's re-marks about the novel's dependency on death, which I want to extend to biogra-phy: "What draws the reader to the novel is the hope of warming his shivering body with a death he reads about." Walter Benjamin, "The Storyteller: Reflections on the Works of Nikolai Leskov," in *Illuminations,* ed. Hannah Arendt, trans. Harry Zohn (New York: Schocken, 1969), 101. He earlier argues that "death is the sanc-tion of everything the storyteller can tell. He has borrowed his authority from death" (94).

[21]   It is worth thinking about the strikingly similar narratives of death offered by vampire tales and near-death accounts. They differ primarily by the context of darkness and satanic forces (and fiction) in the first case; light and divine forces (and ostensible nonfiction) in the second. Some of the AIDS chronicles of the 1990s arguably represent a new autobiographical subgenre in which one can ap-proximate, if never reach, a narrative deathpoint, recounting one's own dying, if not death. For a lucid discussion of death as a major differential of biographi-cal and autobiographical narratives, see Georges May, *L'Autobiographie* (Paris: Presses Universitaires de France, 1979). For a discussion of death as unavailable to any but fictional narrative, see Dorrit Cohn, "Fictional *versus* Historical Lives: Borderlines and Borderline Cases," *Journal of Narrative Technique* 19, no. 1 (Fall 1989): 3–24.

Some literary anecdotes trace a paradoxical fullness bestowed by the void in biography's text. Robert Louis Stevenson wrote *The Master of Ballantrae,* set in Scotland, when he was in Tahiti on assignment from the *New York Times* to write a series of South Pacific travel sketches. Somerset Maugham, who became fascinated by the life of Gauguin in the South Pacific, spent a month in Tahiti in 1917 but wrote the story of his Gauguin, *The Moon and Sixpence,* in a sanatorium in Scotland. Flaubert's *Voyage en Orient* is a product of France. In the single part of the *Voyage* written in the Orient, some pages composed on the Nile, Flaubert spoke of his youth, his memories, Normandy—everything but the voyage on which he was embarked. To tell of Egypt, he had to go back to France. Flaubert's "travel journal" is a renunciation of chronicling travel; writing depends on being elsewhere.[22]

Writing in his metabiographical *Footsteps* about his literal retracing of Robert Louis Stevenson's footsteps in the Cévennes, Richard Holmes inscribes interruption in biography in the figure of a broken bridge: "Even in imagination the gap was there.... You stood at the end of the broken bridge and looked across carefully, objectively, into the unattainable past on the other side. You brought it alive, brought it back, by other sorts of skills and crafts and sensible magic."[23] The gap is inevitable but also necessary to the kind of biography he writes; it is a literary space. It would be fatally bridged if all the facts could be filled in.

Julia Blackburn juxtaposes dream space, historical and geographic distance, and identificatory bridging in a passage where her narrator speaks of her subject Daisy Bates and then of herself:

> She leaves Australia and after five years she comes back to Australia.... As I write this I can see myself standing on the deck of a ship, staring at the sea, the sky, the land...and all three elements seeming to be made out of...layers of mist shifting and moving. I am no longer sure what year it was or where I was

---

[22] See Pierre-Marc Biasi's excellent critical introduction in Gustave Flaubert, *Voyage en Égypte,* ed. Pierre-Marc Biasi (Paris: Grasset, 1991).
[23] Richard Holmes, *Footsteps: Adventures of a Romantic Biographer* (London: Penguin, 1985), 27.

going but I can remember [that]...as I stood there I really felt
for a brief moment that it was possible to become another person just by the fact of departure.[24]

We have here the biographer's identification with a blurred subject,
figured by vaporization, by departure, by the gap of the unknown.
I want to extract these elements—if one can hold on to the equiva-
lent of the holes in a net—because their conjunction recurs in biography. Rephrased as transport and transference and shrouded by
metaphor, they tell the story of death's boatman.

Richard Holmes compares the biographer to "a kind of ferryman,
perhaps even a kind of Charon, crossing back and forth between the
Past and Present, over the dark river of Oblivion."[25] Ferrying in time
like Charon—but also, I would suggest, like the analysand who tries
to sort phantoms from living souls—the biographer always risks drift-
ing into the life of the other. A nexus imposes itself: travel, transference, death; displacement, identification, mourning. In these terms
Holmes brings back Eunice Lipton, the Paris sojourn, the intrusions
of the dead mother, the reconstruction of an artist foremother.

"I know I'm still looking for a hero," Eunice writes from Paris.
"She has to be...a brilliant painter...whose life was full of satisfaction and pleasure" (135). But she is forced to acknowledge: "[Victo-
rine's] life was invisible....For some reason this invisibility makes
me think of my mother" (155). Now, this association of Victorine
and Eunice's mother *through their common obscurity* helps to explain why Eunice seeks to reconstruct a Victorine who is famous,
talented, happy: that foremother could redeem the mother who was
unknown and unfulfilled, and in so doing legitimate the daughter.
The counterpart to Victorine's invisibility is her spectral hold: like
a lost mother, she haunts. The vision of Victorine that visits Eunice
is tinged with the maternal phantom: "She draws me into a state of
wonder and reverie. She looks at me wistfully and brushes the hair
from my face....She smiles....'Find me, Eunice'" (42). Omnipotent

---

[24] Julia Blackburn, *Daisy Bates in the Desert: A Woman's Life among the Aborigines* (New York: Vintage, 1995), 39.
[25] Richard Holmes, *Dr. Johnson and Mr. Savage* (New York: Vintage, 1993), 228.

and vacuous at once, she can never be found. Mother, daughter, and ghost coexist as an infernal trinity, the personae ever collapsed and reconfigured. They echo in Victorine's protean voice, which lapses into Yiddish-inflected English despite an occasionally interjected "mais oui" or "tant pis."

The discursive conflation points to an identificatory resurrection of Victorine, the ghost of Eunice's desire, through the missing figure of the mother. But it is precisely because the mother's place is evacuated that the simulacrum of Victorine must fail as well. It is in a painting of an aged, drunken, derelict Meurent that Eunice locates Victorine's most revealing essence and, more fundamentally, finds reflected the matricidal image of her own inner self: "A pathetic woman, no better than my mother, a sack of a woman bundled in *schmatas*, sagging into the table....Did I do this to my mother? My mother became a heap of rags, all her words gone, her desire shriveled, because of *me*?" (105).

Odd fragments resound from my distant past. The ragged remnants of a woman "bundled in *schmatas*" trail into the tattered phrases of a discarded childhood dialect. "No greater *nachas* could come to your family....Him I don't know....You should've seen the *drek* on sale at Klein's..." (23, 147, 24). And I'm mortified by the scene in which Eunice raises her voice to hail the curator at a French archive from the other side of the room: "'Madame Berthier?' This time I just call across the room. 'Where's Colombes?'...It is as if we are yelling across our backyard fences" (163).

I imagine Eunice's loud New York voice crossed to Paris. The passage reverses. In Queens when the weather got warm the neighbors sat outside gossiping on beach chairs. From across the central courtyard the questions rang out when a car door opened. No package went unnoticed, no arrival unheeded.

Years later, when I hear Eunice's voice in the archives, I recognize the ambivalent identification that brought me to biography. My point is not to invalidate the reservations I have set forth about *Alias Olympia* by conceding an anxiety of origins. But without a negative identification with the book, my misgivings would have lacked the intensity that led me on a roundabout reading course through biography.

The space of identification marks the place of death. Killing her mother, Eunice revives Victorine. But her desire and hope for Victorine can never be other than the eternally repeated memory of the mother's absence.[26]

Once Upon Her Time

October 1997: "I flew to Paris to find a dead writer.... I would probably not have liked her.... Still—[she] is my accomplice." "I'm searching for a hero, and I haven't found one.... Where are the women? I am barren of women.... I know I'm still looking for a hero.... She has to be larger than life, and successful, a brilliant painter...who produced many paintings that have been spirited away by evil men." "So began a quest in which this book is one stage. That was years ago.... [H]ere she is, she who gave birth to unique forms, the Female sculptor.... She is over there, she is waiting, there is not another moment to lose, that face there that cries out in the night, half sealed, A Woman."[27]

What desperate quest, what heroine hunt, what poignant lack motivates the preceding lines? In fact I have constructed there a collage of citations reproduced from three different yet similarly motivated biographies of women by women in order to resituate *Alias Olympia* within the larger project. My sources are, first, Michele Zackheim's *Violette's Embrace,* which appeared in 1996 and is about Violette Leduc, and last, Anne Delbée's *Une Femme,* which dates from 1982; embedded between them is Eunice Lipton's *Alias Olympia,* published in 1992, whose subject, Monet's model and would-be artist, Victorine

---

[26] My thinking about the intertwined structures of identification, violence, and mourning in contemporary women's biographies is indebted to Jessica Benjamin, especially to "The Omnipotent Mother," in *Like Subjects, Love Objects: Essays on Representation and Sexual Difference* (New Haven: Yale University Press, 1995), 129–46; Felman, *What Does a Woman Want?*; Diana Fuss, *Identification Papers* (New York: Routledge, 1995); Eric Santner, *Stranded Objects: Mourning, Memory, and Film in Postwar Germany* (Ithaca: Cornell University Press, 1993).

[27] The citations are taken from, respectively, Michele Zackheim, *Violette's Embrace* (New York: Riverhead, 1996), 1–2; Lipton, *Alias Olympia,* 115, 135; Anne Delbée, *Une Femme* (Paris: Presses de la Renaissance, 1982), 15.

Meurent, we are already well acquainted with. Although each of the three biographies takes a different woman as its subject, we can read them together as part of an overarching project less concerned with specific women's lives than with the problematic writing of these lives. Since the 1970s feminism has been not only claiming biographies of its own but also reclaiming biography after an earlier stage when graphing a woman's life would have inadmissibly rehearsed a tradition of patronizing women's works by conflating them with their days. At stake is a generic appropriation which has three vital characteristics.

First, each biographer has as mission (and I use the word advisedly) to retrieve a lost woman's life. This intent produces a particular kind of life story that I think of as "salvation narrative" or "resurrection biography." In many if not most cases the hope is to recover illustrious foremothers who might be shown to have mimed the success stories of their better-known male counterparts, or to have dared to carve out transgressive models that might now be appropriated to tell new stories. Patriarchal mimics and transgressive inventors alike stand in as female role models. Yet the various lives of these precursors were marked not always by success and renown—however relative these may have been—but also by obscurity and anonymity. We note among my examples of rescued lives those of a writer and a sculptor, but also that of an artist's model who is an artist manqué. We slide easily from here into the non-illustrious cases: biographies of unexceptional women, foremothers nonetheless. In fact the biography of ordinary women constitutes a new subgenre aiming to give anonymity a respectable if not always a proper name. We recall the pseudonymous subject of Susan Cheever's *A Woman's Life: The Story of an Ordinary American and Her Extraordinary Generation*, written in place of her originally planned "biography of a prominent woman."[28]

The aim of salvation biographers might be summarized as the attempt to rescue a woman from the night of time and oblivion. It is not by chance that Delbée in her preface tellingly signs off, "Angers,

---

[28] Cheever, *A Woman's Life*, 8–9. Biographies of anonymous women are an emblematic subset of the New Historical project, launched by the Annales school in France, which focuses on the everyday and the ordinary.

1982, *Night.*"[29] But the salvation biographer strives not only to retrieve a woman but also—and here I move on to the second characteristic of the genre—to represent the quest that led to her. This means that she is telling a double story, though the doubling may become evident either by a single paratextual move (as in a preface or an afterword), intermittently, or in a more sustained manner.

The third characteristic of the genre is in fact a refinement of the second. It follows from the dual nature of the project that the biographer is herself at the very least implicated in the biography; in more extreme instances she may be more tangibly and even clumsily present every step of the way. This is not to deny that every biographer has an imaginative and emotional identification with his or her subject, but simply to say that this identification is not only acknowledged but also intensified—and often foregrounded—in women's salvation biographies. Between biographies that veer toward the autobiographical in the course of the telling and autobiographies that use biography as a screen, there is an entire spectrum of narrative that I have been referring to as "bio-autography": the conjoined story of one's own life and the life of another. To the examples of a biographer's fusing with her biographee that I have already offered, I would add a more elaborated analysis of the French series of biographies published under the rubric "Elle était une fois": a gender play on the opening line of the fairy tale in French, "Il était une fois," and which I translate as "Once upon her time." Since this series will serve as focal point for a number of the pages that follow, some background will be useful before continuing. "Elle était une fois" is a series of twenty-two biographies published between 1987 and 1993 by the publisher Robert Laffont under the direction of the novelist and biographer Marie-Josèphe Guers. Each of these biographies of women "of old," as the series blurb puts it, is written by a contemporary female celebrity. The collection was inaugurated in 1987 by Françoise Sagan's *Sarah Bernhardt: Le Rire incassable,* but the biographers who succeeded Sagan, though all well-known public figures, are not necessarily known as literary personages. Among the authors, politicians, and media personalities who have published in this series are,

---

[29]   Delbée, *Une Femme,* 15.

in addition to Sagan, Françoise Giroud, Catherine Clément, France Huser, Micheline Boudet, Benoîte Groult, Laurence Jyl—and Huguette Bouchardeau, to whom we shall return in some detail in chapters 3 and 4.

This is a collection of books about which a lot can be told by the cover. The back cover of most books in the series juxtaposes copy about biographer and biographee, giving us a twinned bio, and sometimes twin (visual) portraits as well. On most of the covers the series description is reprinted as well, a sort of mini-manifesto or mission statement that is pithy enough to merit quoting in its entirety:

> This is a collection of encounters between a woman of today and a woman of the days of old. One is a writer; the other a singer, a painter, a courtesan, a model, a composer, or an actress. It is a collection of mirror biographies, where two women reflect each other, echo each other, respond to each other. And so there is established between them, across the ages, an extraordinary exchange which renews the laws of the genre and makes of these books something much better than biographies: surprising dialogues between women.[30]

The project articulated here—life writing as an exchange that both modernizes the laws of biography and makes for books superior to biographies that in fact transcend the very category of biography—presents a curiously contradictory claim. That is, the books in this collection both work within the law and are above the law—the law being that of the genre traditionally defined as "the lives of great men," which is to say, the Father's law. The marketing formulation evokes at once models of judicial reform and of infraction. As the series blurb speaks of reforming and transcending the laws of the genre in a single breath, it suggests that the opposition may no longer

---

[30] "C'est une collection de rencontres entre une femme d'aujourd'hui et une femme du temps jadis. L'une écrit, l'autre chante, peint, courtise, pose, compose ou joue. C'est une collection de biographies-miroirs, où deux femmes se reflètent, se font écho, se répondent. Ainsi s'instaure entre elles, par-delà les époques, un échange insolite qui renouvelle les lois du genre et fait de ces livres beaucoup mieux que des biographies: de surprenants dialogues de femmes."

work, and that the old laws have become so inconsistent or dim and hard to read as to be nonfunctional and unrecognizable today.

The split definition of the series project corresponds to a practical dichotomy within the series. Some of the books are dialogues, if only in a purely formal sense (and so apparently comply with the promise of innovating the genre). Sagan's biography of Sarah Bernhardt, for example, is written as an exchange of letters between the writer and the actress, in which a kind of contract is tendered early on by the biographer and duly accepted by the subject: "My dear friend, I accept," replies Bernhardt to Sagan's proposal to collaborate.[31] Nathalie de Saint Phalle writes *Jane Fillion ou la belle d'un seigneur* as exchange as well, though the conversation is more plausible. Her biography of Fillion, who was the model for Albert Cohen's Ariane, imbricates Fillion's life with the story of the literal crossing of their paths.[32]

But many of the biographies in this collection that seeks innovation through author-subject reflexivity mirror only their authors' sentimentality; they are otherwise rather conventional in their approach to the genre, and could be considered above it only because their choice of subject contravenes the canonical sense of biography as the public lives of great men. The series runs from narratives of the lives of already well-known and sometimes even well-biographed women, among them Anaïs Nin, George Sand, and la comtesse de Ségur, to biographies of some very creative women whose talents were never sufficiently acclaimed, like Alma Mahler and Jenny Marx, to lives of women who are sought and celebrated by their biographers primarily for their ability to inspire great men: Jane Fillion and Marie de St.-Exupéry, presented as lover and mother, respectively. Are we so very far from the muse?

I cite these inconsistencies and contradictions not to take issue with the collection per se but rather because the logical contradictions and inconsistencies in its presentation open some chinks through which to view the fundamental problems of women's biography in the form of salvation project. In particular, the legal contradiction announced

---

[31] Françoise Sagan, *Sarah Bernhardt: Le Rire incassable* (Paris: Laffont, 1987), 11.
[32] Nathalie de Saint Phalle, *Jane Fillion ou la belle d'un seigneur* (Paris: Laffont, 1988).

by the series' description (reform or infraction of the Father's law?) suggests not only the uncertain status of women's life stories within the biographical genre, but also the shifting discursive position from which such stories are to be recounted. Speaking *of* but also *as* what has been excluded from the language of exclusion I am also *in*, how can I renew the law without breaking it? And wouldn't breaking the law in this case mean fracturing linguistic and/or narrative forms? Yet the biographies of "Elle était une fois" are less iconoclastic than reflective: indicative of the fundamental difficulties of a salvation project that can't quite decide what to save, how to go about saving, or even whether salvation is feasible.

By way of its very title, "Elle était une fois" leads us into the thick of a very thorny enterprise. A collection that calls itself "Elle était une fois" clearly aims to put the heroine back into the text by way of inserting her into the formulaic fairy-tale opening. The substitution of "elle" for "il" plays on the impersonal neuter expression, reminding us once again that the neuter in language is never gender neutral, as grammar would have it, but is culturally gendered male. In other words—those of the formula I play with in my rough translation— "Once upon a time" is not just any old time but *his* time, man's time. There has not been enough time in legend for her, for woman. It is time to open the tale to, and by, her.

Correlatively, however—if perhaps unwittingly—the new formula relegates the lives of illustrious women to legend, puts them under the banner of fairy tale. The feminine greatness sought, and perhaps even the possibility of recovering it, are cast in the flickering light of illusion.

Logically, of course, we recognize that the gender switch denaturalizes the ritual opening, reminds us that men's biographies too are imaginary tales: by restoring the notion of male gender to the neuter impersonal "il," we restore the possibility of meaning to the ritualized opening of fairy tales. If "he" once was where once "there" was (if *il était une fois*), then the genre we know as the lives of men might well be a fairy tale too. But I am of course playing devil's advocate here. If instead of fastidiously bending language, I listen to its effects, then I know empirically (my ear tells me) that the force and context of the unexpected "elle était une fois" makes for a statement sharply focused on women and biography: a statement that vacillates between sheer optimism and hardheaded pessimism, determination and cynicism, possibility and impossibility.

Here is the point at which Guers's project meets my own, at the intersection of feminism and biography, in this space of sometimes naïve hope emblematized by the fairy tale retold in the feminine. Since the 1970s, feminism has sought not only to recuperate biographies of its own (to retrieve buried lives and to reinvent biographical models and plots) but also, and in vital association with this project, to revalidate biography as a genre: to rehabilitate it in the public eye. On the heels of the death of the author comes the birth of (often literary) women's biography. But it is clear that the newfound legitimacy of such biography is not unqualified. We might summarize its problematic status by paraphrasing the question asked by Michelle Perrot about the history of women in the 1980s: Is women's biography possible?[33]

I have in mind less the material problem of what can be learned about specific women's lives than the problematic writing of these lives—problematic not only on the metaphysical grounds so well surveyed by Carolyn Heilbrun and Shoshana Felman, among others (the inaccessibility of plots on which to hang our stories, and of a language in which to begin to think them),[34] but also on the metapsychical grounds I earlier raised. That is, what story shall be written in the place of undocumented lives, and what shall be its modes of reconstruction? And when identification and engagement with biographical subjects whose stories are inaudible or illegible replace ostensibly objective discursive modes sanctioned by time and tradition, how do biographers avoid speaking for their missing subjects in their eagerness to save their stories? The contemporary feminist biographer's tendency to identify intimately with her subject, to retrace origins to her, to think back through her, is, we have seen, often conceived in terms of relation.[35]

---

[33] Michelle Perrot, ed., *Une Histoire des femmes est-elle possible?* (Paris: Rivage, 1984).

[34] See especially Heilbrun, *Writing a Woman's Life,* and Felman, *What Does a Woman Want?*

[35] Again, the biographer's identification with the biographee is a defining characteristic of feminist biography but is not limited to it. Autobiography has always stamped other literary genres. According to a Renaissance aphorism (ascribed to Cosimo de' Medici), "Every painter paints himself." For Paul Valéry, "there is no

Salvation biographies construct nurturing or, alternatively, competitive relationships between biographer and biographee. They create alter egos. Carol Ascher compares the writing of her life of Simone de Beauvoir to "the attitude one takes when hovering over the sick."[36] Sara Ruddick writes that Virginia Woolf "changed [her] life" and explains, "Before my encounter with Woolf, I was fragmented and anxious."[37] Leah Blatt Glasser relates, "I travel into the lives of other women and...find what I need to make my words whole."[38] The transferential relationship implied by these bio-autographical cases suggests a similarity to psychoanalytic therapy. Bell Gale Chevigny has suggested that women writing biographies of women often act out and even rewrite their relationships to their own mothers in the process, so that the foremother taken as subject is always a shadow of the mother: "My point is that when we are the writing daughters of mothers who did not write or otherwise articulate our aspirations for autonomy, we will probably be tempted in writing to create our own maternal, mirroring sanctions and precedents."[39] Might the writing process instead become the maternalizing relationship? The mother in the text could well turn out to be the text as mother: a mother generated by textual relations with the author-daughter.

Writing against a certain tide—we might call it a blood-tide—that crested in the 1980s, Christine Planté, like Linda Nochlin before her,

---

theory that is not a carefully prepared fragment of an autobiography" (*Œuvres*, ed. Jean Hytier, vol. 1 [Paris: Gallimard (Pléiade), 1987], 1320). Nietzsche calls any great philosophy "a confession on the part of its author and a kind of involuntary and unconscious memoir" (*Beyond Good and Evil*, trans. R. J. Hollingdale [Harmondsworth: Penguin, 1973], 19). And Borges writes: "Through the years, [a man] peoples a space with images of provinces, kingdoms, mountains, bays, ships, islands, fishes, rooms, tools, stars, horses, and people. Shortly before his death, he discovers that the patient labyrinth of lines traces the image of his face" (epilogue, in *Dreamtigers* [Austin: University of Texas Press, 1964], 93). The biographer Richard Holmes speaks of biography as a "haunting" that could lead to madness if an analytic distance is not imposed between biographer and subject (*Footsteps*, 66).
[36] Carol Ascher, "On 'Clearing the Air': My Letter to Simone de Beauvoir," in *Between Women: Biographers, Novelists, Critics, Teachers, and Artists Write about Their Work on Women*, ed. Carol Ascher, Louise DeSalvo, and Sara Ruddick (Boston: Beacon Press, 1984), 90.
[37] Sara Ruddick, "New Combinations: Learning from Virginia Woolf," ibid., 137.
[38] Leah Blatt Glasser, "'She Is the One You Call Sister': Discovering Mary Wilkins Freeman," ibid., 216.
[39] Bell Gale Chevigny, "Daughters Writing: Towards a Theory of Women's Biography," ibid., 372.

seeks to bring sociopolitical analysis to the sometimes mystifying metaphorics of cultural mothers. Recontextualizing Virginia Woolf's reflections about Shakespeare's sister, she reminds us that Balzac's sister was not a great writer either. For Planté, however, it is much more useful to explore the fundamental conditions that formed her as she was than to indulge in a tautological lament about her unrealized greatness.[40] Christa Wolf similarly questions what we might think of as the omnipotent foremother, in the form of goddess myths:

> It is worth thinking about, why women today feel they must derive part of their self-esteem and a justification of their claims from the fact that civilization begins with the worship of women. How does it help us to know that the ancient Greeks gradually replace "mother right" with "father right"? ... Doesn't this harking back to an irretrievable ancient past reveal more clearly than anything else the desperate plight in which women see themselves today?[41]

Wolf is here probing the myth that has been called, in an eponymous essay collection, *The Lost Tradition: Mothers and Daughters in Literature*.[42] The connections between the feminist biographical project and the mission statement articulated by the introduction ("The Lost Mother") to *The Lost Tradition* are manifest: "tracking our roots back to ancient mothers whose origins are the earth itself but whose traces are as dust."[43]

The mother-foremother figure reasserts itself in Phyllis Rose's introduction to *The Norton Book of Women's Lives*. Rose quite rightly suggests that Virginia Woolf's aphorism "A woman writing thinks back through her mothers" could serve as "the motto for the whole postmodern moment in the literature of women's lives," and she goes

---

[40]   Christine Planté, *La Petite Sœur de Balzac* (Paris: Seuil, 1984). The passing references are to Virginia Woolf, *A Room of One's Own* (London: Harcourt Brace Jovanovich, 1929), and Linda Nochlin, "Why Have There Been No Great Woman Artists?" in *Women, Art, Power, and Other Essays* (London: Thames & Hudson, 1991), chap. 7.

[41]   Christa Wolf, *Cassandra*, trans. Jan von Heurck (London: Virago, 1984), 195.

[42]   Cathy Davidson and E. M. Broner, *The Lost Tradition: Mothers and Daughters in Literature* (New York: Frederick Ungar, 1980).

[43]   Ibid., 2.

on to refer to Simone de Beauvoir, Mary McCarthy, Virginia Woolf, and Anaïs Nin as "the mothers of the literature of women's lives."[44]

As I reread Woolf through Phyllis Rose, I am struck by the realization that Woolf's originally metaphoric use of mothers to express the idea of feminine precursors (what would be covered by the term "foremothers" today) is no longer metaphoric. That is, as Woolf has been adopted as the mother of us all, her founding metaphor has become perfectly transparent, which is to say, wraithlike, or dead. Current cultural discourses (feminist, literary, scholarly) slide us unthinkingly from the concept of mothers to foremothers. Annie Ernaux closes the memoir of her mother, *Une Femme*, with the passing statement, left without explanation: "She died eight days before Simone de Beauvoir."[45] It is as if a double timeline and a superimposed history were always implied. The implication, as Freud famously asserted, is that if the father is uncertain, the mother is known;[46] the lives of our foremothers are (or could be) as accessible as the mother's life. But perhaps this unexamined slippage, along with the assumptions that support it, need to be thought out. Do we in fact have better access to the mother's life than to that of a foremother whose story is lost in the night of time? In other words—to refine my earlier question—is a biography of the mother (conceived in the literal as well as figurative sense) possible?

When a woman becomes biographer of her mother, she faces the specter of a foremother. When a woman becomes biographer of a foremother, her mother's ghost is never far away—but this mother is not necessarily a model, as Lipton makes clear and Bouchardeau will later confirm. Tossed from Scylla to Charybdis and from Charybdis back to Scylla, the woman biographer navigates lost time and ambivalent identifications with no sign of a safe course out.

The double bind may be usefully explored with the words of U.S. Supreme Court Justice Ruth Bader Ginsburg. Upon accepting her

[44] Phyllis Rose, ed., *The Norton Book of Women's Lives* (New York: Norton, 1993), 23–24. Rose slightly misquotes Woolf, whose exact words (about writing women) are "For we think back through our mothers if we are women." Woolf, *A Room of One's Own*, 79.

[45] Annie Ernaux, *Une Femme* (Paris: Gallimard, 1987), 105.

[46] Sigmund Freud, "Family Romances," in *The Standard Edition of the Complete Psychological Works of Sigmund Freud*, vol. 9, ed. James Strachey et al. (London: Hogarth Press, 1959), 235–41.

appointment to the Court, Ginsburg invoked her mother in order to represent her own aspirations: "I pray that I may be all that she would have been had she lived in an age when women could aspire and achieve."[47] I want to zero in on Ginsburg's recourse to the conditional in her framing of these poignant and troubling words. While this conditional clearly marks a realization, a cogito—that is, the recognition of socioeconomic conditions that make it difficult to use a simple indicative to speak of the mother—it also bears the mark of a certain (perhaps inevitable) shame that accompanies the expected expression of humility. For the conditional is the marker not only of hypothesis but also of the unreal, of dreams, and even of phantasms. According to Maurice Grevisse, the conditional can indicate "the imagination somehow transporting events into the realm of fiction," and he notes the existence, "in particular, of a 'pre-ludic' conditional, used by children in proposing imaginary play scenarios."[48]

Similarly, Ginsburg situates herself in the imaginary place where her mother was not able to be: that is, in a space where her mother was missing; she identifies herself with an original absence. She cannot aspire to be what her mother *was*—historical conditions prevent this—but rather what her mother *would have been*; we are plunged into hypothesis, unreality, play, the fairy tale. If history and culture make it impossible to aspire to what she was, they make it illusory to aspire to what she might have been. "I pray that I may be all that she would have been." Can we not hear in Ginsburg's "all that she would have been" an echo of the series title "Elle était une fois"—that is, the dream of a fairy-tale return to a place and time that never were? A wish to be "all that she would have been" could be told in other words as "once upon her time." At the core of the matter is a temporal problem. Impossible to say what she was; impossible to say that *she was* ("elle était"); one can only return to what was, *once upon her time* ("[ce qu']elle était une fois"), which is tantamount to saying *what she would have been*. We cannot return to her in her time but only to a phantasmatic "once upon her time."

---

[47]   Ruth Bader Ginsburg cited by Joan Biskopik in "High Court's Justice with a Cause," *Washington Post,* April 17, 1995.
[48]   Maurice Grevisse, *Le Bon Usage* (Gembloux, Belgium: Duculot, 1975), 734–35.

Speaking generally with the help of Ginsburg's and Bouchardeau's wise words, we might think of salvation biography as imaginary biography inseparable from a sense of the mother's story as missing. Wanting precursors, the mother's biography wants as well. A perception of the mother's story as incomplete or deficient creates the need to resurrect a foremother who might redeem the maternal lack. But the sought-after foremother can only be reconstructed as the foreshadow of the mother's lack. The daughter's quest then resembles a neoromantic quest for an imaginary object ("[la recherche d']un bien inconnu"), as Chateaubriand famously phrased it.[49] So in fact each of the two recovery missions mirrors the doom of the other. "Elle était une fois"—indeed, a collection of mirror biographies.

Thinking back through the foremother biographies we have considered, I suspect that the silent slide to the foremother—what I earlier described as a "dead metaphor"—is an elision of the mother, or, in crueler terms, a ritual murder. So a cycle of mourning is set. If, as Mark Rothko's biographer James Breslin has suggested, every biographer's identification with the subject represents a kind of mourning, then perhaps contemporary feminist biography can be understood generically as a mourning for woman's place in culture.[50] Since such mourning knows no beginning and no end (for any given biographer there is no time before the loss, and it can never be resolved), we could think of it as a form of melancholia, the name Freud originally gave to chronic mourning and later generalized as the identification with a lost object that founds all of the work of grieving.

---

[49] See François-René de Chateaubriand, *René*, in *Atala-René*, ed. Gérard Gengembre (Paris: Pocket, 1996), 111.

[50] I am extending to a broader context Rachel Blau duPlessis's analysis of a component of her personal voice: "a mourning for the place of the female in culture" (*The Pink Guitar* [New York: Vintage, 1990], vii). On biography's more general similarities to mourning, see James E. B. Breslin, "Terminating Mark Rothko: Biography Is Mourning in Reverse," *New York Times Book Review*, July 24, 1994, 19–20, and Breslin's afterword to his *Mark Rothko: A Biography* (Chicago: University of Chicago Press, 1993), 545–58. It is worth thinking about the extent to which contemporary women's writing about mothers is dominated by the experience of maternal death and so itself constitutes a form of mourning. Many of the canonical works in the genre—Simone de Beauvoir's *Une Mort très douce* and Annie Ernaux's *Une Femme* are prime examples—burgeon into memoir from a mother's death, while others—notable examples are Marie Cardinal's *Les Mots pour le dire* and Nathalie Sarraute's *Enfance*—are texts of mourning elicited not by literal death but by perceived maternal absence or inadequacy.

For Judith Butler rethinking Freud, "identifications substitute for object relations, and identifications are the consequence of loss, [so] gender identification is a kind of melancholia."[51] Though Butler is directing her words to a discussion of heterosexual and homosexual object choice, it is helpful to borrow them for their pertinence to our consideration of women's identification with idealized (and so impossible) maternal figures: a loss that preserves the loved object, internalized, and also the prohibition on it (because of cultural devaluation in this case). To pose alternatives to the impossibly anguished genre of idealized or imaginary biography—that is, to write women's biography otherwise—may require from the start a sacrifice of the dream of transparency in order to confront the story of a woman's life as always already lost, and forever irretrievable within conventional frameworks.

Cat's Cradle

August 1998: "To pull some threads loosely together I'd like to make a net—much more a collection of holes tied together than a sack to catch fish. In it I will put some metaphors: the space of dreaming, the breach of leaving, the gap in time...death's form in the mirror. So the writing of women's lives ends with a sack of holes. This is the beginning. The rest—the string—is writing."

The last paragraph reproduces the words I used to close an early conference version of this chapter. Julian Barnes provided the closing analogy, but a listener's question complicated his binarism for me: made me see that biography, like a net, is not simply *either* a bunch of holes *or* a container. It is also a safety net used by performers whose work puts them constantly at risk. Biography, literally a *lifeline,* is that safety net we draw between our lives and the perils of exposure to cut a free fall to self.

The text of this chapter has stretched and ripped and re-formed since then, aided by comments and reading suggestions. One listener

---

[51] See Judith Butler, *Gender Trouble: Feminism and the Subversion of Identity* (New York: Routledge, 1999), 80. Butler is looking back at Freud's "Mourning and Melancholia" and *The Ego and the Id.*

signaled the need for a connecting thread; another turned me toward Shoshana Felman's postulation of a "bond of reading" linking women's missing stories.[52] Rereading and revising, I have thought about the irony of a missing thread in this text that had generated so many threads and strands and strings of metaphor. Spools and cords and skeins proliferated—evidently enough rope to hang myself with—but not a single continuous filament to follow through the labyrinth. And I thought that perhaps here, without my realizing it, my unconscious *had* followed a thread, and that the constant twists and turns and loose ends were its very defining features. It was a lifeline, an Ariadne's thread, a spider's web, a fisherman's net, a high wire: a string kaleidoscope whose pattern was constantly being unraveled and redesigned.

A game I remember from childhood, cat's cradle, formalizes such a play of metamorphoses. It involves two or more players who alternately take from each other's fingers a string design that is in the process modified constantly. It is a kind of weaving and unweaving rewoven with each alternation. It emphasizes neither the web nor the spider artist but instead a collaborative process of expression. If Barthes's "hyphology" or theory of the web featured a practice of *rereading*, and Miller's "arachnology" one of *overreading*, cat's cradle may be characterized by a practice of *interreading*. As such it emblematizes the hybrid life writing of bio-autography.

When I first connected string play and lifelines, I indulged in recollections: names and patterns, such as "cradle," "manger," "hourglass"—and a piece of string whose ends I knotted together and used to prod the memory in my fingertips. But I wanted to know more. I turned to the *OED*, where I found the following representative quotation: "1823 Lamb Weaving those ingenious parentheses called cat-cradles."

Seeking an attribution of significance to the game, I looked back to the most obvious source for one who came of age in the 1970s:

---

[52] Felman argues: "*As women*...we have a story that by definition cannot be self-present to us, a story that, in other words, is not a story, but *must become* a story. And it cannot *become* a story except through the *bond of reading*, that is, through the *story of the Other* (the story read by other women, the story of other women, the story of women told by others)." Felman, *What Does a Woman Want?* 14.

Kurt Vonnegut's *Cat's Cradle*. A rereading was disappointing. The novel is negatively disposed toward its eponymous string figure, which is centrally exploited to represent "the sticky nets of human futility hung up on a moonless night to dry," or, more concisely, "the meaninglessness of it all."[53] For Vonnegut, but also for the *OED*, cat's cradle is a metaphor embracing qualities ranging from caprice and indecision to insignificance and even absurdity.

I spent some time with old manuals of children's games. I learned from Kathleen Haddon that cat's cradles are found from "the arctic north... to the coral islands of the Pacific" and are highly informative for the anthropologists who collect them.[54] Iris Vinton traced string figures back to the Stone Age. Theories about their origins differ tremendously, and range from aboriginal games to old Scottish cribs made with brass knobs for weaving a net of strings to keep babies safe from leaping cats, to networks of nautical rope constructed for the purpose of "catting" or storing the ship's anchor. Most intriguing were the fanciful references and strange anecdotes of the manuals' annotations: "ingenious parentheses" that could be used to frame as much as to marginalize.[55]

---

[53] Kurt Vonnegut, *Cat's Cradle* (New York: Delacorte, 1963), 137, 140.
[54] Mrs. O. H. T. Rishbeth (Kathleen Haddon), it turns out, was not the home-bound woman I must admit I originally supposed her to be by the title of her book, *String Games for Beginners* (1934; rpt. Cambridge: W. Heffer & Sons, 1958), and its early prose: "There is the obvious tying up of parcels, and also the hardly less obvious rigging of a boat—for rope is but glorified string. Some of you may remember the old-fashioned string bags which our grandmothers used, and almost everybody has seen a fish-net....Wherever there are sailors there are knots, and any Boy Scout or Girl Guide will know some of these." Just as I was locking Mrs. Rishbeth into conventional domesticity, there was an abrupt twist in her narrative: "I once arrived alone at a village up the Fly river in Papua where no white woman had been before, and as I did not know the language I wondered at first what to do. Then, remembering my string, I sat down on the ground and began to make some cat's cradles" (5–6). Kathleen Haddon (1888–1961), it turns out, was a zoologist by training, although Cambridge did not formally bestow her 1911 degree until women were granted the privilege of receiving degrees in 1948. She held an academic post, wrote research papers and books, and accompanied her father, the noted anthropologist Alfred Haddon, when he did field research in the Torres Straits and Papua, serving as assistant and photographer. See Henry Rishbeth, "Kathleen Haddon," in *Bulletin of the International String Figure Association* 6 (1999): 1–16.
[55] Iris Vinton, *The Folkways Omnibus of Children's Games* (Harrisburg, Pa.: Stackpole Books, 1970), 201; subsequent references are provided in the text. See also the *Bulletin of String Figures Association* (1978–93), and the *Bulletin of the International String Figure Association* (1994—).

Let me illustrate. Vinton describes the most basic cat's cradle figure, the cradle transformed into a manger and back again by a mere shift of the hands. And then she offers an odd detail: "On the island of Crete in the old days, just such a cradle, big and made of stout rope, was used to capture and entrap a bull" (203). Although there is iconographic evidence for the trapping of bulls in huge rope snares, the thought of such an animal charging through a cat's cradle—like the more tired image of a bull in a china shop—is fantastic, trails into a network of associations.

In the days when bulls were caught in cat's cradles on the island of Crete, a woman loved a man who slew a bull-man reigning in a maze built by a gifted artificer. She led her lover to safety with a string given her by the architect. Her mother's passion for a bull, lured to her as she lay hidden in heifer skins sewn seductively by the future maze builder, had engendered the slain monster. Later the same artist, architect of the mother's and daughter's desire and punisher of both, won a contest that required threading a string through a conch shell. He attached it to a tiny ant, who wove its way through the shell. Is there a way to weave similarly through this story that spirals through successive generations—a way to tie Ariadne's thread to her mother's story through the labyrinth and the Minotaur, through the stitched cowhides and the bull from the sea, through the ropes of the ancient Cretan bull snares? I want to know more about Pasiphaë than is told by the story of Minos punished by a grotesque cuckoldry for neglecting to sacrifice a bull to Poseidon. Why did the queen contract a passion for a bull? Did Minos not satisfy her? What did Pasiphaë feel while she waited for the bull in her bovine disguise? What did she think when she saw her monstrous progeny? My questions continue. But Pasiphaë's story can't be told. It is literally full of holes, as we realize when we muse on the punctilios of the bull-heifer-woman coupling, the technical inconceivability of aligning all the holes in such a tangled web of deception.[56]

Pasiphaë's story and Ariadne's as well are characterized by lack. Ironically they are offered to fill a blank, given *in lieu of* another

[56] For a thorough account of the legend, see Sarah P. Morris, *Daidalos and the Origins of Greek Art* (Princeton: Princeton University Press, 1992). For a poet's musing on the place of women in this legend and others, see Diane Fahey, *Metamorphoses* (Sydney: Dangaroo Press, 1988).

absent story, in Racine's version of the other daughter's spiral. When urged to name her despair, Phèdre responds by indirection, explaining the withholding of her narrative by oblique references to her mother's and her sister's stories.[57] But both tell of displacement, interruption, and loss: in Pasiphaë's case the deviations of love, and in Ariadne's a lover's abandonment. One might in fact say, reading Racine with Felman and thinking back through Lipton, that Phèdre tells her own story as missing, as knowable only through and as the juxtaposed gaps in the mother's and sister's story. The bull snare, unknotted into Ariadne's thread, is refigured as the penultimate tangle of reins in which the object of Phèdre's incestuous passion is caught and broken and lost.

Imagine a cat's cradle strung out in time, its threads twisting future and past in an ever-shifting fabrication of presence. At a given moment it might resemble an ant in a shell, winding slender threads through spirals of time connecting labyrinthine narratives of loss. Or it might look something like Ruth Bader Ginsburg's earlier cited double vision of her mother as a once and future self. Alternatively, it might entangle disparate storylines in time. Imagine, on the one hand, the daughters: Ruth with Eunice, Ariadne, and Phèdre; on the other, the mothers: Mrs. Bader with Trudy and Pasiphaë. Between the hands, as the lines start to cross and to interweave, there is a coiled line, a maze, a welter of stitched cowhides. A cow hides a woman, a woman in cow's clothing, a sack of a woman bundled in *schmatas:* the tissue of desire, biography's text, become a shriveled heap of rags. With such frayed bits of string and a knot we would net a school of fish or snare a bull, rescue love or unkill life. In such a cradle, spun from the loose ends of our mothers' shrouds, we rock our dreams to sleep.

---

[57] "Your fatal hatred Venus! Oh, your wrath!/Into what aberrations did Love cast/My mother!" ["O haine de Vénus! O fatale colère!/Dans quels égarements l'amour jeta ma mere!"] (Racine, *Phèdre,* trans. Margaret Rawlings [New York: Dutton, 1962]; Racine, *Phèdre,* ed. Boris Donné [Paris: GF, 2000], 1.3.249–50). "Ariadne, my sister, by what Love/Were you wounded and left to die alone/Upon that shore!" ["Ariane, ma sœur! de quel amour blessée/Vous mourûtes aux bords où vous fûtes laissée?"] (ibid. 1.3.253–54).

Unwrapping the Mummy

In Search of Kuchuk Hanem

As Michel Foucault has observed, the nineteenth century was "haunted by the theme of the hermaphrodite."[1] Such a haunting must be understood above all as the expression of a certain ambivalence, for if the century was medically and scientifically dedicated to the binary attribution of sex, it was also, simultaneously, oneirically and artistically compelled to perform a more whimsical dance on the divide.

My focus here, unlike Foucault's, is not on the figure of the hermaphrodite per se but rather on the ulterior dynamic of ambivalence and indecision about sexuality and gender that was responsible for making the hermaphrodite such a powerful figure in the nineteenth-century imaginary. Such an ambivalence that juxtaposes a horror of and a flirtation with sexual difference manifests itself, beyond its graphic representation in the hermaphrodite, in myriad figures including the hysteric, the dandy, and the fetishist.[2]

In what follows, my theoretical subject is an indecision, an uncertainty, an ambivalence about sexual difference; my theme the

[1] Michel Foucault, intro. to *Herculine Barbin: Being the Recently Discovered Memoirs of a Nineteenth-Century French Hermaphrodite*, trans. Richard McDougall (New York: Pantheon, 1980), xvii.
[2] On the hysteric, the dandy, and the fetishist as examples of a cultural working-through of sexual difference, see, respectively, Janet Beizer, *Ventriloquized Bodies: Narratives of Hysteria in Nineteenth-Century France* (Ithaca: Cornell University Press, 1994); Jessica R. Feldman, *Gender on the Divide: The Dandy in Modernist Literature* (Ithaca: Cornell University Press, 1993); Emily Apter, *Feminizing the Fetish* (Ithaca: Cornell University Press, 1991).

fetish, as it plays itself out in corresponding texts by Gustave Flaubert and Louise Colet; and my ulterior purpose an allegorized reflection on loss and recovery as motor forces of contemporary women's biography. It may be useful first, however, to rehearse the classical Freudian concept of fetishism and to note its later, more abstract reformulation.[3]

For Freud, fetishism is a perversion resulting from the castration complex: responding, that is, to the phantasy of castration produced, from childhood on, in explanation of anatomical difference between the sexes (understood in terms of the presence or absence of a penis).[4] More specifically, the fetish is a substitute that preserves, even as it confirms, a particular loss: the loss of belief in the mother's phallus. It is worth emphasizing Freud's insistence, throughout the essay, on the indecision, contradiction, and compromise involved in the structure of fetish formation: the child "retains this belief [in the woman having a phallus] but he also gives it up" (216). Putting aside the thematic associations of the fetish with shoes, feet, fur, and of course the phallus, we can trace its appearance in Freud's text as a psychic "oscillat[ion] between two assumptions" and as a "vehicle both of denying and of asseverating"—in other words, as a structure of thought mixing disavowal and recognition (218).

Octave Mannoni later revised the anatomical thematics of psychoanalytic fetishism while retaining its logic, in this way accentuating the deep structure of Freud's thinking. For Mannoni, the double-bind structure of fetishistic thinking is summarized by the formula "I know, but still..." ["Je sais bien, mais quand meme..."]—with the fetish acting out, as it were, the "still."[5]

As I move on to Flaubert and Colet, I pursue a rhetoric of presence and absence, appearance and disappearance, discovery and loss, in which each term in every binary couple refuses the other

---

[3] My focus here is on psychoanalytic fetishism. There are, of course, other studies of fetishism, notably Karl Marx's. For a brief history of fetishism, see Apter, *Feminizing the Fetish,* chap. 1, and the essays in Emily Apter and William Pietz, eds., *Fetishism as Cultural Discourse* (Ithaca: Cornell University Press, 1993).
[4] See in particular Freud's 1927 essay "Fetishism," in *Sexuality and the Psychology of Love,* ed. Philip Rieff (New York: Collier Books, 1963), 214–19; subsequent references are provided in the text.
[5] Octave Mannoni, "Je sais bien, mais quand même...," in *Clefs pour l'imaginaire ou l'autre scène* (Paris: Seuil, 1969), 9–33.

it nonetheless admits. My immediate context is the search for the elusive courtesan Kuchuk Hanem, but my larger intent is to begin to explore, through the specific frame of this story, that broader quest for the lost narratives of women's lives that has been the focal point of much recent feminist history and biography. As I speculate on the gendering of the fetish and of fetishistic thinking, I mean also to open some questions about the potentially fetishistic logic of certain contemporary forays into a feminist past—forays that interest me all the more because I am necessarily implicated in such quests by my own work on women's biography. As we shall see, if the fetish by its very nature poses questions about cultural perceptions and representations of sex and gender, then contemporary gender theory, as it asks out loud who is speaking, who is looking, and whose gaze is perceiving or assigning gender, productively multiplies such puzzles for us.

Kuchuk Hanem, already "a very famous courtesan" when Flaubert wrote home about her from the Orient in 1850, has been handed down to posterity as "Flaubert's courtesan" with all the attendant accoutrements of infamy and legend.[6] Her name, emblematic of the seductions of the Orient for nineteenth-century travelers and their audiences, has more recently been used to stand for the violation of women's voices and bodies by patriarchal culture and the imperialist silencing of the East by its Western colonizers.[7] By one of those increasingly familiar paradoxes, as she is taken to embody a protest

---

[6]   Gustave Flaubert, *Correspondance*, ed. Jean Bruneau, 6 vols. (Paris: Gallimard, 1973–2007), 1:605. The quotation is from a letter to Louis Bouilhet of March 13, 1850. Subsequent references to the *Correspondance* are provided in the text, cited by volume and page.

[7]   See, for example, Edward Said's comments on Flaubert's representation of Kuchuk Hanem: "Flaubert's encounter with an Egyptian courtesan produced a widely influential model of the Oriental woman.... *He* spoke for and represented her. He was foreign, comparatively wealthy, male, and these were historical facts of domination that allowed him not only to possess Kuchuk Hanem physically but to speak for her.... My argument is that Flaubert's situation of strength in relation to Kuchuk Hanem was not an isolated instance. It fairly stands for the pattern of relative strength between East and West, and the discourse about the Orient that it enabled" (*Orientalism* [New York: Vintage, 1979], 6). Maryline Lukacher has more recently spoken of the record of Flaubert's adventure with Kuchuk Hanem as "the appropriation of the Oriental woman by the Occidental imagination" ("Fictions biographiques: Flaubert et *Le Voyage en Égypte*," *Revue des sciences humaines* 263 [July–September 2001]: 187).

against the imperialism of gender or race, Kuchuk Hanem's own woman's body and voice and her own Egyptian identity are inevitably evacuated. This rather postmodern alienation from and by her own representation (what becomes a legend most, we might say) is strangely anticipated, included in the nineteenth-century descriptions of her as always displaced, not visible even when home, not quite present to herself.

Émile Auriant reports the pilgrimage of a certain Louis Pascal who, a decade after Flaubert, travels to Egypt, wends his way to Esna, and finds Kuchuk Hanem's house—but reinhabited by another courtesan.[8] Louis Bouilhet writes a poem called "Kuchiuk-Hanem, Souvenir" in 1851, but the courtesan is completely outside both Bouilhet's memory and his poem, which is based solely on Flaubert's experience as described in a letter (2:1139n). The dislocation is compounded when Flaubert reads Bouilhet's verse invoking Kuchuk—"In your Esna house, what are you doing now…,"—and corrects him: "But poor Kouchiouk is no longer in Esna, she is back in Cairo! No matter, for me, she will always be in Esna" (2:777).

When Flaubert initially meets the courtesan in Esna in 1850, she is already transplanted, having been deported upriver from Cairo in a purge of *almehs*, or dancing girls. On his return trip, when he stops for a second visit, she is absent for him in the sense that the renewed experience doesn't exactly reproduce the first, represents a falling away. She looks tired, appears to have been ill, has only a handkerchief covering her head, is not wearing her jewels. Her failure to fulfill the promise of memory is summarily transcribed by Flaubert as absence: "The house, the courtyard, the staircase in ruins, everything is there—but *she* is no longer there, above us, with her torso bare, gleaming in the sun—we hear her voice."[9]

---

[8] See Émile Auriant, *Koutchouk-Hanem, l'Almée de Flaubert* (Paris: Mercure de France, 1943), 31–32.

[9] Gustave Flaubert, *Voyage en Égypte*, ed. Pierre-Marc de Biasi (Paris: Grasset, 1991), 362; subsequent references are provided in the text. Charles Bernheimer reads this passage as indicative of an elegiac poetry of reminiscence in Flaubert in which "memory and forgetting are held together in a kind of fetishistic suspension" (*Figures of Ill Repute* [Cambridge: Harvard University Press, 1989], 138). The story of Kuchuk Hanem (and, more generally, prostitution and its narration in Flaubert) is for Bernheimer an integral component of a fundamental structure of loss which at once denies and affirms—*veils*—a knowledge of female sexuality

For Flaubert's traveling companion, Maxime Du Camp, absence gnaws at Kuchuk Hanem from the very beginning. Even the first visit is de-realized, has the quality of a visitation: "At the top of the stairs, Koutchouk-Hanem was waiting for me. I saw her as I raised my head; it was like an apparition."[10] Kuchuk seems to elude representation. Even the transliteration of her name is mobile. In the course of my research I counted no fewer than eight different spellings in my various sources, and found inconsistent renditions of her name even within a single source. It is as if her identity could not be fixed even long enough to reach the stability implied by naming and spelling.

Let me state at the outset that I won't try to find Kuchuk Hanem. I make no attempt to restore her body or to retrieve her voice. My purpose is to use Kuchuk Hanem to think with: to think about and to critique women's salvation narratives. I'll be looking here at one more voyage to Egypt, one more visitor seeking Kuchuk Hanem with Western eyes—but the eyes of a woman who is, in the process, herself under observation. With the mediation of Francine du Plessix Gray's biography of the writer Louise Colet (who was also, incidentally,

---

and sexual difference (129–56). For Ali Behdad as well, Flaubert's adventure with Kuchuk Hanem epitomizes his Orientalist encounter and constitutes—indeed crystallizes—an experience of loss; he is "the victim of a pathological search for the lost object" (*Belated Travelers: Orientalism in the Age of Colonial Dissolution* [Durham: Duke University Press, 1994], 68)—albeit a self-conscious victim—condemned to "repeat...his experience of loss in a chain of metonymic signification" (70). And for Maryline Lukacher, Flaubert's entire voyage to Egypt is lived under the aegis of loss: the condemnation of the manuscript of *La Tentation de Saint Antoine* by his friends, his father's recent death, his mother's bereavement when he departs ("Fictions biographiques," 183–84). I highlight these critical accounts of Kuchuk Hanem as embodying an object or experience of loss because my discussion, as it unfolds, will come to question the language of loss which shrouds not only the courtesan but the discourse that narrates, theorizes, and metacritically represents her.

[10] "En haut des degrés, Koutchouk-Hanem m'attendait. Je la vis en levant la tête; *ce fut comme une apparition*." See Maxime Du Camp, *Le Nil*, in *Un Voyageur en Egypte vers 1850: "Le Nil" de Maxime Du Camp*, ed. Michel Dewachter and Daniel Oster (Paris: Sand/Conti, 1987), 130, emphasis added; subsequent references are given in the text. As critics have well observed, Flaubert appears to have lifted this phrase from Du Camp for *L'Éducation sentimentale*. Fifteen years after Du Camp relates his first sight of the courtesan, Frédéric describes his first vision of Madame Arnoux: "It was like an apparition" ["Ce fut comme une apparition"]. Gustave Flaubert, *L'Éducation sentimentale*, in *Œuvres complètes*, ed. Jean Bruneau and Bernard Masson, vol. 2 (Paris: Seuil, 1964), 9.

Flaubert's second-most-celebrated mistress), I focus on the late-twentieth-century biographer's glance at Colet at the specific moment when she contemplates Flaubert watching Kuchuk Hanem, two decades after the fact, through her own Egyptian journey. My focus is the viewing process rather than the object viewed: the course and metamorphoses of a chain of gazes. Or, if we speak in symbolic rather than narratological terms, the chain may be collapsed into a series of concentric frames: the outermost circle—what I am writing here today—encloses Francine du Plessix Gray's biography of Louise Colet (specifically, Gray's account of Colet's trip to Egypt), which in turn englobes Colet's narrative of her trip, *Les Pays lumineux: Voyage en Orient* (republished as *Les Pays lumineux: Voyage d'une femme de lettres en Haute Égypte*), which frames the elusive—the finally silent and invisible—Kuchuk Hanem.

Now, one of the features of such an infinitely regressive and recessive symbolic structure—that is, a representation *mise en abyme*—is that each circle reflects and reproduces all the others. I take this as license to begin at a random place, with the closing statement of Gray's preface to her *Rage and Fire: A Life of Louise Colet.* Gray describes a vivid tableau that shows an aging Flaubert, in 1879, at home one evening before a roaring fire with his good friend and chief disciple Guy de Maupassant and a suitcase full of old letters. As the night wears on, Flaubert proceeds to burn pile upon pile of letters, notably one packet bound with a narrow ribbon and including with the letters a silk slipper, a faded handkerchief, and a withered rose. Gray closes her preface, and opens her biography, with this manifesto: "I believe that those last missives...were the many hundreds of letters written to Flaubert by Louise Colet. That is why I have written this book. To reinstate a colleague into the annals of her time. To do her justice. To resurrect yet another woman whose memory has been erased by the caprices of men."[11] Gray's words, though referring specifically to Louise Colet, might serve as a more general mission statement for the genre I call "salvation narrative," whose aims—in remodulated terms I borrow from Gray—are to resurrect women, to reinstate colleagues, and to undo erasure. I take Gray's words as a departure point

---

[11]   Francine du Plessix Gray, *Rage and Fire: A Life of Louise Colet* (New York: Simon and Schuster, 1994), 16.

for my own inquiry into and critique of a genre I find both riveting and fraught with peril.

First, a brief detour past the milestones of the Colet-Flaubert liaison. It was in 1846 in the studio of the sculptor James Pradier that they met, then went on to become lovers and correspondents. She was a prizewinning poet, novelist, and playwright eleven years his senior; he was twenty-five and unknown. They corresponded and very occasionally trysted for the next year and a half until Flaubert, distressed by his lover's urgings that they meet, and meet more often, sent her a letter of rupture in March 1848. In late October 1849 Flaubert left for the Orient. Though he passed through Paris on his way to Marseilles, his point of departure from France, he did not contact Louise Colet. She, however, kept track of his passage through Paris—and in fact of his entire journey—by means of newspaper accounts, rumor, and friendly gossip. Colet's journal entries indicate that she thought often and amorously of Flaubert during his Oriental sojourn. Their correspondence and liaison recommenced in July 1851, when she sought him out upon his return from the East. It ended definitively by his unilateral decision in the spring of 1854. Although she was later linked with some of the most creative men of her time, Colet's journal entries suggest that she never forgot and in a sense never extricated herself from her involvement with Flaubert.[12]

In October 1869—twenty years to the month after Flaubert—Colet leaves for Egypt to cover the opening of the Suez Canal for *Le Siècle* (France's leading progressive daily at the time) and to take notes for what will become the posthumous travelogue of her own Egyptian saga. Colet's *Les Pays lumineux* isn't actually written until 1875, shortly before her death. The dreary narrative, not quite illuminated by its title, reads like a cross between a Blue Guide and a Woody Allen script: Colet goes on endless sightseeing tours but seems to engage only with eunuchs, harems, and her own state of ill health. I begin with a passage that is the dark heart of *Les Pays lumineux.* The scene she describes unfolds on board the ship that will take her up the Nile as it lies at its moorings the night before departure.

---

[12] For an extended reading of the Flaubert-Colet correspondence, see Beizer, *Ventriloquized Bodies*, pt. 2.

In her bed that night Colet is visited by a vampiric figure, whom she identifies without naming. This is clearly Flaubert's phantom double, made in the image of a memory undead, a past that refuses to stay buried, and returns to feed on the present: "The dead image of a being beloved in my blind youth, buried in my heart for over twenty years, was suddenly revived in the form of a dominating and brutal being."[13] Fixing her with his gaze, he mounts her, penetrates her body with his teeth:

> Opaque and heavy as an animal mass, the obstinate specter sat on my burning chest. The round porthole through which two huge stars shone represented his head with its startled eyes, alternately bold and cowering in shadow. I closed my eyes to avoid seeing it.... But seeing it no longer, I sensed its harsh and importune presence all the more; were those not its hands that choked my whimpering throat, and was that not its foul mouth that covered my languishing body with bites? (205–6)

Continuing her Gothic reportage, Colet describes waking from her encounter with the incubus only to enter another nightmare state:

> An unbearable itching succeeded the bites, as if its nails had torn into me.... [S]itting up, I lit one of the burned-out candles that I had placed under my pillow beside a box of matches. Then I saw, crawling on my white nightshirt like black crabs, five or six of those horrible insects called cockroaches, others making their way in a slow processional on the gilded molding of my cabin's paneling; I sat stark upright in terror, and, shaking loose the creatures that were upon me, I crushed them beneath the heel of my slipper. An unbearable stench arose from these dead bodies, viscous and sticky as woodlice. I grabbed a flacon from my travel bag and poured its essence here and there. All of a sudden two rats leapt out of the bag that held sugar and pastilles.... The idea

---

[13] Louise Colet, *Les Pays lumineux: Voyage en Orient* (Paris: E. Dentu, 1879), 205–7; subsequent references are provided in the text. See also Muriel Augry's re-edition of *Les Pays lumineux* (Paris: Cosmopole, 2001), with its helpful background essay, chronology, and bibliography.

of being delivered in the dark to the contact of field mice, cock-roaches, mosquitoes, and flies terrified me. (206)

This text is extraordinary not merely because it reproduces with un-canny precision the kind of animal phantasms Charcot was at the same moment in time reporting in his Salpêtrière patients (and that Freud would later describe in the case history of Frau Emmy von N.), but because Colet steps into the dual role of patient and physician.[14] Hysterics characteristically cannot speak their story; they deliver themselves over to others in a desperate plea to be deciphered. But Colet here practices dream interpretation, offering a reading of the tableau she herself terms "a strange and indefinable hallucination" (204–5). Relating the scene and its aftermath, she recalls feverishly writing all the night long in order to keep her creaturely companions at bay. Quoting at the time of writing from a page in her notebook— "an almost illegible page" (207)—she reproduces the interpretation she made of the vampire hallucination upon awakening:

But why the sudden apparition of this forgotten being? Oh—it is simple, there is nothing supernatural in the evocation of this for-gotten specter. Yesterday, among the motives that determined my excursion in upper Egypt, I thought suddenly that it would be intriguing to find in the shape of a living mummy one of those seductive *almehs* that he used, to tear at and revolt my heart in his travel narratives. The recent nightmare hatched from this idea, without troubling me, without moving me, without the slightest stirring of feelings dead among the ashes. (207–8)

Now, Colet goes to great pains to distinguish between vampire and bug bite, between hallucination and waking horror, framing the vampire alone as phantasm by interpreting it from an analytically distanced, merely nightmarish entomological "reality." She carefully establishes the factuality of the horrific frame by contextualizing it:

---

[14] See Jean Martin Charcot, *L'Hystérie,* ed. E. Trillat (Toulouse: Privat, 1971); and Sigmund Freud and Josef Breuer, *Studies on Hysteria,* vol. 2 of *The Standard Edi-tion of the Complete Works of Sigmund Freud,* ed. James Strachey et al. (London: Hogarth Press, 1955).

she recalls discovering used sheets on the bed in her uncleaned cabin opposite the filthy latrines the evening before, and remembers the morning after, comparing notes with other passengers who survived a similarly odious night.

Nonetheless, I am operating on the assumption that it matters not that the bug and fly and rodent infestation actually happened; these creatures take their place all the same with the vampire in the order of textual phantasm that I will go on to explore. The "illegible page" on which Colet finds her self-analysis inscribed turns out to be surprisingly easy to read—in fact deceptively so. Taking a cue from Colet's metaphor of a nightmare that "hatched" from the idea of seeing a mummified *almeh* ("From this idea the nightmare of a little while ago hatched" [207]), we need to reintegrate the vampire nightmare with the prolific hatching of vermin, and with the *almeh* transformed into mummy. We need to unwrap the mummy, even at the risk of witnessing its core disintegrate before our eyes. To perform such an unwrapping, we must read Colet's text both palimpsestically and mosaically. Approaching palimpsestically, we must consider in its duality a text inscribed over another, even at the risk of finding beneath the proffered text a blank page. Approaching mosaically, we need to fracture Colet's *Voyage en Orient* and then read it with and through and against fragments from both Flaubert's *Voyage en Égypte,* and his letters from and about Egypt.

We may begin by considering once again the courtesan in mummy's clothing who instantly materializes in Colet's thought but proves impossible to track down in the world. We can glimpse if not hold Kuchuk Hanem's fleeting shadow as it crosses the pages of Colet's and Flaubert's earlier writings. It leaves a trace in a letter from Flaubert to Colet written in March 1853. Flaubert here replies to Colet's reactions to his Egypt manuscript, which he had after two years of supplications consented to show her—with not very happy results. We have access to the letter expressing her reactions, as in the case of all but five of her letters to Flaubert, only between the lines of Flaubert's responses. Whatever she has expressed in the vanished letter occasions on the part of her lover a meditation on the unfathomability of women's jealousy.

It becomes evident that Colet has reproached Flaubert, on the one hand, for having neglected to see her on his way to the Orient, and, on the other, for excessively having seen, experienced, enjoyed—and, perhaps especially, written about—Kuchuk Hanem. Flaubert attempts to assuage Colet's resentment by means of a curious reasoning:

> As for Kuchiouk-Hânem, ah! let me reassure you and at the same time rectify your Oriental perceptions. Rest assured that she felt nothing at all; emotionally, take my word for it, and physically even, I strongly doubt it.... The Oriental woman is a machine, and nothing more; she makes no distinction between one man and another.... And as for physical pleasure, even that must be extremely minimal since its very seat, that celebrated button, is cut out very early on. And that is what makes this woman so poetic from a certain point of view: the fact that she is entirely subsumed by nature. (2:282)

Flaubert, of course, is not alone in finding woman naturalized by cultural forces that require erotic sacrifice. He proceeds to elaborate on the poetry of the Orient as embodied by its women:

> What I love...in the Orient is this grandeur that is unaware of itself, and this harmony of disparate things.... This is the true, and therefore poetic Orient: scoundrels in gold-trimmed rags covered with vermin. So forget about the vermin: it glitters in the sun like golden swirls. You tell me that Kuchiouk-Hânem's bedbugs degrade her for you; but that is exactly what enchanted me. Their nauseating odor fused with the odor of her skin dripping with sandalwood. (2:283)

We can follow the vermin trail as it weaves between Flaubert and Colet. Given the infestation in his text and hers, the evident dialogue about Kuchuk Hanem's bedbugs, the indication of disgust on Colet's part (with the inevitable dose of fascination), it strikes me as curious that the noticeable absence in the litany of swarming, scurrying, flying creatures recited in the text of her nightmare is precisely this one. There are rats, mice, flies, cockroaches, crabs, larvae, and mosquitoes pervading the dreamscape, but no bedbugs.

Their absence is revealing. They are in fact incorporated into the text as an unseen presence, for after Colet runs through the catalogue of creatures in attendance, she adds, "What would have happened if I had suspected the myriads of bedbugs, fleas, and white lice whose yet invisible hatching became perceptible in the following days?" (206–7). In this way the bedbugs are marked off as unremarked, made remarkable in their very invisibility.

These creatures that provocatively glitter in Flaubert's narrative creep into Colet's own Egyptian narrative in the form of an "intolerable odor" emanating from the viscous and sticky insects she crushes with her slipper. Such beasts, mislabeled as cockroaches, can only be bedbugs, those miniature vampires which, when crushed, grow redolently viscous and sticky with the blood they have pumped from their supine victims.

Squashed underfoot—under a slipper reminiscent of those "relics" of Colet fetishistically used by Flaubert to remember her during the long periods of their separations—the vampire bug embodies the memory of Flaubert, finally "conquered" at the hands and in the words of his ex-mistress. At the same time it evokes another small blood-engorged body, equally marked as absent, this one metonymically representative of his other ex-mistress, the courtesan Kuchuk Hanem. Associated by Flaubert with lack—that, most concretely, of her excised "button," but also, by extension, of her sexual pleasure, and, finally, of her consciousness and of her will—Kuchuk Hanem comes to materialize absence for Louise Colet as well. When, twenty years after Flaubert, Colet travels to the Orient, she replicates his difficult voyage up the Nile in the phantasmatic hope of sighting the infamous courtesan.

If jealousy motivates Colet's intense interest in Kuchuk Hanem, as Flaubert earlier assumed, I posit that it isn't acting alone but in concert with a strong identification with her Eastern double. Colet's dreamscript contains a series of transformations of Flaubert's Egyptian narrative, with herself cast in the courtesan's role or position. A few examples: Flaubert's account of his first night with Kuchuk Hanem notes his performance of "violent cunnilingus" (2:286–87);[15] Colet's dream deformation shows Flaubert as vampire and reports, "His foul mouth...covered my languishing body with bites" (206).

---

[15]   "Une gamahuchade des plus violentes."

Flaubert recounts a foray outside during Kuchuk Hanem's dancing: "A very bright star shone.... [I]t was only the lit window of Kuchiuk's house" (Flaubert, *Voyage*, 286); Colet's night visitation represents the star, the implied eyes of Flaubert's upturned gaze, and the window as twin stars/eyes studding a porthole/head: "The round porthole through which two huge stars twinkled represented his head with its startled eyes" (205). Flaubert casually mentions Kuchuk Hanem's clitoridectomy ("that celebrated button is cut out very early on" [2:205]); Colet counts her blessings as she compares herself (speaking to herself in the second person here) to intact stone uncut by the sculptor's chisel: "He was not able to cut into your soul, which remained whole like a block of intractable Parian marble, refusing to quiver before the maiming force of this common Pygmalion" (209).

Kuchuk Hanem's genital mutilation never figures directly in Colet's text, though we might read its displacement in her fascinated terror of eunuchs, and in the poem with which she closes *Les Pays lumineux*, "L'Île Éléphantine," one verse of which expresses horrified indignation at the custom of piercing an adolescent girl's lips or nose to mark nubility (323). In fact Colet's dream episode represents a displaced identification with the courtesan's mutilation, notwithstanding her boast of marmoreal wholeness, for the ordeal is accompanied by a loss of voice. "My throat is on fire, and *I have lost my voice*," she writes (196, emphasis added), as prelude to her nightmare, and "the cough that I forced myself to stifle has *cut off my words*" (198, emphasis added). These symptoms give way to the vampire hands of the nightmare, which "strangle her throat," and the accompanying suffering, which "smothers her voice" (205–6).

If Colet is saved from the vermin invasion by writing, as she insists, this is because what could otherwise only be inscribed as itching and gnawing on her body finds expression through the pen:

> I understood that the only way to escape the invasion of these horrible animalcules was to force my mind to exercise and my body to move; continuing to crush and to chase the pests, I opened the trunk that held my books and my travel notes, I set a notebook and a blotter on my vanity table, and each time my constrained pacing across the narrow space of the cabin led me

back to the vanity table, I feverishly noted my impressions of
this long night. (207)

The vampirized blood is converted into a flow of ink; the drained
voice recirculates as letters. Like Philomela, she fashions a tissue
of loss.

I move toward a conclusion by confessing that I am not entirely
comfortable with Colet's writing of loss. Her narrative as it plays out
within mine incessantly evokes absence: Flaubert's withheld manuscript, Colet's vanished letters, the courtesan she cannot find, the
excised clitoris, the elided bedbug, the undead lover, the mummy.
The cumulative conjunction of vampire, courtesan, and bedbug in
the name of lack and loss begins to sound suspiciously like a story
of castration. As this story has unfolded in my own text, it has
evolved within a series of embedding narratives including a report
(Colet's) of a lost voice and cut-off words, and an account (Gray's) of
letters burned and memory erased. In my own narrative, this series of
frames which has at its core the tale of a woman in hiding, revealed
in layers to be cast off one by one, has come to sound a bit like the
stereotypic phantasm of the Oriental woman whose voluptuously
veiled body extends the illusory hope of retrieving a lost object.

Both Flaubert and Colet recounted with vibrant interest a highly
eroticized dance of unveiling observed in Egypt. When the *almeh*
performs the bee dance, she lifts veil after veil of transparent gauze
in a mock search for a buzzing bee—a search, need I add, whose cause
and effect is an alluring striptease. Flaubert and his friend Du Camp,
however, both felt cheated by the bee dance, which they found in
the end to be terribly disappointing. Du Camp spoke for their shared
sense of insufficiency when he remarked, "There was neither bee nor
bee-stung girl" (*Le Nil*, 132).[16]

The futility of imagining the *almeh* unveiled as a lost or found
object may be glimpsed through Colet's grotesque figuration of the
unveiling courtesan as mummy. We recall that her Nile journey was
motivated by the desire to recover "in the shape of a living mummy
one of those seductive *almehs* that [Flaubert] used, to tear at and

---

[16] "Il n'y eut ni abeille ni jeune fille piquée."

revolt my heart in his travel narratives" (207). Colet's reply to Flaubert and Du Camp's fantasy of unwrapping the *almeh* to find both
girl and bee together might well be that when the veils are removed,
what is revealed can only be nothing—no thing, or death. For the
mummy is the ultimate fetish: a simultaneous denial and avowal of
a lack, an illusory substitute for something that is simply not there
(in Freud's sense, the maternal phallus; in the mummy's case, life). It
is true that Colet's mummy is not perfectly analogous to the Freudian fetish, for when the mummy simulates life in death, it produces
the illusion of a presence *that once was,* while when the fetish flirts
with the possibility of a maternal phallus, it produces an illusion that
is pure phantasm.[17]

The analogy may be usefully flawed, however. I am not sure that
the fetish acts predictably in Colet's regendered rhetoric of difference, with its recurrent play of absence and presence, death and life,
lack and abundance, oblivion and memory, illegibility and clarity.
I am told we have come a long way since Freud. We know that female
castration is a male phantasm, a defense against the horror of sexual
difference—a fetish. But what changes when we are listening to a
woman talking about clitoridectomy? How does the reality of what
is sometimes called female castration figure in the formation of the
fetish and other phantasms for women and for men? Is Colet's bedbug a female fetish? Is the fetish the same animal when it replaces
an organ rightfully owned and lost?[18] If not, how do we then regender

[17] As Bernheimer argues, Freud is implicated in the perversion he calls fetishism,
in so far as he equates female difference with a lost penis: "When Freud calls castration a fact he is in effect taking as the basis of factuality his own hypothesized
sexual theory of children. He strategically, or unconsciously, forgets what he took
to be the genesis of this theory, the actual perception of difference, and proposes as
factual what is in fact a theoretical fetish, a veil that obscures the facts" ("'Castration' as Fetish," *Paragraph* 14, no. 1 [March 1991]: 3).
[18] Flippancy aside, this query seems to me to be at the heart of the question of female fetishism. Ever since psychoanalysis and feminism began to take each other
seriously, female fetishism has been a theoretical area in need of reinvention.
For some other work on the subject, see Apter, *Feminizing the Fetish;* Sarah Kofman, "Ça cloche," in *Les Fins de l'homme: À partir du travail de Jacques Derrida*
(Paris: Galilée, 1981), 89–116; and Naomi Schor, "Female Fetishism: The Case of
George Sand," in *The Female Body in Western Culture,* ed. Susan Rubin Suleiman (Cambridge: Harvard University Press, 1986), 363–72; see, too, Geoffrey A.
Dudley, "A Rare Case of Female Fetishism," *International Journal of Sexology* 8,
no. 1 (August 1954): 32–34, for an interesting early note.

scenarios of presence and loss? How do we retrieve or retrace the frayed threads of life narratives dropped or lost or cut along the way? I can only end anticlimactically. My own unveiling of the *almeh* or unwrapping of the mummy reveals no bee and no sting, to paraphrase Du Camp—just a lot of loose ends.

I close with these ends proudly loosed. I don't propose to gather and reweave them, and I don't recommend that they be bound in any way. Such a task would imply a fundamental deficiency that could or should be filled in or covered over, as if by a narrative loincloth. Women's biography risks being fetishized in much the same way plaiting and weaving were fetishized by Freud, who described them as women's (only) inventions, designed to conceal genital lack. When we write the lives of women as stories of what our mothers should have been, we are not so much inventing narratives to which we might aspire, as grieving phantasmatic loss. When we project upon our mothers' lives a story we ourselves have not yet assumed, we too, like Freud, are weaving a genital braid—or unweaving it in frustration because it doesn't measure up. If Penelope's unweaving may stand as an allegory for the plotlessness of women's lives, as Carolyn Heilbrun once argued,[19] it does not necessarily follow that we should aspire to a finished tapestry.

[19]   Carolyn Heilbrun, "What Was Penelope Unweaving?" in *Hamlet's Mother and Other Women* (New York: Columbia University Press, 1990), 111. See chapter 5 for some further reflections on this metaphor.

WRITING ORIGINS

George Sand as the Story of Our Life

The absence of a feminine literary tradition resounds in postmodern writing about women's lives. We have seen how Virginia Woolf's musing that "we think back through our mothers if we are women" has been appropriated by biographers and other seekers of a "lost tradition" of feminine creativity as motif if not refrain and often dirge.[1] In what follows I consider more closely, in a very specific context of the feminist biographical enterprise, the slide from literal to figurative mother, from childhood nurturer to intellectual precursor.[2] If, as I suggest, the lives of mothers and the lives of foremothers play out in narratives that cannot today be conceptualized separately, might

---

[1] Virginia Woolf, *A Room of One's Own* (New York: Harvest, 1957), 79. A good example of the attempt to retrieve a hypothetical lost tradition is the collection I refer to in chapter 1, *The Lost Tradition: Mothers and Daughters in Literature,* ed. Cathy N. Davidson and E. M. Broner (New York: Frederick Ungar, 1980). For a more recent critique of nostalgia for a feminine literary tradition, see Lynne Huffer, *Maternal Pasts, Feminist Futures: Nostalgia, Ethics, and the Question of Difference* (Stanford: Stanford University Press, 1998). Although Woolf's original statement was metaphorical, the metaphor was not yet dead, so that the mother's material shadow was not far. See Evelyne Ender, "A Writer's Birthpains: Virginia Woolf and the Mother's Share," in *Families,* ed. Werner Senn (Tübingen: Gunter Narr Verlag, 1996), 257–72, for an incisive articulation of the literal along with the figurative mother's share in Woolf's writing.

[2] The metaphorical transparency, the certitude of knowability, is opposed to the father's obscurity. "'Pater semper incertus est,' while the mother is 'certissima,'" as the old law popularized by Freud put it. Sigmund Freud, "Family Romances," in *The Standard Edition of the Complete Psychological Works of Sigmund Freud,* vol. 9, ed. James Strachey et al. (London: Hogarth Press, 1959), 239.

an understanding of their cultural entanglement help to resolve what appears to be a natural confusion? These questions direct my readings, necessarily imbricated, of three texts whose intersections dramatically play out the mother-foremother dynamic at stake in the rhetoric of women's life writing.

Bouchardeau's Rose, Bouchardeau's George, Sand's Aurore's Sophie

In 1990 the writer and politician Huguette Bouchardeau published two biographies. *George Sand: La Lune et les sabots,* a biography that frames Sand's literal and figurative maternity, was followed six months later by *Rose Noël,* a memoir of Bouchardeau's mother. Nearly a century and a half earlier, George Sand had dispersed a memoir of her mother, Sophie, in the pages of her autobiography, *Histoire de ma vie.* If the Sophie memoir is a model for Bouchardeau's *Rose Noël,* and Sand as biographer daughter is a foremother to Bouchardeau, we can explore Bouchardeau's double investment as daughter in her two-pronged biographical venture. By moving back to *Histoire de ma vie* through Bouchardeau's contemporary feminist focus— reading Sand's text first through Rose-colored glasses, as it were—I hope usefully to exaggerate an inevitably anachronistic reading, and in the process, to pose questions about the aspirations and limits of a retrospective feminist vision.[3]

In *La Lune et les sabots,* Huguette Bouchardeau portrays a Sand "hungry for maternity" ["avide de maternité" (116)]. "Sand herself strove steadfastly to compose this image in *Story of My Life,*" Bouchardeau insists, perhaps a bit defensively ["C'est [Sand] elle-même

[3] References are to the following editions of Bouchardeau's and Sand's works and are provided in the text: Huguette Bouchardeau, *George Sand: La Lune et les sabots* (Paris: Laffont, 1990), and *Rose Noël* (Paris: Seghers, 1990) (hereafter cited as *LS* and *RN,* respectively); George Sand, *Histoire de ma vie* in *Œuvres autobiographiques,* 2 vols., ed. Georges Lubin (Paris: Gallimard, 1970–71) (hereafter cited as *Histoire*). Translations of Bouchardeau are my own; translations of *Histoire de ma vie* are my modifications of *Story of My Life: The Autobiography of George Sand,* a group translation edited by Thelma Jurgrau (Albany: State University of New York Press, 1991).

qui a voulu, avec obstination, composer cette image dans *Histoire de ma vie*" (116)]. Bouchardeau is certainly not alone among Sand's biographers and critics in focusing on the writer as literal and figurative mother to a mixed brood of children and lovers in need of protection. Her presentation of Sand is remarkable, rather, in its dogged insistence on a perspective she otherwise implicitly complicates. After all, as she elsewhere reminds us, Sand's construction of her image as daughter was persistent: "All her life, Aurore will strive to unknot the tangled threads of her ancestry" ["Toute son existence, Aurore cherchera à dénouer la trame emmêlée de ses ascendances" (*LS*, 15)]. In fact Bouchardeau's portrait of the author as a young girl exposes scars of daughterhood no accession to maternity could ever expunge.[4] Quoting the words Sand attributes to her grandmother in *Histoire de ma vie*, Bouchardeau borrows her ornithological metaphors (metaphors to which we will have ample occasion to return). Aurore here appears as fledgling chased by her mother from the nest: "Your mother...is so uncivilized that she loves her children as birds do, with great care and ardor during early infancy, but when they have wings, when it is a matter of reasoning and using instinctive tenderness, she flies to another tree and pecks at them, chasing them away" (*Story*, 803) ["Ta mère...est si inculte qu'elle aime ses petits à la manière des oiseaux, avec de grands soins et de grandes ardeurs pour la première enfance; mais quand ils ont des ailes, quand il s'agit de raisonner et d'utiliser la tendresse instinctive, elle vole sur un autre arbre et les chasse à coups de becs" (*LS*, 29; *Histoire*, 1:1111)]. Torn between grandmother and mother, pecked out of the nest, preoccupied by genealogy her entire life, George Sand remains nonetheless quintessentially "mother" in Bouchardeau's biography. The Sand perversely inscribed as omnimaternal by this narration that is so resistant to the surging filiality it describes, can be reread in tandem with Bouchardeau's other biography. In *Rose Noël* as in *La Lune et les sabots*, Bouchardeau writes a life of the woman who is her own stiff-beaked mother.

---

[4] Sand herself repeatedly has us hear echoes of daughterhood in motherhood, beginning with accounts of her own childhood play and continuing with recollections and reflections prompted by caring for her daughter, son, and grandchildren.

A familiar discourse of maternity supplies the vocabulary for the earliest representations of Rose: "dwelling, fountain, cradle...blanket and nourishment" ["habitacle, fontaine, berceau...enveloppe et nourriture" (*RN*, 14)]. Later representations echo Sand's descriptions of the volatile Sophie: "The mother blackbird is in her nest....Outside all is danger. In a few weeks, the babies will venture out from branch to branch, the mother will once again walk on the lawn. Mother birds do one day leave the nest" ["La merlette est au nid.... Tout l'extérieur est danger. Dans quelques semaines, les petits s'aventureront de branche en branche, la merlette se promènera à nouveau sur la pelouse. Les mères-oiseaux, elles, quittent un jour le nid" (*RN*, 161–62)]. The allegorical becomes more insistently explicit when Bouchardeau describes her mother's love of babies transformed into impatience with growing children: "Right away, from the moment we left her arms, she expected us to be worldly and independent. A real mother bird" ["Vite, du moment où nous quittions ses bras, elle nous voulait dégourdis et indépendants. Une mère-oiseau" (*RN*, 203)].[5]

Like Aurore, Huguette is a birdling to be warmed, nourished, and then pecked out of the nest. The overarching metaphors set up a relationship of Huguette to Rose Noël analogous to Aurore's relationship to her mother, Sophie: each is daughter to an inconstant mother. If Sand nonetheless remains Mother for Bouchardeau writing her life, it is, I would suggest, chiefly because there is an unspoken intertextual relationship in which Bouchardeau as author of her mother's life plays daughter to Sand as illustrious predecessor author of her mother's life.

Let me try to tease out this relationship by turning back to *Rose Noël.* One of the motifs of this biography is the mother's reticence, her awkwardness in language. "A quiet woman" ["Une silencieuse" (*RN*, 19)], she is suspicious of eloquence, misspells, declares reading a sin (*RN*, 19, 139, 165). The daughter as biographer self-consciously refuses the position of sociologist, ethnologist, or judge but cannot

---

[5]   The image continues when Bouchardeau relates her adolescent reaction to the unraveling fabric of her parents' relationship: "Fear for us little ones that the protective nest might collapse" ["De la peur pour nous, les petits, que le nid protecteur ne s'effondrât" (*RN*, 111)].

avoid that of mourner. With traces of frustration, Bouchardeau re-counts her mother's foray into public speaking in rather fraught cir-cumstances. In 1973, when Bouchardeau is active in the movement to legalize abortion, the group she works with organizes an open forum to publicize testimony from older women who resorted to abortion as a means of birth control. She secures her mother's con-sent to participate, to make public the sordid details she has previ-ously evoked for her daughter, though even then in a halting and unfinished fashion—"by bits and pieces torn from silence...not able to find the words to finish"—tears taking the place of words ["par bribes arrachées au silence...les mots lui manquaient pour dire la suite" (*RN*, 64)]. But when she rises to speak, Rose can only summon "a few discreet words that made her past sound banal" ["quelques mots pudiques qui banalisaient le passé" (*RN*, 65)], and Huguette is left to lament the "antiseptic reduction" of her story. She grieves her mother's failure to serve as witness to her era or even to her own past: "I regretted her inability to communicate to these women, who could have been her granddaughters, the harshness of olden times" ["J'ai déploré qu'elle ne pût communiquer à ces femmes, qui avaient l'âge d'être ces petites-filles, la dureté des temps anciens" (*RN*, 65)].

Sand, certainly, speaks volumes about her own times and her own experiences (though she has been reproached from some quarters for omitting the most intimate ones).[6] And so I would suggest that Bouchardeau takes Sand as a dually determined mother. Huguette's identification with Aurore as a daughter who becomes George Sand and goes on to write a mother's life is the keystone of Sand's spiritual motherhood for Bouchardeau. She can then replace her own mother, Rose, with a very literate foremother.

The terms of exchange are critical. Rose and George, both grounded by Bouchardeau in maternity, each carry a differently charged version of it. Rose incarnates the excessive maternal body, while George, figure for the mother, translates flesh into word. "Disfigured" and "invaded" by maternity, Rose literally overflows; after each birth her abun-dant milk nourishes a neighbor's child along with her own (*RN*, 12).

---

[6] Michael Sheringham, for instance, speaks of the "sanitization" of Rousseau's legacy in autobiographers such as Sand (*French Autobiography: Devices and De-sires, Rousseau to Perec* [Oxford: Clarendon Press, 1993], 116).

Only the infant Huguette cannot digest this milk, develops "a milk intolerance" ["une maladie de lait" (*RN*, 14)] that she will later attribute to a nauseating submersion in the warm white torrent of maternal nourishment. Later on, the proximity of her mother's menstruating body will fill the adolescent Huguette with a similar disgust, a sense of drowning in the intimacy of her mother's physicality (*RN*, 183). She will cling to bookish pleasures, to the inessential but irrepressible flow of words ["paroles irrépressibles et inutiles" (*RN*, 165)], in the face of her mother's "condemnation of garrulous thinking, of the gift of wordiness" ["condamnation des pensées volubiles, des facilités verbeuses" (*RN*, 19)].

Sand's words—Sand as the word or spirit of maternity rather than its flesh—will relieve Rose's materiality. The toxic milk, the noxious blood will be discharged as words. This transformation can work because it is only partial; Sand as writer can redeem Rose because in Bouchardeau's narrative she is—last and foremost, albeit abstractly—mother. Bouchardeau's biography of George Sand comes to a close with an evaluation:

> Some of her works are studied in school. Some well deserve to be once again embraced by a circle of nonscholarly readers. Her letters still have a fine, glowing intensity. "I will never be a sage or a scholar," she would say. "I'm a woman, my gifts are love, and pity, and rage."
>
> [Certains de ses ouvrages s'étudient dans les classes. Certains mériteraient bien de retrouver la chaleur et l'amitié de lecteurs non scolaires. Ses lettres brûlent toujours, belles, vivantes. "Je ne serai jamais ni un sage ni un savant," avait-elle dit. "Je suis femme, j'ai des tendresses, des pitiés et des colères." (*LS*, 263)]

Cautious praise for Sand's works yields to unqualified admiration for her letters, here consigned to "life" rather than to "work." Giving the last word to a passage from the letters in which Sand identifies with womanly emotion, the biography anchors her in a woman's—and, implicitly, a mother's—life. Sand's words can then redeem Rose's silence. More crucially, perhaps, they can legitimize Bouchardeau's writing by reconstructing a minimalist maternal lineage.

It is worth thinking about the nostalgia component implicit in the mission of (fore)mother biography (which we have seen named "mirror biography" by the cover description of the series "Elle était une fois," in which *La Lune et les sabots* appears).[7] Such nostalgia may well be a better mirror of the present than the past, a result of what I described earlier as a feminist anxiety about not having the dubious privilege of a patriarchally styled anxiety of influence.[8] A word of warning, then, to be picked up later; for now, only some questions elicited by a vague unrest. As a feminist writing today, how does one read and write lives in retrospect and yet respect the silences of the past? What does one seek and reasonably expect to find, and what methods will permit this? What would a retrospective feminist reading that did not do violence to the past in fact look like? Can we begin to imagine a salvation project that would recover even fragments of a life without imposing another consciousness—the sensibility of another age—in its place?

Sand, too, sought lost traces of a maternal past. One of the declared motivations for her autobiography is the effort to retrieve and preserve bits of her mother's unrecorded life: "I shall take up [her] story again when I can pick up its traces" (117) ["Je reprendrai [son] histoire où il me sera possible de la retrouver" (*Histoire* 1:75)]. With Sand's Aurore, we confront once again the intertwined issues of missing maternal origins, mourning, and a coming to writing. Such a nexus evokes a contemporary feminist project and has been appropriated by more than one. My intent in identifying these apparently similar structures at the outset is to go on to trace their divergences in the course of my reading of Sand's writing of her mother's life.[9]

---

[7] See chapter 1.

[8] Sandra Gilbert and Susan Gubar argued, in *The Madwoman in the Attic* (New Haven: Yale University Press, 1979), for a feminine "anxiety of authorship" as opposed to the Bloomian "anxiety of influence." (See Harold Bloom, *The Anxiety of Influence* [New York: Oxford University Press, 1973].) Since women in patriarchal society don't have a heritage of female precursors, they cannot suffer from the authority of earlier women creators, but instead struggle with the isolation, obscurity, and alienation of creating in and against a world of male models. Some thirty years after Gilbert and Gubar, I speak of an anxiety that is logically more contemporary, more mediated by what is now a critical tradition of anxiety about gendered precursors.

[9] Lynne Huffer asks the leading question, "How does a daughter write about...a mother without consigning the mother to the absence, invisibility, and silence on

Weighing the Mail

As every reader of *Histoire de ma vie* knows too well, the first five hundred pages of the autobiography are essentially given over to the reproduction of letters from the author's father, Maurice, written largely to his mother, from Paris or from his tours with the Napoleonic forces. I think I speak for most readers when I say that we scale this wall of letters (if we don't skirt it) in order to move on to more gripping, more passionate, more dynamic, more affect-laden pages of the text. Readers' speculations on the rather outrageous inclusion of a block of foreign material in what is ostensibly the narrative of Sand's life range from the cynical to the pious. Is she leaning on her paternal legacy for extra copy, self-authorization, or reflected glory? Or, rather, is she honoring her resolve to monumentalize the father she barely knew—"no pun intended, the real author of the story of my life" (169) ["sans jeu de mots, le véritable auteur de l'histoire de ma vie" (1:156)]—by posthumously restoring his scriptoral role?[10] If so, her extensive revision of his letters suggests an attempt to rewrite genealogy, to place herself in the position of textual and familial generatrix. If the epistolary effect has been well covered by critical reaction (most famously by Pontmartin's quip that Sand's autobiography would better have been titled "Story of My Life before My Birth" ["Histoire de ma vie avant ma naissance"]),[11] it has

---

which a certain conception of writing traditionally depends?" (*Maternal Pasts,* 4). My sense, with Huffer, is that contemporary writing about mothers does indeed consign them to absence and silence *in the very attempt to give them presence and voice.* I want to argue, however, that Sand's writing about her mother differs from this pattern in that she seeks to maintain and even to celebrate silence, in this way perhaps paradoxically establishing maternal presence in and through the unvoiced.

[10] Naomi Schor argues, using Mary Mason's more general observations on women's autobiography, that Sand gives her father a prominent place in the writing of her autobiography as a woman seeking an identity through alterity, and further, that Sand's aesthetics of idealism should be linked to the idealization of her father. As my own argument evolves, it will become clear that I disagree with Schor's contention that Sand favors the paternal branch of her tree and repeats the "matricidal gesture" of her biographers. Naomi Schor, *George Sand and Idealism* (New York: Columbia University Press, 1993), 160–65. For a summary of the various reasons proposed for Sand's inclusion of her father's letters, see Janet Hiddleston, *George Sand and Autobiography: A Reading of Histoire de ma vie* (Oxford: Legenda [European Humanities Research Center], 1999), 25–26.

[11] Georges Lubin, intro. to Sand, *Histoire de ma vie,* 1:xxi.

perhaps not been accurately measured. Whether we align ourselves with what Naomi Schor has called "the fatherists" or "the motherists" in assessing Sand's creative origins,[12] we can begin to weigh the significance of Sand's epistolary appropriation only after considering the other side of the balance.

I turn now from paternal to maternal epistolarity, and to a single letter that exists as event rather than as object. The scene in question takes place at a point when Aurore would have been somewhere between nine and ten, when her grandmother was clearly gaining ascendancy in the pitched custody battle with her daughter-in-law. She has more or less bought out Sophie's maternal interests with educational and financial advantages for Aurore in Nohant, and a pension for Sophie and her older daughter, Caroline, in Paris. The end of Sophie's month-long visit to Nohant coincides with her daughter's dawning knowledge that the estrangement is to be permanent. The moment that interests me unfolds between the eve and day of Sophie's departure and is situated—not coincidentally, I think—almost at full center of the autobiography.

Striving desperately to deny the custody arrangement, daughter and mother create a shared entrepreneurial fantasy. They will, together with Caroline, open a boutique (*une maison de modes*) in Paris. Poor but happy together, they will eke out a modest living making hats and dresses.[13] The grandmother will be out of the picture. With nightfall, however, comes doubt. By her bedtime, Aurore is overcome with anxiety, terrified by the lack of reassuring maternal glances cast in her direction. She determines to stay awake until her mother has finished her grandmother's lengthy bedtime ritual so that she can see her once more and reconfirm their plans. On the chance that the farewell scene she envisions will be interrupted, she sets about composing a long letter to Sophie. By the time of writing the autobiography, the childhood message is long since forgotten, but the

---

12   Schor, *George Sand and Idealism*, 244n7.
13   Aurore arrives at an early correlation of money with loss, as she begins to understand that she must part ways with her mother in order to retain access to her heritage: "I consequently acquired a great scorn for money before I even knew what it was, and also a haunting fear of the wealth with which I was threatened" (467) ["Il en résulta pour moi un grand mépris pour l'argent, avant que je susse ce que ce pouvait être, et une sorte de terreur vague de la richesse dont j'étais menacée" (1:604)].

passion remains: "What was in that letter? I don't remember any-more....My heart overflowed onto the paper, so to speak,...for my tears literally watered the page, forcing me at every instant to retrace the letters they washed away" (571) ["Qu'y avait-il dans cette lettre? Je ne m'en souviens plus....Mon cœur y coulait à flots pour ainsi dire,...car mes larmes l'arrosèrent littéralement, et à chaque instant j'étais forcée de retracer les lettres effacées par mes pleurs" (1:759)]. It is as if the force of this letter written from the body cancels out the content of its message in memory, just as the child's heart drowns her text: tears erase words.

Aurore then constructs a child's version of a detective story. She furtively plants the letter in back of a picture of her paternal grandfa-ther that hangs behind the door to her mother's room (and that serves as reminder that the grandmother can never be entirely out of the pic-ture). In place of an address, she leaves instructions for her mother: "Put your answer behind this same portrait of Dupin Senior. I will find it tomorrow when you are gone" (572) ["Place ta réponse der-rière ce même portrait du vieux Dupin. Je la trouverai demain quand tu seras partie" (1:760)]. To signal the letter's existence, she hangs her mother's nightcap on the portrait, and pins inside the nightcap a note: "Shake the portrait" (572) ["Secoue le portrait" (1:760)]. Later still that night, unable to sleep, she creeps to her mother's bed and finds her in tears reading the letter. The anguished conversation that follows exposes the dressmaker plan as fantasy. Desolate, Aurore se-cures her mother's promise to leave an answer to her letter before departing the next day, and goes back to her bed to finish a sleepless night. The next day Sophie packs her bags and returns to Paris. Au-rore finds no letter. She is bereft, stricken less by the absence of her mother than by the emotional abandonment: "My mother felt more passion than affection for me" (573) ["Ma mère avait pour moi...plus de passion que de tendresse" (1:762)].

Much could be and has been said about this plaintive scene. I will limit myself here to a few questions about the narration of this absent letter. At issue is not the truth value of the memory but the narrative value of the report. First, one might ask what remains to be said in a letter. Whatever Sophie might have tried to write to her daughter has already been communicated by the bedside tears, the embraces, the futile explanations and excuses. Again, it is perhaps not so much the content of the message as its material function (its position as an extension of the mother) that counts. Second, one wonders why the adult narrator looking back at the missing letter comes uncharacteristically to a hasty conclusion unfavorable to the mother. Let us look back at the text. The facts recounted are scant: Aurore did not find a letter in the designated hiding place when she was finally able to search the room unobserved many hours after Sophie's departure. Now, as we have seen, Aurore's letter and the elaborately conceived instructions for a response were, like an inverted purloined letter, so ostentatiously hidden as to be patently obvious. The narrative opens a space to suggest that someone (one of the maids cleaning the mother's room? the grandmother, alerted by one of the maids?) might in fact have intercepted the letter—but it does not make the suggestion explicit. On other occasions when the mother's fidelity, devotion, and attention have been impugned, every effort is made on the part of the narrator to seek justifications or alternative explanations, however implausible. Why not now?

Perhaps in this case that which is emotionally unthinkable is narratologically imperative. That is, the mother is and must remain she who doesn't write letters. Again, what is at stake is the structure of narrative and not of truth. A myth of maternal near-illiteracy is deliberately, indeed proudly (though apparently quite falsely), unfolded throughout the text, beginning in and against the context of paternal letters. In one of the bits of narrative that fill in the gaps between Maurice's letters to his mother, Sand marvels at a rare letter to him from Sophie: "At this time she did not know how to write well enough to do more than make herself understood.... [O]nly a lover's eyes could decipher her unintelligible scrawl and understand the passionate outbursts that had not managed to find the right form in words" (310) ["C'est tout au plus si à cette époque elle savait écrire assez pour se faire comprendre.... [I]l fallait les yeux d'un amant pour déchiffrer ce petit grimoire et comprendre ces élans d'un sentiment passionné qui ne pouvait trouver de forme pour s'exprimer" (1:365)]. But Georges Lubin categorically dismisses Sand's report: "A fiction" ["Roman"]. His description of Sophie's letters of this period sharply contradicts Sand's picture of ignorance and illiteracy: "The letters that Sophie wrote...are not at all those of an illiterate, and her spelling as well as her writing are certainly equal to Maurice's" ["Les lettres que [Sophie] écrivait...ne sont pas du tout d'une illettrée, et tant l'orthographe que l'écriture valent bien celles de Maurice" (1:1331n)].

But we should not leap too quickly to assumptions of filial denigration on Sand's part. The story is more nuanced, and Sophie's alleged deficiencies are offset by rare and magical gifts. Sand attributes her aesthetic initiation to her mother's influence in early childhood and, more specifically, recalls Sophie's incantatory use of a language she ostensibly cannot spell or write or even wholly speak:

> My mother instinctively and very ingenuously opened the world of beauty to me by acquainting me from my very early years with all her impressions....Objects which I might not have noticed on my own revealed their beauty to me, as if my mother had had a magic key to open my mind to the untutored but profound sentiment she had for them herself....I do not, however, remember my mother ever *crafting a sentence.* I do not believe she had the means to do it, for if she knew how to write at this time, it was with difficulty, and she did not pride herself on a vain and useless sense of spelling. And yet she spoke purely, as birds sing without having learned to sing. (436–37)

> [Ma mère m'ouvrait instinctivement et tout naïvement le monde du beau en m'associant dès l'âge le plus tendre à toutes ses impressions....[D]es objets, que je n'eusse peut-être pas remarqués de moi-même, me révélaient leur beauté, comme si ma mère avait eu une clef magique pour ouvrir mon esprit au sentiment inculte mais profond qu'elle en avait elle-même.... Et pourtant je ne me rappelle pas que ma mère m'ait jamais fait *une phrase.* Je crois qu'elle en eût été bien empêchée, car c'est à peine si elle savait écrire à cette époque, et elle ne se piquait point d'une vaine et inutile orthographe. Et pourtant elle parlait purement, comme les oiseaux chantent sans avoir appris à chanter. (1:556–57)]

Despite the temporal qualifier ("à cette époque"), and although we come to hear bits of letters Sophie writes to Aurore from Paris, although too we are told that she teaches the peasant child Liset to read and write, I want to argue that in a sense fundamental to the narrative of Sand's autobiography, her mother is preinscribed as the one who did not write a letter.

How then do we balance the epistolary scales? The father's letters weigh heavy, as if their density might compensate for the inevitable abstraction of a man who died before his daughter's fifth birthday; they weigh the sheaf of paper they are printed on, the leaves we must turn to get to what follows, the concreteness of place-names and action and description. They weigh swashbuckling romance, filial love and devotion, patrician bloodlines and Napoleonic glory. Documentation could be put in the balance, although some of it is ersatz. The mother's letter weighs absence and waiting. It weighs its impact on Aurore's life, reminiscent of the effect on Emma Bovary's life of the Vaubyessard ball, which leaves a hole like a chasm that a storm, in a single night, hollows out in the mountains.[14]

What does an unwritten letter weigh? Empirically speaking, only the paper it is not written on. But it may be that this very lightness is a generative and transformative force to be reckoned with.[15] In his meditation on lightness, Italo Calvino reflects on a story by Kafka, "Der Kübelreiter" (The Knight of the Bucket). The narrator, a man unsuccessfully seeking to fill his bucket with coal in a wartime

[14]   "Her visit to La Vaubyessard had opened a breach in her life, like one of those great crevasses that a storm can tear across the face of a mountain in the course of a single night" ["Son voyage à la Vaubyessard avait fait un trou dans sa vie, à la manière de ces grandes crevasses qu'un orage, en une seule nuit, creuse quelquefois dans les montagnes"]. Gustave Flaubert, *Madame Bovary* (Paris: Flammarion, 1986), 116; translation from Flaubert, *Madame Bovary*, trans. Francis Steegmuller (New York: Random House, 1957), 63.

[15]   Yvette Bozon-Scalzetti suggests that for Sand, "writing always means writing to the absent mother" ["Écrire, c'est toujours écrire à la mère absente"]: that is, absence is the motor force of writing. Yvette Bozon-Scalzetti, "Vérité de la fiction et fiction de la vérité dans *Histoire de ma vie*: Le Projet autobiographique de George Sand," in *Nineteenth-Century French Studies* 13 (Summer–Fall 1984): 111, 113. It is difficult to acknowledge the volume of critical material devoted to *Histoire de ma vie*. I simply mention here a few studies whose focus on the mother's and/or Sand's coming to writing have borne fruit for my own harvest: Philippe Berthier, "Corambé: Interprétation d'un mythe," in *George Sand*, ed. Simone Vierne (Paris: Sedes, 1983), 7–20; Bozon-Scalzetti, "Vérité"; Béatrice Didier, "Femme/Identité/Écriture: À Propos De L'*Histoire de ma vie* de George Sand," *Revue des Sciences Humaines* 42 (October–December 1977): 561–76; Lucienne Frappier-Mazur, "Nostalgie, dédoublement et écriture dans *Histoire de ma vie*," *Nineteenth-Century French Studies* 17 (Spring–Summer 1989): 265–75; Hiddleston, *George Sand and Autobiography*.

winter, is finally borne off by the empty bucket into the night sky. Calvino suggests that the bucket, "symbol of privation and desire and seeking," tells of "privation that is transformed into lightness, and makes possible... flight."[16] Two brief chapters after the desolation provoked by Sophie's missing letter, Aurore invents the volatile Corambé in her mother's image—in other words, transforms privation into muse—and makes her (as yet unwritten) literary debut.[17]

We can begin to map Sand's coming to writing, following the path she provides through a landscape that is lushly paradoxical. Sand's *Histoire* both discourages a postmodern matrilineal derivation of her writing and resists an alignment with a paternal legacy of letters read in contrast to maternal song or even silence. One writes, the other sings. Yet the partition is neither conventionally hierarchized nor simply gender-bound in this text in which the mother's birdsong must be weighed not just against the father's correspondence but against the epistolary talents of a paternal grandmother who is compared to Madame de Sévigné.[18]

Genealogies

Jane Gallop reminds us that there is a tradition of women writing letters, and that such women are first and foremost "Ladies," noblewomen like Madame de Sévigné—and Aurore de Saxe, we might interpolate—then, later, members of the bourgeoisie, but not women

---

[16] Italo Calvino, "Lightness," in *Six Memos for the Next Millennium* (New York: Vintage, 1988), 28.

[17] "And then, I also had to complement it at times with a woman's garb, because what I had loved best and understood best until then was a woman—my mother. So s/he often appeared to me with female features" (605) ["Et puis, il me fallait le compléter en le vêtant en femme à l'occasion, car ce que j'avais le mieux aimé, le mieux compris jusqu'alors, c'était une femme, c'était ma mère. Ce fut donc souvent sous les traits d'une femme qu'il m'apparut" (1:813)].

[18] Maurice, whose own letters repeatedly anticipate, reflect on, dote on his mother's epistles, writes: "Your letter is charming, and I am not the first to tell you that you write like Sévigné" (203) ["Ta lettre est charmante, et je ne serai pas le premier à te dire que tu écris comme Sévigné" (1:207)]. Sand's narrative of her grandmother's talents borrows the comparison: "She spent her life writing letters—which were, I must say, almost as good as those of Mme. de Sévigné (100) ["Elle passait sa vie à écrire des lettres qui valaient presque, il faut le dire, celles de madame de Sévigné" (1:50)].

of the people, women like—again we can interpolate—Sophie Delaborde Dupin.[19] I want to keep this class contextualization firmly in mind while reflecting on the central role given to a nonwriting mother in Sand's mythology of her genesis as writer. For here, as at almost every point at which a gender issue seems to be at stake in *Histoire de ma vie*, it is underwritten by class lines.

Sand's description of Sophie as "this untutored nature" (469) ["cette nature inculte" (1:606)] is cast from the perspective of the very cultured woman who is her grandmother: "My grandmother often watched her with a sort of curiosity" (469) ["Ma grande-mère l'observait souvent avec une sorte de curiosité" (1:606)]. And Sand goes on to attribute her mother's lack of cultivation to what we would today call socioeconomic factors: "My mother was a great artist who had missed her calling for a lack of training.... [H]aving had no education, she was ignorant" (469) ["Ma mère était une grand artiste manquée faute de développement.... [E]lle n'avait rien appris, elle ne savait rien" (1:606)]. According to Sand's account, Sophie's own apprehensions about her intellectual and cultural deficiencies were grounded in her social rather than her gender position: "What tormented her, in relation to my father, was the superiority of intelligence and education which she attributed to society women" (470) ["Ce qui la tourmentait, par rapport à mon père, c'était la supériorité d'intelligence et d'éducation qu'elle supposait aux femmes du monde" (1:608)].

At several points in her text Sand laments the lost traces, the unrecorded history of her mother's life, but her unlettered mother is each time inscribed in the obscure annals of her class. The amputated narration of her mother's immediate family is placed in a wider social context:

> If I have not said more [on behalf of my maternal grandfather], it is because I do not know any more. My mother hardly spoke of her parents.... Who was her paternal grandfather? She knew nothing of him, nor did I. And her grandmother? Nothing more. Clearly the genealogies of ordinary people cannot compete with

19 Jane Gallop, "The Other Woman," in *Thinking through the Body* (New York: Columbia University Press, 1988), 160–78.

those of the rich and powerful in this world. No title, no escutcheon, no painting preserves the memory of these obscure generations who spend time on this earth without leaving a trace. The poor die entirely. (114)

[Si je n'en dis pas davantage [sur le compte de mon grand-père maternel] c'est que je n'en sais pas davantage. Ma mère ne parlait presque pas de ses parents.... Qui était son grand-père paternel? Elle n'en savait rien, ni moi non plus. Et sa grand-mère? Pas davantage. Voilà où les généalogies plébéiennes ne peuvent lutter contre celles des riches et des puissants de ce monde.... Aucun titre, aucun emblème, aucune peinture ne conserve le souvenir de ces générations obscures qui passent sur la terre et n'y laissent point de traces. Le pauvre meurt tout entier. (1:71)]]

She couches the imperative to record her own lineage in a more broadly based exhortation to the people:

Artisans, who are beginning to understand all things, peasants who are learning to write, don't forget your departed ones any longer.... The trowel, the pickaxe, or the pruning hook are symbols just as beautiful as the horn, the tower, or the bell.... Write your stories, all of you who have understood your lives and probed your hearts. For no other reason do I write mine and am I about to tell you the story of my forebears. (86)

[Artisans, qui commencez à tout comprendre, paysans, qui commencez à savoir écrire, n'oubliez donc plus vos morts.... La truelle, la pioche ou la serpe sont d'aussi beaux attributs que le cor, la tour ou la cloche.... Écrivez votre histoire, vous tous qui avez compris votre vie et sondé votre cœur. Ce n'est pas à d'autres fins que j'écris la mienne, et que je vais raconter celle de mes parents. (1:28–29)]][20]

---

[20]   Sand goes so far as to propose a very modern kind of social history derived from fragments of the social record: "History...makes use of everything: a merchant's bill, a cookbook, a laundry list." (119) ["L'histoire se sert...de tout, d'une note de marchand, d'un livre de cuisine, d'un mémoire de blanchisseuse" (1:79)]. In passing, it is worth recalling that Derrida links the birth of writing (in the common

Sand begins her autobiography with a lengthy narrative genealogy—most famously of her father's line, but also, less directly, of her mother's. Seeking to correct the emphasis of biographers who have obscured her maternal lineage behind her illustrious paternal line, Sand proclaims: "One is not only the offspring of one's father, one is also a little, I believe, that of one's mother" (77) ["On n'est pas seulement l'enfant de son père, on est aussi un peu, je crois, celui de sa mère" (1:15)]. When she continues, it becomes clear that what is at stake in the recuperative gesture she is shaping is class: "If my father was...next of kin to Charles X and Louis XVIII, it is no less true that my bloodlines are tied to the people in a way as intimate and direct" (77) ["Si, (du côté paternel) je me trouve...proche parente de Charles X et de Louis XVIII, il n'en est pas moins vrai que je tiens au peuple par le sang, d'une manière tout aussi intime et directe" (1:15–16)]. She goes on to present her maternal grandfather, Antoine Delaborde, *maître oiselier*, and her maternal godfather, also a bird seller. There follows a lengthy "digression" (79–81; 1:18–22) from ancestry to ornithological affinity to bird lore, which Sand abruptly closes along with this first chapter in order to go on, in chapters 2 and 3, to an elaboration of the paternal bloodline: "But it is time to close this treatise on birds and return to the one on my birth" (81) ["Mais il est temps de clore ce chapitre des oiseaux et d'en revenir à celui de ma naissance" (1:22)].

When we follow the path of birds throughout Sand's autobiography, however, it becomes clear that she is not in fact departing from the history of her heritage and birth by telling stories about birds, but rather tracing a storyline that is metaphorically and metonymically continuous with her matrilineage. If the second and third chapters constitute a kind of narrative family tree, discursively schematizing the paternal line, chapter 1 takes a different but parallel iconographic approach: it presents a narrative family totem, anecdotally emblematizing the maternal line.[21]

---

sense of the term) with genealogical anxiety. Jacques Derrida, *Of Grammatology*, trans. Gayatri Chakravorty Spivak (Baltimore: Johns Hopkins University Press, 1974), 124.

[21]   In the words of Béatrice Didier, "The bird is the maternal totem" ["L'oiseau, c'est le totem maternel"] ("Femme/Identité/Ecriture," 564).

After noting her descent from a line of bird sellers, Sand goes on to describe her mother's birdlike nature, along with the special power over birds that is her maternal legacy. She extols the moral and aesthetic superiority of winged creatures, and particularly admires their domesticity and talent for nurturing, on the one hand, and their dexterity, grace, and artistry, on the other. She then launches into a series of ornithological anecdotes, the first and longest of which is worth lingering on for its condensation of the bird's place in her life narrative.

Jonquille and Agathe are two baby warblers rescued by Sand from different nests and tenderly nurtured by her. One day, however, Sand, busy writing a novel, tires of tending to live feathers and turns back to her quill. The (slightly) older of the two birds then learns to gather food, not to feed herself but to nourish the younger. Although the narrative emphasis is on the remarkable nurturing capability of the older bird, who, herself still a fledgling, takes on an "adoptive daughter" ["fille adoptive"], and on the inseparability of adoptive mother and daughter forever after, the anecdote also more quietly illustrates maternal and filial ambivalence. The bird impeccably performs the maternal role that the text everywhere demands, but Sand, here playing the bird-woman role usually performed by Sophie, shadows and modifies the mother bird part, abandoning the requisite solicitude. Her background role in the anecdote discreetly represents the darker side of that recurrent figure of a tender mother bird who will come to peck her growing babies out of the nest (1:1111).[22]

---

[22] Although it is Sophie who, in her mother-in-law's not disinterested characterization, is predominantly identified with the inconstant mother bird, the image returns several times in association with different characters in the course of *Histoire*. One of Aurore's two maids, Rose (chosen by and identified with Sophie), is similarly described by Sand: "I think she was one of those good mother hens that care for their young most tenderly as long as the chicks can sleep under their wings, but who peck at them freely the moment they begin to fly and run about on their own" (583) ["Je pense qu'elle était de la nature de ces bonnes couveuses qui soignent tendrement leurs petits tant qu'ils peuvent dormir sous leur aile, mais qui ne leur épargnent pas les coups de bec quand ils commencent à voler et à courir seuls" (1:777–78)]. Sand's close friend the actress Marie Dorval portrays herself as mother in like terms: "'My children,' she said, 'claim I loved them less and less as they grew up. That isn't true, but it is true I loved them differently....Only little children are worth being brooded and fussed over in that way'" (972) ["Mes enfants, disait-elle, prétendent que je les ai moins aimés à la mesure qu'ils grandissaient. Cela n'est pas vrai; mais il est bien certain que je les

Rather tangentially, the anecdote presents what is, I would argue, its veritable silent heart: the image of Sand's desk as amalgamated dining/writing table. She writes:

> One day I was writing some novel or other which intrigued me a little....But, finally, appetite won out, and Jonquille, land- ing...on my table, came to obliterate the last word at the end of my pen, while Agathe...beat her wings at my side and stretched her wide-open beak with desperate cries. I was in the middle of the dénouement....I pointed out to her that...she had under her nose some excellent food in a pretty dish. (79–80)

> [Un jour, j'écrivais je ne sais quel roman qui me passionnait un peu....Mais enfin l'appétit se réveilla, et Jonquille, sau- tant...sur ma table, vint effacer le dernier mot au bout de ma plume, tandis qu'Agathe...battait des ailes et allongeait de mon côté son bec entrouvert avec des cris désespérés. J'étais au milieu de mon dénouement....Je lui fis observer...qu'elle avait sous le bec une excellente pâtée dans une jolie soucoupe. (1:18–19)]

---

ai aimés autrement....Il n'y a que les petits enfants qui soient dignes d'être choyés et couvés ainsi" (2:238)]. Most curious, in the network of mother bird images, is the poem Maurice includes in a letter to his mother, along with an imprecation to continue caring for his illegitimate son, Aurore's half-brother Hippolyte. He writes: "Oh, no, we must not abandon that little creature....Let us not justify that terrible pronouncement on the human species delivered through the mouths of young birds: "Our mothers shall raise us, / Every chick, as many as we are. / Had we been born to humankind, / We might be left at someone's door" (231) ["Oh! non, il ne faut pas abandonner cette faible créature....Ne justifions pas cette sen- tence terrible pour l'espèce humaine, que l'on fait prononcer à de jeunes oiseaux: "Nous allons tous, tant que nous sommes, / Par notre mère être élevés. / Peut-être si nous étions hommes, / Serions-nous aux enfants trouvés" (1:248)]. Sand's cita- tion of her father's praise of his mother's open-minded munificence and support of family bonds resonates ironically with her subsequent rejection of Hippolyte's counterpart, Aurore's half-sister Caroline, Sophie's first child (of an other—and perhaps illegitimate—bed). It also resounds ironically in the context of the disrup- tion of the Sophie/Caroline/Aurore family caused by the grandmother's custody of Aurore. In *Teverino*, a novel to which Sand refers the reader in the course of expounding on Aurore's winged matrilineage, the bird-girl Madeleine is accused of misusing food to lure young birds to her, seductively disrupting bird families. Though Madeleine is a much more sympathetic character than is her accuser, a misguided priest, the charge takes its place in a vast network of ambivalently imagined nurturing.

Here, in the opening chapter of her autobiography, Sand situates herself as writer between bird and pen. Yet the issue raised for me by this tableau is not that of a woman torn between motherhood and work but that of a writer bound to both feathers and quills, striving to join matter to spirit in the act of writing. Her paper, marked by pen strokes and brushed by tail feathers, emblematically links creativity to its material sources. Her desk is the site not of a struggle but of a suture—of the material to the spiritual, of labor to art, of the people to the aristocracy.

The Birds

For W. S. Merwin, birds take a primeval place in the human imagination as "our elders, our originals, our predecessors in life and death."[23] For George Sand reconstructing her maternal ancestry, Merwin's words are literalized. Her bird seller forebears have uncanny affinities with the creatures they handle (though it is unclear whether proximity breeds affinity, and metonymy metaphor, or vice versa). Through mother, grandfather, godfather—all the birdlike progenitors of her biological and spiritual line—Sand persistently claims her birthright as the daughter of her mother and a daughter of the people. Her lower-class maternal line is routinely juxtaposed to her noble paternal lineage in terms of a chain riveting Aurore to Sophie to the originary plebeian ancestor, coded as bird seller. Cautioning Aurore about her marginal position in aristocratic circles, Sophie predicts, "They'll never forgive you for being my daughter and for having a bird seller as a grandfather" (570) ["On ne t'y pardonnera pas d'être ma fille et d'avoir eu un grand-père marchand d'oiseaux" (1:757)]. Speaking of her grandmother's patrician rejection of her half-sister Caroline, Sand asks, "But wasn't I also the daughter of Sophie Delaborde, granddaughter of a bird seller?" (500) ["Mais n'étais-je pas, moi aussi, la fille de Sophie Delaborde, la petite-fille du marchand d'oiseaux?"

---

[23] W. S. Merwin, "'Where Late the Sweet Birds Sang,'" review of *Birds in Literature* by Leonard Lutwack, *New York Review of Books*, August 11, 1994, 40. Lutwack's *Birds in Literature* (Gainesville: University Press of Florida, 1994) provides a panoramic survey of the literary uses of birds.

(1:650)]. The legacy is so consistently brokered by a bird mediator that it becomes difficult to separate its constituent threads—bird/ mother/people—threads on which Sand hangs her self-portrait of the artist.[24]

Birds are musicians and poets. "The bird-man is the artist" (79), Sand proclaims at the beginning of her book ["L'homme-oiseau, c'est l'artiste" (1:18)]. If Sophie sings like a bird but knows no notes, has an aptitude for all the arts but cultivates none (1:606–8), loves botany but mocks the erudition of botanical names (1:774–75), what is her relationship to the figure of the artist? More pointedly, how do we configure the birdlike Sophie with her more anchored artist daughter? Sand gives the reader (and, more critically, herself) a way back from the artist to Sophie through the mediation of Corambé. Sand explains the advent of Corambé as a messianistic coming: "I did what humanity had done before me. I searched for a mediator, an intermediary, a man-god" (604) ["Je fis ce que l'humanité avait fait avant moi. Je cherchai un médiateur, un intermédiare, un Dieu-homme" (1:811)]. But Corambé crosses categories, fuses the religious with the aesthetic and the social. As compellingly, if less concisely, Sand's text tells us that Corambé mediates many relationships, not only that between deity and humanity. The story of her life is the story of how Sand comes to reconcile the contradictions of her situation: ideal and real, spirit and matter, art and labor, aristocratic and popular, daughter and mother (and so on). In abstract terms, Corambé is the name of the myth by which we may read the process of reconciliation.

A fantasy figure who emerges bearing Sophie's facial features precisely when she fades from view, Corambé, another creature of the air, part tender mother, part god, part muse, is also perhaps the finest

---

[24]   Toward quite another end, Henry James mentions Sand's derivation from bird folk ("this young girl, the daughter of a bird-catcher"). Although he doesn't make the connection explicit, his note of her maternal ancestry prepares his choice of metaphor to convey her verbal facility: "She wrote as a bird sings; but unlike most birds, she found it unnecessary to indulge, by way of prelude, in twitterings and vocal exercises; she broke out at once with her full volume of expression." Henry James, "George Sand," in *Literary Criticism: French Writers* (New York: Library of America, 1984), 709, 717. See Evelyne Ender's insightful analysis of James's figuration of Sand in chapter 2 of her *Sexing the Mind* (Ithaca: Cornell University Press, 1995).

feathered avatar of Sand's aviary. Let me state plainly: I do not mean to claim that Corambé *is* a bird, but rather that Corambé embodies many of the characteristics that Sand otherwise assigns to birds, shares their company on the page, cohabits the same semantic universe. Metaphorically coequal with a bird, Corambé is created from a child's improvised "nest" of ideas: "S/he makes a nest with whatever straw can be gathered" (604) ["Il se fait un nid avec les fétus qu'il peut rassembler" (1:812)]. S/he "flies away" when Aurore, writing *Indiana,* begins to impose a form on her vague reveries: "My poor *Corambé* took flight forever as soon as I started to feel in a mood to persevere with a given subject" (925) ["Mon pauvre *Corambé* s'envola pour toujours, dès que j'eus commencé à me sentir dans cette veine de persévérance sur un sujet donné" (2:165)].

When, at the height of her need and its attendant adoration, Aurore erects a cult to Corambé, she decorates an altar with flowers, shells, and birds' nests, and makes a ritual of reverse sacrifices. Animals, most prominently birds, are brought to the shrine to be liberated: "For the duration of my secret ritual, I was able every day to deliver up, in honor of Corambé, a swallow, a redbreast, a goldfinch, even a house sparrow" (610) ["Tant que dura mon culte mystérieux, je pus tous les jours délivrer, en l'honneur de Corambé, une hirondelle, un rouge-gorge, un chardonneret, voire un moineau franc" (1:820)].

An affinity with birds is an initial structural sign of what is in fact a dynamic derivation of Corambé from Sophie's line.[25] Hatched in the void left by the missing letter, Corambé embodies and enables the fantasy life that the absent Sophie can no longer support. What Sand calls "the novel of Corambé" (622) ["le roman de Corambé" (1:839)] occupies the space from which Sophie is missing: "I still nursed an ill-fated desire for my absent mother. But there was no hope left for our cherished novel" (628) ["Je nourrissais toujours au fond de mon cœur une sorte de passion malheureuse pour ma mère absente. De notre cher roman, il n'était plus question" (1:848)]. One "roman" replaces another, and Corambé, taking up residence in Aurore's

---

25 As Philippe Berthier aptly remarks, "Each time Aurore delivers a baby bird for and through the grace of Corambé, it's as if she's delivering her mother" ["Chaque fois qu'Aurore délivre un petit oiseau pour et par Corambé, c'est un peu de sa mère qu'elle délivre"] ("Corambé," 15).

wounded soul, takes on the role of comforter and consoler as well as that of surrogate secret sharer of fantasy: "Corambé consoled and healed ceaselessly" (606) ["Corambé consolait et réparait sans cesse" (1:813)]. Corambé's powers of solace are especially called for when Aurore's pain is inflicted by any manner of ill that others speak or think of Sophie, and by deprivation of her proximity. When she is confined to her room in Nohant for preferring to live with her mother in Paris, Aurore is soothed by Corambé's presence: "So I spent three days in an assiduous tête-à-tête with Corambé. I related my sorrows to him, and he consoled me" (630) ["Je passai donc ces trois jours dans un tête-à-tête assidu avec Corambé. Je lui racontai mes peines, et il m'en consola" (1:851)]. Once released, Aurore goes to help an old peasant woman gather wood, fantasizing about doing similar laborious chores for her mother, while in the background she hears blackbirds singing: "That evening the song of the blackbird seemed to be Corambé's own voice that sustained and encouraged me" (631) ["Ce soir-là ce chant me parut la voix même de Corambé qui me soutenait et m'encourageait" (1:853)]. Again we find Corambé faded into the fused voices of birds, mother, people.

Corambé serves, then, as a continuation of Sophie, but also, in more negative terms and times, as a compensation for her. The comforts of Corambé can allay Sophie's absence, neglect, or insufficiency. In the wake of her mother's letterless departure, Aurore begins to understand Sophie's imperfections: "My mother felt more passion than affection for me....It was as if her soul had gaping lacks, unknown to her" (573) ["Ma mère avait pour moi...plus de passion que de tendresse. Il se faisait dans son âme comme de grandes lacunes dont elle ne pouvait se rendre compte" (1:762)]. Filling in for the once idealized Sophie, Corambé will be venerated for precisely those qualities Aurore comes to acknowledge as Sophie's lacks: "I think I was becoming a little like that poor crazy man who was looking for affection. I asked for it from the woods, the plants, the sunshine, the animals, and heaven knows what invisible being, who existed only in my dreams" (610) ["Je crois que j'étais devenue un peu comme ce pauvre fou qui cherchait la tendresse. Je la demandais aux bois, aux plantes, au soleil, aux animaux, et à je ne sais quel être invisible qui n'existait que dans mes rêves" (1:820)]. When creating Corambé, Aurore strives to form an accessible and so, necessarily, an imperfect god, a god made, imperfectly, in Sophie's image, but the nature of whose imperfections are made to enhance Sophie's image: "For that reason, I wished it to have a few of our failings and weaknesses. I looked for a failing which would be consistent with its perfection, and I chose excessive kindness and indulgence" (605) ["À cet effet, je souhaitais qu'il eût quelques-unes de nos erreurs et de nos faiblesses. Je cherchai celle qui pourrait se concilier avec sa perfection, et je trouvai l'excès de l'indulgence et de la bonté" (1:813)]. Like Sophie, Corambé will be flawed, but in a way that will serve to counteract her flaws. Such defects, by any other name, might be considered virtues. Aurore's godhead is generous to a fault, and overindulgent, like a phantasmatic good mother. S/he takes a place in a succession of good mother figures that stretches from Sophie to God to Corambé to the nun Marie Alicia, "my chosen mother" (679) ["la mère de mon choix" (1:925)].[26] This is not to say that Corambé *is* Sophie, any more than Sophie is a bird. With Béatrice Didier, I would argue that "Corambé is Proteus" ["Corambé, c'est Protée"][27]—but I imagine a limited proteanism, a net of associations and characteristics that stream into one another and recreate a multitude of shifting but related patterns.

Supplementing but never supplanting Sophie, Corambé retains her lost or desired or idealized characteristics. I have in mind particularly her diffused connection to writing. What Aurore calls "the novel of Corambé" ["le roman de Corambé"] replaces the co-authored fiction, "our cherished novel" ["notre cher roman"], in the literal sense of a novel as well as a fantasy, because Sophie, somewhat paradoxically in view of her identity as not-writer of letters, *is* in Aurore's mind her connection to writing. We can best tease out the threads of Sophie's

---

[26]   The passage in full is quite clear about the derivation and place of such figures in Aurore's life: "I needed someone to cherish and place in my thoughts above all other beings; to imagine perfection, tranquillity, power, and fairness through that being; to venerate an object superior to me and to give heartfelt, assiduous worship to something like God or Corambé. This something took on the grave and serene features of Marie-Alicia. She was my ideal, my holy love, my chosen mother" (679) ["J'avais besoin de chérir quelqu'un et de le placer dans ma pensée habituelle au-dessus de tous les autres êtres, de rêver en lui la perfection, le calme, la force, la justice; de vénérer enfin un objet supérieur à moi, et de rendre dans mon cœur un culte assidu à quelque chose comme Dieu ou comme *Corambé*. Ce quelque chose prenait les traits graves et sereins de Marie-Alicia. C'était mon idéal, mon saint amour, c'était la mère de mon choix" (1:925)].
[27]   Didier, "Femme/Identité/Ecriture," 571.

paradoxical status by way of Corambé's related identity as writing and (simultaneously) not-writing.

Alternately and sometimes all at once, Corambé functions for Aurore as muse, companion, co-author, subject, character, and title of a cycle of fictions. Child of contradiction—child of writing *as* contradiction—Corambé is born for Aurore in the gap between the patronage and censure of writing represented by the schism between grandmother and mother.

A bit of chronology:

1. At age twelve, shortly after the non-receipt of Sophie's letter, Aurore begins to write, to great acclaim at Nohant: "My grandmother had the kindness to declare...that they [her *descriptions*] were masterpieces" (601) ["Ma grand-mère eut la bonté de déclarer...que c'était des chefs-d'oeuvre" (1:806)].

2. Paris reacts less positively than Nohant: "One of my *descriptions* was sent to my mother, to show her how clever I had become; she replied, '*Your beautiful phrases really made me laugh; I hope you're not going to start to talk that way*'" (602) ["On envoya à ma mère une de mes *descriptions* pour lui faire voir comme je devenais habile et savante; elle me répondit: *Tes belles phrases m'ont bien fait rire, j'espère que tu ne vas pas te mettre à parler comme ça*" (1:808)].

3. Aurore concurs with Sophie's evaluation, and acts (almost) accordingly: "I therefore stopped *writing*, but the need to invent and compose tormented me nonetheless" (202) ["Je cessai donc d'*écrire*, mais le besoin d'inventer et de composer ne m'en tourmentait pas moins" (1:808)].

4. Aurore names her "médiateur" for the first time four pages later.

"Corambé" is the writing born when the twelve-year-old Aurore stops *writing*. It is best contrasted to what Sand calls "a fixed form, a logical outline" (603) ["une forme arrêtée, un plan régulier" (1:809)], and is best described, in terms borrowed from her text, as invention, fantasy, composition, and dream: "a permanent dream, as disconnected, as incoherent as the dreams of sleep" (622) ["un rêve permanent, aussi décousu, aussi incohérent que les rêves du sommeil"

(1:839)]. Thinking back to her twelve-year-old experiments with writing, Sand muses on the incommensurability of imagination and emotion with their apprehension in art: "The soul holds something that transcends form" (601) ["Il y a dans l'âme quelque chose de plus que dans la forme" (1:806)]. Linked to Sophie's condemnation of her *writing*, the "writing" embodied by Corambé (which I will henceforth call by that name) is a dense poetic narrative that is all the more malleable for its lack of visible traces. Unformulated and unanchored, it is emotionally charged, capricious, changeable, ethereal, and volatile—all characteristics inherited from Sophie.[28] At the time when Aurore feels most severed from her mother, Corambé replaces maternal nurturing yet continues to attach Aurore to her mother.

Most critically, Corambé plays for Aurore a role derivative of what the object relations analyst Christopher Bollas calls "the first human aesthetic": the infant experience of maternal handling as a process of transformation.[29] For Bollas, this first human (maternal) aesthetic is reenacted in all later aesthetic encounters. The "aesthetic moment" (which covers a range of experiences of rapt attention such as "a christian's conversion experience, a listener's rapture in a symphony...the uncanny pleasure of being held by a poem, a composition, a painting" [31–32]) is a "fundamentally wordless occasion" characterized by "the density of the subject's feeling and the fundamentally non-representational knowledge of being embraced by the aesthetic object" (31). Although this aesthetic, grounded in being and touching rather than saying, eventually yields to language and form, adult aesthetic reaction will always bear traces of the mother's

---

[28] "He was of too tenuous an essence to bend to the demands of form" ["Il était d'une essence trop subtile pour se plier aux exigences de la forme"]. She goes on to describe the incompatibility of *writing* with "those thousands of beings who lulled me every day as pleasant daydreams, those vague figures, those half-distinct voices that floated around me like paintings brought to life behind transparent veils" (925) ["ces milliers d'êtres qui me berçaient tous les jours de leurs agréables divagations, ces figures à moitié nettes, ces voix à moitié distinctes qui flottaient autour de moi comme un tableau animé derrière un voile transparent" (2:165)].

[29] Bollas uses the term "transformational object," which is grounded in the more conventional object relations term "transitional object," to insist on the idea of creative process inherent in early childhood experience of the other. See Christopher Bollas, *The Shadow of the Object: Psychoanalysis of the Unthought Known* (New York: Columbia University Press, 1987), especially chaps. 1 and 2; subsequent references are provided in the text.

original touch.[30] As adults, Bollas argues, we continue to bear the mark and the style of the mother's handling. Internalized, the structure of the maternal aesthetic transforms us well beyond encounters with art; even character is "an aesthetics of being" (35). Sand seems to anticipate a similar derivation of character and belief from early childhood handling when she writes:

> What is sure, what cannot be disputed in good faith after one has read the story of my childhood, is that I did not choose my opinions out of caprice, or because of artistic fancy, as has been said; they were the inevitable outcome of my early sorrows, my most sacred affections, the very circumstances of my life. (585)

> [Ce que l'on ne contestera pas...après avoir lu l'histoire de mon enfance, c'est que le choix de mes opinions n'a point été un caprice, une fantaisie d'artiste, comme on l'a dit: il a été le résultat inévitable de mes premières douleurs, de mes plus saintes affections, de ma situation même dans la vie. (I, 781)]

Her convictions, her caprices—Corambé, that abiding "fantaisie d'artiste" first in a line of replacements (what Bollas would call secondary transformational objects)—must be traced to the preverbal maternal aesthetic (the first transformational object).[31]

Though Corambé is an interim structure, filling a creative space between mother and future *writing*, all of Sand's texts to come will be ruled by the Corambé principle.[32] Sand as writer has a double

---

[30]   It is tempting to speculate on a connection between Sand's ongoing generativity—her unwillingness to hold on to her writing—and her first memory (which she presents as a kind of *cogito*) of being dropped at the age of two, by a maid to whom her mother had entrusted her (1:530).

[31]   Not unrelated to my sense of Corambé as transformational object is Lucienne Frappier-Mazur's suggestion that Aurore's dolls are transitional objects ("Nostalgie," 266–67).

[32]   Sand reports: "When I reached the age when one laughs at one's own naïveté, I returned Corambé to his proper place; that is, I reintegrated him into my imagination, among my dreams; but he continued to occupy a central position, and all the fictions that continued to form around him always emanated from that principal fiction" ["Quand je fus dans l'âge où l'on rit de sa propre naïveté, je remis Corambé à sa véritable place: c'est-à-dire que je le réintégrai, dans mon imagination, parmi les songes; mais il en occupa toujours le centre, et toutes les fictions qui continuèrent à se former autour de lui émanèrent toujours de cette fiction

imperative, a dual allegiance to Corambé which leaves two sets of traces: on the one hand, the trails of an abstract winged being who evokes spiritual and emotional flight, and on the other, the tracks of a material plumed creature who builds nests, digs for food, and bears feathers that can be plucked for a variety of utilitarian purposes, including writing implements, dresses, and fancy hats. *Writing* for Sand will always have an obligation to retain Sophie's part: to derive its sources from the purely and proudly unwritten, the soul untrammeled by any form. But it must also retain a material element, a manual component that is somewhat incongruously also derived from the working-class Sophie.[33] That is why the image of Sand seated at her desk between birds and quills seems to me fundamental. She must somehow keep the two imagined together, strive to reaffix the feather to the bird, as it were. She must retain the feather in the wing of her writing, as if to exorcise the bad conscience of the privileged woman writer whom Annie Leclerc describes as a spoiled woman, "a woman who was able to pick up the quill without having had to pluck it from the wing of a bird" ["femme pour qui la plume est venue en ses doigts sans qu'il lui faille l'arracher à l'aile de l'oiseau"].[34]

Sophie, not a goose-girl but a once and (phantasmatically) future *modiste,* would have handled feathers constantly in the course of her daily labor. This component of labor in and with the material world is later diffused as the blood of Sand's *writing:*

> To be an artist! Yes, I had wanted to be one...above all, to reconcile myself with myself. I could not bear to be idle and useless,

---

principale" [2:166]]. The adult writer retains a nostalgia for Corambé, whose flight is experienced as a loss: "I did not consider myself as having been cured of a mental aberration, but rather deprived of a faculty" [926] ["Je ne me crus donc pas guérie d'une maladie intellectuelle, mais, au contraire, privée d'une faculté" [2:167]].
[33] Isabelle Naginski discusses this material element in slightly different terms: "When [Sand] compared her art to the sewing of a hem, she was not so much reducing the artistic to the domestic as attempting to incorporate it into a vital and rich system in which the values of life were praised, its exuberant flow accepted generously and enjoyed." Naginski further argues that there is in Sand's writing a conscious and coherent articulation of a literary aesthetic, "a genuine 'prosaics' of the novel"—a wonderfully insightful term that we must understand in reference to an aesthetics not only of narrative but also of the commonplace, or quotidian. Isabelle Hoog Naginski, *George Sand: Writing for Her Life* (New Brunswick, N.J.: Rutgers University Press, 1991), 225.
[34] Annie Leclerc, "La Lettre d'amour," in *La Venue à l'écriture* by Hélène Cixous, Madeleine Gagnon, and Annie Leclerc (Paris: Union générale d'éditions, 1977), 138.

leaning, in my position as master, on the shoulders of the workers. If I could have dug the earth, I would have joined them....I would not, by preference, have chosen the literary profession....I would have preferred to live by the labor of my hands. (936)

[Etre artiste! oui, je l'avais voulu...avant tout, pour me récon- cilier avec moi-même, que je ne pouvais souffrir oisive et in- utile, pesant, à l'état de *maître,* sur les épaules des travailleurs. Si j'avais pu piocher la terre, je m'y serais mise avec eux....Par goût, je n'aurais pas choisi la profession littéraire....J'aurais voulu vivre du travail de mes mains. (2:181–82)]

Born of this legacy of labor fused with unlettered spirit soaring un- bound, Corambé is preserved in *writing.*

Corambé is not uncontested, however. There is a latent tension throughout *Histoire de ma vie* between the idea of raw spirit, or inspi- ration, and that of platitude, or mechanical repetition. The ethereal form of Aurore's first religious ideal, the mysterious cult of Corambé whose liturgy takes the form of a cycle of "songs" and whose altar is graced by the flight and song of birds (1:820–21), must be contrasted to the prosaic Christianity imposed on the adolescent Aurore, epito- mized by the catechism which she learns and repeats "like a parrot" (623) ["comme un perroquet" (1:840)].

Borne on the wing and the tongue of birds, an incipient reflection on language scattered through the pages of *Histoire de ma vie* fol- lows romanticism in privileging the unheard and the amorphous— "those half-distinct voices" (925) ["ces voix à moitié distinctes" (2:165)] that curiously characterize the otherwise musical eloquence of Corambé.[35] Yet it anticipates modernism in pursuing impressions of the already said. Aurore's youthful "parroting" of the catechism finds an echo in the squawking parrot never far from the convent teacher nicknamed "La Comtesse" for her foolish well-born airs: "At her window, or in front of her door, lived, scratched, and squawked at the sun the sole object of her affection—an old, gray, threadbare parrot, a surly beast on whom we heaped our insults and disdain"

[35]   As Sand reminds the reader on more than one occasion, "true poems reside in the soul's sanctuary, and they never emerge" (926) ["les vrais poèmes sont dans le sanctuaire de l'âme et...ils n'en sortent jamais" (2:166)]. On Corambé's eloquence and musicality, see, for example, 1:813, 853.

(669) ["A sa fenêtre ou devant sa porte, vivait, grattait et piaillait au soleil l'unique objet de ses amours, un vieux perroquet gris tout râpé, maussade bête que nous accablions de nos dédains et de nos insultes" (1:910)]. "La Comtesse," ever attentive to the constant shrieking and the constrained garden circuits of her chained "Jacquot," may recall, by contrast, the humbler bird lady of this text, Sophie, and the silent intimacy that she shares with creatures of the air.

Sophie's tacit eloquence is reflected elsewhere in association with maternity. Sand reveals Aurore's first pregnancy in a few words followed by a tableau: Aurore is confined to bed rest for six weeks. It is a very cold midwinter; her room is opened up to hordes of assorted freezing, starving birds. They take turns coming in from the cold to defrost and feed, and wheel madly about her bed. Presiding at this annunciation is a multiple and shifting ornithological presence in place of the Holy Dove.

For the child Aurore, there is an unprobed linking of birds, language, and death. Two anecdotes relate events that occur when she accompanies her mother to her father's military post in Spain at age four. It is when she watches pigeons being killed in the kitchen of an inn that she first grasps what the word "death" signifies: "This, however, was not what gave me a clear idea of death; I needed another spectacle to understand what that was....I knew the word and not the thing" (439) ["Je ne me fis pourtant pas pour cela une idée nette de la mort, et il me fallut un autre spectacle pour comprendre ce que c'était....Je connaissais le mot et non la chose" (1:560)]. Almost immediately following the text of the slaughter of the pigeons comes the account of a talking magpie in a cage at another inn. Upon hearing the magpie's repeated decree *"Muera, muera!"* the awed child is plunged into a fearsome fairy-tale world of talking birds (1:562). The adult narrator knows what the child cannot about the machine of language: "It did not occur to me that the words were mechanical and that the poor bird did not understand the meaning. To my mind, because he talked, he had to think and reason" (440) ["Je ne me rendis pas du tout compte de cette parole mécanique dont le pauvre oiseau ne comprenait pas le sens: puisqu'il parlait, il devait penser et raisonner, selon moi" (1:563)].

A child confuses the mechanical "parroting" of a word with human linguistic consciousness. The intervening awareness of an adult narrator introduces a potential element of irony. But the irony is undercut by the significant positioning of the anecdote immediately after the child's apprenticeship of the conformity of death's "word" and "thing," and shortly before the narrated deaths of her infant brother and her father. A magpie speaks the word of death—a "parole méca-nique," to be sure—yet in this case, the *jacquot* is a bird of death: it speaks a word of death that *is* the thing of death. There is material here for an extended meditation on language, irony, and sincerity.

Flaubert, of course, more famously delivered an extensive reflection on similar material—language, irony, sincerity, tenderness, and parrots—in *Un Cœur simple*.[36] His summary of the tale recalls its plot:

> The story of an obscure life, that of a poor girl ... tender as freshly baked bread. She loves, in this order: a man, the children of her mistress, her nephew, an old man she nurses, then her parrot; when the parrot dies, she has it stuffed and then, dying in turn, she confuses the parrot with the Holy Ghost.
>
> [Le récit d'une vie obscure, celle d'une pauvre fille ... tendre comme du pain frais. Elle aime successivement un homme, les enfants de sa maîtresse, un neveu, un vieillard qu'elle soigne, puis son per-roquet; quand le perroquet est mort, elle le fait empailler et, mou-rant à son tour, elle confond le perroquet avec le Saint-Esprit.][37]

An inventory of parallels between *Un Cœur simple* and *Histoire de ma vie* is inescapable, though it vastly oversimplifies a complex web of texts. Briefly, then:

1. Tales of love and loss; serial attachments
FLAUBERT: Félicité loves a man, Théodore; her mistress's children, Paul and Virginie; her nephew, Victor; passing soldiers, victims of cholera, Polish refugees; le père Colmiche; a parrot; God.

---

[36] For two readings of *Un Cœur simple* that persuasively argue for accommodat-ing both linguistic irony and simplicity of heart, see Ross Chambers, "An Invita-tion to Love: Simplicity of Heart and Textual Duplicity in 'Un Cœur simple,'" in *Story and Situation: Narrative Seduction and the Power of Fiction* (Minneapolis: University of Minnesota Press, 1984), 123–50; and Nathaniel Wing, "Reading Sim-plicity: Flaubert's 'Un Cœur simple,'" in *Nineteenth-Century French Studies* 21 (Fall–Winter 1992–93): 88–101.
[37] Flaubert to Mme. Roger des Genettes, June 19, 1876, cited by Pierre-Marc de Biasi in his introduction to Gustave Flaubert, *Trois contes* (Paris: Seuil, 1993), 249–50.

SAND: Aurore loves her mother, Sophie; Corambé; God; the nun, Marie Alicia; writing.

2. Ornithological apotheoses

FLAUBERT: Félicité's love for the parrot Loulou might in less simple terms be called idolatry. She conflates the parrot with the Holy Spirit, by way of the Dove. In a dying hallucinatory moment she offers the parrot (now dead and stuffed) to God on a street altar set up for Corpus Christi. Her dying vision transforms the parrot into God.

SAND: Aurore's cult of Corambé conflates her imaginary companion with Christ and the spirit of writing. She liberates birds as reverse sacrificial offerings to her deity. She erects a forest shrine to Corambé that is discovered by her playmate Louiset, who mistakes it for a Corpus Christi altar.

3. Language, parrots, and other birds

FLAUBERT: Writes with a borrowed stuffed parrot on his desk. A lifelong obsession with issues of originality and imitation in language crystallizes in the figure of a parrot. An early plan gives Félicité a supernatural power over animals. This narrows to an affinity with a bird. Flaubert read in Maury that "the soul leaving its mortal remains has always been represented by the image of a bird flying away" ["c'est toujours sous l'image d'un oiseau qui s'envole, qu'on s'est représenté l'âme quittant sa dépouille mortelle"].[38] (See Julian Barnes for a full inventory of Flaubertian parrots.)[39]

SAND: Writes with live warblers on her desk. A childhood conviction that real poetry is unwritten liberates her pen. Only Sophie and Corambé are (silently) eloquent. The rest is chatter. Parrots

---

[38] Cited by Peter Michael Wetherill in his introduction to Gustave Flaubert, *Trois Contes* (Paris: Garnier, 1988), 50; from Alfred Maury, *Croyances et légendes du moyen âge* (Paris: Champion, 1896), 272.

[39] On parrots in Flaubert, see not only the most famous source, Julian Barnes, *Flaubert's Parrot* (New York: Knopf, 1985), but also Philippe Bonnefis, "Exposition d'un perroquet," *Revue des sciences humaines* 181 (January–March 1981): 59–78. Martin Bidney points out parallels between parrots and other images in *Un Cœur simple* and *Histoire de ma vie* in "Parrots, Pictures, Rays, Perfumes: Epiphanies in George Sand and Flaubert," *Studies in Short Fiction* 22 (Spring 1985): 209–17. I owe to Bidney an awareness of the Countess's parrot in *Histoire*.

and magpies and writers chatter. Sophie has a supernatural power over birds. Magpies and pigeons have an early association with death. When Corambé takes flight, inspiration dies.

The Purloined Parrot

To purloin, says Lacan, is not, etymologically speaking, to steal but rather to prolong, to divert, or to put a(long)side.[40] Similarly, the subtitle of this chapter does not refer to literary theft or imitation. I don't seek particularly to establish influence or even to reverse established patterns of influence. I don't want to pursue concepts of priority and belatedness. I don't wish to claim that Sand's was the original and Flaubert's the copied parrot—or, for that matter, that a primitive parrot conceived by Sand was later refined by Flaubert. (Remember: Sand's "parrot" was a magpie, a pigeon, a warbler, a robin, a finch, a mother, and so on—and only tangentially a parrot.) Rather than suggest theft or plagiarism or, more politely, borrowing of bird images, I want to follow lateral intertextual migration patterns. I want to propose juxtaposing parrots and warblers and magpies, the cult of Loulou and the cult of Corambé, reading Flaubert and Sand in correspondence.

Flaubert's self-acknowledged debt to Sand for *Un Cœur simple* has been consistently understood (if most often disputed) as owing to her part in their correspondence: the influence or effect of her letter writing on his literary writing.[41] In turning now to Sand with Flaubert, I want to read together, through the lenses of the Sand-Flaubert correspondence, *Histoire de ma vie* and *Un Cœur simple*. My point is not to trace the influence or effect of one writer on another but to look at each as reader of the other, and to consider the effects of this prodigious early readership on later readers.

[40] Jacques Lacan, "Seminar on the Purloined Letter," in *The Purloined Poe*, ed. John P. Muller and William J. Richardson (Baltimore: Johns Hopkins University Press, 1988), 43.
[41] For a history and critique of critical attempts to disparage Sand's influence on Flaubert, see Naomi Schor, "Il et elle: Nohant et Croisset," in *George Sand: Une Correspondance*, ed. Nicole Mozet (Paris: Christian Pirot, 1994), 269–82, and chapter 6 ("Living On: Flaubert's Idealism") of her *George Sand and Idealism*. Schor's is one of the few voices raised (with Biasi's, briefly in his introduction to *Trois Contes*) in support of the effect of Sand's writing on Flaubert's.

Une Vie, Mon Cœur simple
(Sand and Flaubert in Correspondence)

CHRONOLOGY

1847–1854: Sand writes *Histoire de ma vie.*

1855: Flaubert reads *Histoire de ma vie* serially published in *La Presse.* "Every day I read George Sand and consistently I feel indignant for a good quarter hour" ["Tous les jours je lis du George Sand et je m'indigne regulièrement pendant un bon quart d'heure"], he writes (letter to Louis Bouilhet, May 30, 1855)].[42]

1857: Sand and Flaubert first meet at the theater.

1863: First exchange of letters.

1866: The correspondence takes off. Flaubert writes to Sand (September 22, 1866): "I have read straight through the ten volumes of your *Histoire de ma vie* (I already knew about two-thirds of it, but in fragments only). What struck me the most is the convent life. I have many thoughts about it, which I'll remember to tell you" ["J'ai lu, d'une traite, les 10 volumes de l'*Histoire de ma vie* dont je connaissais les deux tiers environ, mais par fragments. Ce qui m'a le plus frappé c'est la vie de couvent. J'ai sur tout cela quantité d'observations à vous soumettre qui me reviendront"].

January 1, 1869, Flaubert to Sand: "I found the Goncourts in a state of frenzied admiration for a book called *Histoire de ma vie* by G. Sand—which goes to show that they are stronger in good taste than in erudition" ["J'ai trouvé les De Goncourt dans l'admiration

---

[42] All quotations from the Sand-Flaubert correspondence are from *Gustave Flaubert–George Sand: Correspondance,* ed. Alphonse Jacobs (Paris: Flammarion, 1981), and are cited in the text by reference to date; the translations, which I have occasionally modified, are from *Flaubert–Sand: The Correspondence,* trans. Francis Steegmuller and Barbara Bray (London: HarperCollins, 1993). Quotations from Flaubert's other correspondence are from Gustave Flaubert, *Correspondance,* ed. Jean Bruneau, 6 vols. (Paris: Gallimard [Pléiade], 1973–2007), and are provided in the text by reference to date and recipient.

frénétique (sic) d'un ouvrage intitulé *Histoire de ma vie* par G. Sand. Ce qui prouve de leur part plus de bon goût que d'érudition"].[43]

February 23–24, 1869, Flaubert to Sand: "You say some very true things about the unknowing inner life of children. Anyone who could see clearly into their little brains would discover the roots of human genius, the origin of the Gods, the sap that determines subsequent actions, etc....The child and the barbarian (the primitive) do not distinguish reality from fantasy. I remember very clearly that when I was five or six I wanted to 'send my heart' to a little girl I was in love with (I mean my *physical* heart). I pictured it lying on a bed of straw in a basket—the sort of hamper they put oysters in. But no one has gone as far as you in these analyses. Your *Histoire de ma vie* has pages on the subject that are extraordinarily profound" ["Vous me dites des choses bien vraies sur *l'inscience* des enfants. Celui qui lirait nettement dans ces petits cerveaux y saisirait les racines même [*sic*] du génie humain, l'origine des Dieux, la sève qui produit plus tard les actions....L'enfant et le barbare (le primitif) ne distinguent pas le réel du fantastique. Je me souviens très nettement qu'à cinq ou six ans je voulais 'envoyer mon cœur' à une petite fille dont j'étais amoureux (je dis mon cœur *matériel*). Je le voyais au milieu de la paille, dans une bourriche, une bourriche d'huîtres! Mais personne n'a été si loin que vous dans ces analyses. Il y a dans l'*Histoire de ma vie*, des pages là-dessus, qui sont d'une profondeur démesurée"].

October 10, 1871, Sand to Flaubert: "But we need to find the link, the reconciliation, between your truths of reason and my truths of feeling" ["Mais il faudrait trouver le lien et l'accord entre tes vérités de raison et mes vérités de sentiment"].

March 1876: Flaubert begins to write a text he originally called *Histoire d'un cœur simple*.

January 15, 1876, Sand to Flaubert: "When people's natures contrast on certain points it's difficult for them to comprehend each other, and

---

[43] Since the last volume of *Histoire de ma vie* had been published in 1855, the Goncourts, coming to the work only in 1869, were not exemplars of erudition, according to Flaubert.

I fear you will understand me no better now than before" ["Les natures opposées sur certains points se pénètrent difficilement et je crains que tu ne comprennes pas mieux aujourd'hui que l'autre fois"].

February 6, 1876, Flaubert to Sand: "Here, I think, is the essential difference between us. . . . You, always, in whatever you do, begin with a great leap toward heaven, and then you return to earth. You start from the *a priori*, from theory, from the ideal. . . . I, poor wretch, remain glued to the earth. . . . [E]verything disturbs me, everything lacerates and ravages me, though I make every effort to soar" ["Voici, je crois, ce qui nous sépare essentiellement. . . . Vous, du premier bond, en toutes choses, vous montez au ciel, et de là vous descendez sur la terre. Vous partez de l'*a priori*, de la théorie, de l'idéal. . . . Moi . . . tout m'émeut, me déchire, me ravage et je fais des efforts pour monter"].

May 29, 1876, Flaubert to Sand: "You will see from my *Histoire d'un cœur simple* (in which you will recognize your own direct influence) that I am not as obstinate as you think. I believe you will like the moral tendency, or rather the underlying humanity, of this little work" ["Vous verrez par mon *Histoire d'un cœur simple* où vous reconnaîtrez votre influence immédiate que je ne suis pas si entêté que vous le croyez. Je crois que la tendance morale, ou plutôt le dessous humain de cette petite oeuvre vous sera agréable!"].

June 8, 1876: Death of George Sand.

August 1876: Flaubert finishes *Un Cœur simple.*

April 1877: Flaubert sends a copy of *Un Cœur simple* to Maurice Sand, inscribed, "To Maurice Sand, in memory of your dear illustrious mother" ["À Maurice Sand, en pensant profondément à sa chère et illustre mère"].

August 29, 1877, Flaubert to Maurice Sand: "You speak to me of your dear illustrious mother! . . . How I miss her! How I need her! I began *Un Cœur simple* for her alone, solely to please her" ["Vous me parlez de votre chère et illustre maman! . . . [C]omme je la regrette! Comme j'en ai besoin! J'avais commencé *Un Cœur simple* à son intérêt exclusif, uniquement pour lui plaire"].

By way of this selective chronology I want to propose a map for reading the relationship between Sand's *Histoire de ma vie* and Flaubert's *Histoire d'un cœur simple* across the Sand-Flaubert *Correspondance*. Let me highlight and briefly develop some milestones of the suggested itinerary:

1. Flaubert's reading of Sand—most notably of her autobiography—undergoes a sea change once their correspondence is under way. His initial indignation turns to admiration—indeed, fascination ("j'ai lu, d'une traite"; "ce qui m'a...frappé"; "quantité d'observations"; "des pages...d'une profondeur démesurée").

2. Flaubert emphasizes the correspondences between puerility and simplicity ("l'enfant et...le primitif")—conditions that engender both human genius and idolatry—and lauds Sand's trailblazing analyses of the spiritual region that children and simple people cohabit ("they don't distinguish the real from the fantastic") ["ne distinguent pas le réel du fantastique"].

3. Flaubert offers a personal anecdote from his own childhood that dovetails with his joined comments on Sand's epistolary musings about her grandchildren and her representation of childhood in the autobiography. How does his unusual self-exposure (the revelation of his own simple heart) (a) affect a reading of *Un Cœur simple*, and (b) modify a reading of his reading of *Histoire de ma vie*?

4. Sand's title, *Histoire de ma vie*, and Flaubert's working title, *Histoire d'un cœur simple*, draw her autobiography and his tale together by their remarkably evocative structural similarity. The most obvious (and not surprising) difference is her possessive article as opposed to his indefinite article. But her choice of the less emotional word "life" as against his metonymic substitution of a "heart" for a "life" results in an unexpected chiasmus.

5. A recurrent and apparently underlying difference (of opinion, of approach) that is at once philosophical, epistemological, aesthetic, and temperamental is somehow harmonized if not neutralized in the course of the correspondence. Flaubert is less *headstrong* ("entêté": literally, *in his head*) than Sand would

have believed; she will be pleased by the *moral tendency,* or the *human grounding* of his tale. Given the emphasis, on both sides of the correspondence, on the lack of desire and in fact of ability that each has to be changed by or to change the other, I want to understand what Flaubert calls Sand's *influence* on his *Histoire* less as persuasion or as pressure than as a quite literal *inflow:* something of Sand has flowed into Flaubert's *Cœur simple.*

Together this series of points charts an evolution that can be summarized by its two endpoints: Flaubert's reading of Sand's work has changed; Sand's reading of Flaubert's work is about to change. But "change" is perhaps too strong a term for the modulation I want to explore: a mutual adaptation in two rather determined people of a certain age (the ripe period of their epistolary relationship finds Sand between sixty-two and seventy-two, Flaubert between forty-five and fifty-five). At issue is not only a shifting recognition of the other but also an alteration in self-perception that may best be described as a reading effect: an effect *of* reading and *of being read* that brings about an effect *on* reading.

Sand's influence, Flaubert's lessening bullheadedness, the new moral tendency or human grounding of his work in progress, Sand's anticipated reading pleasure and implied approval all suggest modifications of positions taken in a larger debate. At the core of the correspondence is an ongoing dialogue about how the self engages with writing, and with which of its constituent parts it is advisable to do so. The relative roles played by head, soul, body, and heart in the aesthetic process are debated. As the letters progress and as the correspondents advance in age, as the country enters a time of war and each of them enters an epoch of private loss, the conversation comes to linger with increasing frequency on the heart.[44]

---

[44] Among Sand's losses during the high years of the correspondence with Flaubert (1866–1876) were the deaths of her close friends Charles Duveyrier, François Rollinat, Armand Barbès, Charles Duvernet, and Jules Boucoiran; of her friend and daughter-in-law's father, Luigi Calamatta, and her ex-husband, Casimir Dudevant; and her own declining health. Flaubert's losses during these years included the deaths of friends Louis Bouilhet, Sainte-Beuve, Jules Duplant, Jules de Goncourt, and Ernest Feydeau; the deaths of his mother and of former lover Louise Colet; and his own financial debacle, with its attendant intestinal and nervous problems. Martine Reid has observed in the *Correspondance* a "connivence" that springs

TOPOLOGY

November 12–13, 1866, Flaubert to Sand: "How many of the dead we have in our hearts! Each of us carries his necropolis within him" ["Comme nous en avons dans le cœur, de ces morts! Chacun de nous porte en soi sa nécropole"].

December 5–6, 1866, Flaubert to Sand: "I feel an unconquerable aversion to putting anything of my heart on paper" ["J'éprouve une répulsion invincible à mettre sur le papier quelque chose de mon cœur"].

December 7, 1866, Sand to Flaubert: "Not put any of one's heart into what one writes? I don't, I simply do not understand. For my part I don't see how one can put anything else. Can one separate one's mind from one's heart?—are they two different things? Can limits be set to what one feels, can one's being be split in two?" ["Ne rien mettre de son cœur dans ce qu'on écrit? Je ne comprends pas du tout, oh mais, du tout. Moi il me semble qu'on ne peut pas y mettre autre chose. Est-ce qu'on peut séparer son esprit de son cœur, est-ce que c'est quelque chose de différent? est-ce que la sensation même peut se limiter, est-que l'être peut se scinder?"]

December 15–16, 1866, Flaubert to Sand: "I expressed myself badly when I told you 'one shouldn't write with one's heart.' What I meant was: don't put your own personality on stage....What you have to do is transport yourself, by an intellectual effort, into your Characters— not attract them to yourself" ["Je me suis mal exprimé en vous disant 'qu'il ne fallait pas écrire avec son cœur.' J'ai voulu dire: ne pas mettre sa personnalité en scène...Il faut, par un effort d'esprit, se transporter dans les Personnages et non les attirer à soi"].

January 23–24, 1867, Flaubert to Sand: "I believe the heart does not grow old. In some people it even expands with age....I get emotional

---

from a discourse of death and illness: "Mourning, melancholy, and a whining discussion of illness are the beating heart of the reflections Sand confides to Flaubert, and Flaubert to Sand" ["Deuil, mélancolie, nosographie grincheuse rythment les confidences de Sand à Flaubert et de Flaubert à Sand"]. Martine Reid, "Flaubert et Sand en correspondance," *Poétique* 85 (February 1991): 60.

over nothing. Everything troubles me, agitates me. To me, everything is like the north wind to the reed" ["Je crois que le cœur ne vieillit pas. Il y a même des gens chez qui il augmente avec l'âge....Il ne faut rien pour m'émouvoir. Tout me trouble et m'agite. Tout m'est aquilon comme au roseau"].

March 17, 1870, Sand to Flaubert: "You're defenseless against sorrow, like all who are tenderhearted" ["Tu es faible devant le chagrin comme tous ceux qui sont tendres"].

September 10, 1870, Flaubert to Sand: "I feel I'm drowning in sorrow—in cascades, rivers, oceans of it....I feel my heart is withered and dry" ["Ce sont comme des cataractes, des fleuves, des océans de tristesse qui déferlent sur moi....Je me sens le cœur desséché"].

October 26, 1872, Sand to Flaubert: "Please, please, listen to me! You're keeping an exuberant nature shut up in jail! You're trying to turn a kind and tender heart into a dedicated misanthropist" ["Je t'en supplie, écoute-moi! tu enfermes une nature exubérante dans une geôle. Tu fais, d'un cœur tendre et indulgent, un misanthrope de parti pris"].

January 12, 1876, Sand to Flaubert: "It's all one to me whether someone represents nonliving things realistically or poetically, but it's a different matter when it comes to the impulses of the human heart.... [S]upreme impartiality is antihuman, and a novel ought above all to be human" ["Peignez en réaliste ou en poète les choses inertes, cela m'est égal; mais, quand on aborde les mouvements du cœur humain, c'est autre chose....[L]a suprême impartialité est une chose antihumaine et un roman doit être humain avant tout"].

January 15, 1876, Sand to Flaubert: "In short, abandon the conventions of the realists and return to true reality...in which the desire for good nevertheless has a place and a use" ["Enfin, quitte le convenu des réalistes et reviens à la vraie réalité...où la volonté du bien trouve quand même sa place et son emploi"].

Paired with the earlier chronology, this brief topology clarifies Flaubert's allusion (in his letter of May 29, 1876) to Sand's "recognizable influence" on *Un Cœur simple,* and circuitously connects it with *Histoire de ma vie.* It is clear that Flaubert's attribution of influence to Sand in terms of the moral and human foundations of a text answers Sand's letter of January 12 which invokes precisely human and moral grounds and a vocabulary of good and evil to counsel against realist detachment in all matters that touch on the pulsing of the human heart—the seat, in Sand's terminology, not only of emotion but also of identity and self-presence. For Flaubert, Sand's "influence" on *Un Cœur simple*—the "human" and "moral" source of her anticipated pleasure—can, then, be traced to the heart, to her discourse of the heart. Now, if the heart is a recurrent object of discussion in the correspondence, it also plays a prominent and often graphic role in Sand's life story, particularly where the effects of her mother's exile are concerned. Alternately shattered, incinerated, erupting, or otherwise reacting, it is rarely relegated to the wings of description.[45]

I want to argue that Flaubert is reading Sand's *Histoire de ma vie,* reading it as a very focused *histoire de cœur,* a story of love and loss, when he writes *Un Cœur simple.* When we turn back to Flaubert's praise of *Histoire de ma vie* in his letter to Sand of February 23–24, 1869, we note a telling association of ideas. Flaubert marvels at the fecundity of children's unknowing (*inscience*); equates it with similar imaginative properties in the simple (*le primitif*); illustrates his point by relating the story of his own childhood plan to send his heart as a gift; and *at this point invokes Sand* ("No one has gone as far as you in these analyses. Your *Histoire de ma vie* has pages on the subject that are extraordinarily profound" ["Mais personne n'a été si loin que vous dans ces analyses. Il y a dans l'*Histoire de ma vie,* des pages là-dessus, qui sont d'une profondeur démesurées"]). It seems terribly important to note here not only that Félicité is implicitly linked to Aurore (*le primitif, l'enfant*), but also that they are linked *through Flaubert's own simple heart*—so that (for example) Félicité's attempts to locate her nephew's house on a map, Aurore's scheme to establish herself

---

[45] A few examples of the vagaries of this heart: "I was hardly awake when grief found me again, and my heart broke at the idea that my mother had left" (573) ["A peine fus-je éveillé que je retrouvai mon chagrin, et que mon cœur se brisa à l'idée que ma mère était partie" (1:761–62)]; "I felt like a fire had raged through me and left a searing emptiness where my heart should have been" (634) ["J'avais comme une énorme brûlure intérieure et comme un vide cuisant à la place du cœur" (1:858)]; and the earlier cited "My heart overflowed onto the paper" (571) ["Mon cœur y coulait à flots" (1:759)].

as a dressmaker, and Gustave's imagined delivery of a heart on ice are coequal fantasies. That Flaubert's praise of *Histoire de ma vie* is mediated by and referenced to the story of his heart suggests a direct contextual link. If, as I suggested earlier, Flaubert's allusion to influence might be interpreted as an influx, we can recall Sand's account of Aurore's devastated letter to Sophie on the eve of Sophie's departure: "My heart overflowed onto the paper, so to speak" ["Mon cœur y coulait à flots pour ainsi dire"]. Something from Sand flowed into Flaubert's *Cœur simple:* perhaps the heart of her *Histoire.*

But Flaubert can read Sand's *Histoire* as a tale of love and abnegation—as, precisely, L'*Histoire d'un cœur simple*—only once Sand has "read" Flaubert.[46] The *Correspondance* presents, among other things, a reading of Flaubert by Sand, in the course of which Flaubert comes to reread himself, comes to take stock of the depths that love and grief, if not reason, can plumb. He expresses an extraordinary degree of resignation in some of the letters, an acceptance of the mysterious linkages between art and emotion and personality: "I can have no temperament other than my own. Nor any aesthetic other than the one that proceeds from it" ["Je ne peux pas avoir un autre tempérament que le mien. Ni une autre esthétique que celle qui en est la conséquence" (February 6, 1876)].[47]

Flaubert's reading of Sand's *Histoire* (something between a reading and a rewriting, which we could call, in Barthes's sense, a writerly reading) would then simultaneously represent an oblique self-reading, a version of his own *histoire.* Although it may surprise that the series of losses and reattachments that define Félicité's story begins with

---

[46]   In her letter to Flaubert of October 25, 1871, Sand summarizes a philosophy of life and love as sacrifice: "To love, to sacrifice oneself, never to withdraw unless the sacrifice comes to harm the people it's meant to benefit, and then to sacrifice oneself again in the hope of serving a true cause, love.... Love and pity together go together. There you have the not very elaborate mechanics of my philosophy" ["Aimer, se sacrifier, ne se reprendre que quand le sacrifice est nuisible à ceux qui en sont l'objet, et se sacrifier encore, dans l'espoir de servir une cause vraie, l'amour.... Aimer et plaindre ne se séparent pas. Et voilà le mécanisme peu compliqué de ma pensée"].

[47]   Flaubert here echoes Sand's thoughts on the connection of personality and aesthetics. Her words, briefly recalled: "What cannot be disputed...is that [my opinions]...were the inevitable outcome of my early sorrows, my most sacred affections, the very circumstances of my life" (585) ["Ce que l'on ne contestera pas...c'est que le choix de mes opinions...a été le résultat inévitable de mes premières douleurs, de mes plus saintes affections, de ma situation même dans la vie" (1:781)].

a suitor, bypassing the founding maternal loss of Aurore's story—a loss that would have been particularly resonant for Flaubert during the period when he wrote *Un Cœur simple,* in the aftermath of his own mother's death—I would suggest that Flaubert's text doesn't so much ignore as displace maternal loss, playing it out indirectly through its Sandian intertext. In this rather unusual case of doubling, both Sand's *Histoire* (with its dominant plot of filial suffering) and its author come to stand in for maternal loss.[48]

Sand, in a similar vein, may well have reencountered her mother in the course of her correspondence with Flaubert. In fact, Sophie's much-awaited letter may finally surface in the Sand-Flaubert correspondence. I speak here of a letter whose form is neither authentic nor phantasmatic but rather, phantomatic. As a child suffering from the banishment of her mother and sister, Aurore acts out her ambivalence with a coveted doll she is given in a futile gesture of compensation by her grandmother:

> My first impulse was of intense pleasure. I took the little creature in my arms, smiled at her pretty smile, and held her like a young mother holds her newborn. But as I gazed at her and rocked her against my heart, the memories of the previous night came back to me. I thought of my mother and my sister, of my grandmother's harshness, and threw the doll away from me. But as the poor thing was still smiling, I picked her up again, held her some more, and soaked her with my tears, *abandoning myself to an illusion of maternal love that my aggrieved feeling of filial love intensified all the more sharply.* (502)

> [Le premier mouvement fut un vif plaisir; je pris la petite créature dans mes bras, son joli rire provoqua le mien, et je l'embrassai comme une jeune mère embrasse son nouveau-né.

---

[48] Following Sand's burial (at which time Flaubert was, we know, in the middle of writing *Un Cœur simple*), he confessed to Maurice: "It seemed to me that I was burying my mother a second time" ["Il m'a semblé que j'enterrais ma mère une seconde fois"]. Cited by Jacobs in *Correspondance,* 535 (trans. 399). That Sand played a maternal role for Flaubert is amply manifested in the course of the correspondence, not only by Flaubert's testimony to this effect but also by her well-evidenced patience, forbearance, and steadfast presence in the face of his multiple revisions, reschedulings, and generalized volatility.

• Mais, tout en la regardant en la berçant sur mon cœur, mes souvenirs de la veille se ranimèrent. Je pensai à ma mère, à ma soeur, à la dureté de ma grand-mère, et je jetai la poupée loin de moi. Mais comme elle riait toujours...je la repris, je la caressai encore et je l'arrosai de mes larmes, *m'abandonnant à l'illusion d'un amour maternel qu'excitait plus vivement en moi le sentiment contristé de l'amour filial.* (1:653–54; emphasis added)]

I would suggest that it is this *fort-da* dynamic of a filial wound regenerating maternal soothing in the person of the wounded daughter (who can then *be* what she wants to *have*)—much more than the age difference—that is responsible for Sand's molding, consoling, modulating posture opposite Flaubert in so much of their correspondence. And if, as I want to argue, the ghost of Sophie's letter haunts the correspondence with Flaubert, it is most perceptible in the continuing process of modulation and transformation that moves Flaubert to write to Sand of one particular epistle in these terms: "Your good letter...so lovingly maternal, has me deep in thought" ["Votre bonne lettre,...si tendrement maternelle, m'a fait beaucoup réfléchir" (December 31, 1875)].

Epilogue

> For the heart is a stubborn organ.
> TENNESSEE WILLIAMS

Let me return to my first and final subject. For I proposed mapping the relationship between Sand's *Histoire* and Flaubert's, across their correspondence, as a detour that would lead to a rereading of *Histoire de ma vie,* and through that, to a reconsideration of the fraught enterprise (then and now) of retrieving a mother's life. The clearly delicate project of approaching Sand's text through Flaubert's may be worth the accompanying set of risks, the ink spilled in caveats, and the indirection, if it has legibly charted a salvation experiment whose crux is to preserve silences in the narration of past lives. Sand's *Histoire* is a model for this sort of venture, in light of the privileged role of the unspoken in her text. Following from the maternal link with true poetry, through the unspoken, there is in Sand's wordy autobiography a conviction of reticence, whose paradoxically generative role in her voluminous work and loquacious style has been insufficiently explored.

What I have attempted, then, in seeking to defer to silence is a lateral rather than a retrospective reading of Sand's story. Reading in patches, mosaically and occlusively rather than holistically, for pattern in fragmentation instead of in linear shape, I have sought to place texts alongside each other in a relationship of *purloinment* rather than one of priority and belatedness. In the process, what may emerge instead of a reconstruction is a series of reverberations, recollections, and modulations.

To juxtapose Flaubert and Sand for versions of a heart whose passions drown out words is less to trace writing influence than to propose a reading strategy that answers to the reservations about reconstruction, retrospection, and anachronism which I have raised. Sand seeks to retrieve a mother's life in the course of writing her own, and meets a nearly blank record. Bouchardeau reconstructs her mother's past and must fill in the spaces of her mother's reticence—or let Sand do it symbolically for her. I want instead to suggest that by reading laterally rather than retrospectively (letting the texts read each other), we might not only respect the unspoken but come to valorize it, as Sand did. Paradoxically, for those of us now accustomed to the notion of women writers thinking back through the mother, this would mean, as Sand's story makes clear, deriving a woman's writing from and through and even thanks to her mother's silence.

I close with what remains a map, a map for reading Aurore and Félicité and Gustave together for stories of a simple heart: a child's heart, a servant's heart, a writer's heart, a heart that washes words away with tears, a heart delivered, like an oyster packed in straw, offered, like a worm-devoured parrot, to the gods.

4

A Different Story

In Dialogue with Huguette Bouchardeau

In late July 1999, two months after finishing the essay on George
Sand and Huguette Bouchardeau that became chapter 3, I interviewed
Bouchardeau in Paris. We met late one summer afternoon and chatted
for an hour or so in the breakfast room of her hotel.[1] Bouchardeau's
responses to the questions I posed sketched a story that was not quite
what I had been expecting, and that in fact departed from the one
I had already framed in my writing. (In a nutshell, I argue in chapter 3
that Bouchardeau's biography, *George Sand: La Lune et les sabots*,
and the memoir about her biological mother, *Rose Noël*, published
six months later, were twin mother books. I propose there that Sand,
as biographer of her mother in *Histoire de ma vie*, was foremother to

[1] After retiring from national politics, Bouchardeau made her home for years in
Aigues-Vives, in the Doubs, where she led a largely literary life, having founded
a publishing company, HB Éditions, and also served as mayor of the town. Currently she lives in Paris. To recapitulate briefly the highlights of her earlier career:
Born in 1935, Bouchardeau was brought up in a working-class family as one of six
brothers and sisters. She is an *agrégée de philosophie*, and taught for many years at
the lycée and university levels before turning her active affiliation with the PSU
(Parti socialiste unifié) into a political career that included serving as national
secretary of the PSU, candidate for president of the Republic, minister of the environment, president of the European Council of Ministers of the Environment,
and deputy for the Doubs. She has long been a strong feminist activist, working
particularly in the pro-choice movement. She is also a prolific writer, having published numerous biographies, novels, and autobiographical works in addition to a
few political pamphlets. For an analytic study of her writing, see Raylene Ramsay,
*French Women in Politics: Writing Power, Paternal Legitimization, and Maternal
Legacies* (New York: Berghahn Books, 2003).

Bouchardeau, who would then be doubly invested as daughter in her dual biographical venture.) The differences in our ways of telling the story disturbed and intrigued me—sequentially, in that order—and eventually reoriented my thinking, and my writing of the remaining chapters. Although I transcribed, translated, and edited the interview tape almost immediately after my meeting with Bouchardeau, I wrote the discussion of the material several years later, for reasons that form the heart of my discussion.

Interview with Huguette Bouchardeau, July 27, 1999, Paris

JB: I've read much of your writing, but [the works that are] especially interesting to me within the context of my own project are *Rose Noël* and *La Lune et les sabots*, and particularly the near overlap of their publication—which might be total chance, I guess...

HB: It's funny because... when I finished the writing of *George Sand*, which was a work that had been commissioned by an editor—

JB: I thought so...

HB: That's right. So, I had a great desire to write—I don't know why—but I had a great desire to write a book about my mother.

JB: Ahh...

HB: And, my mother, who was a very simple woman, said to me, "Oh, but that isn't... you know, it isn't at all the same story." [laughter] And so... it was very different. Because the book about George Sand was an accumulation of documents, a lot of reading, especially the entire correspondence of George Sand.... And so I was leaving a work where I had explored a lot of documentary material, mined a lot of documentary material, and here I wanted to write a book... this book about my mother came to me with great facility. It was like a rest, like... and it was like a gift I was giving to my mother. And so I wrote it without forcing myself, without inflicting a labor upon myself, it was... I wrote it just like that; I would have a table surface, on a plane, on a train; I wrote short sections that way, and then, later, I put them together, but it was...it was really a completely different kind of writing. And this seemed restful to me, compared to the other.

JB: Oh, I see. But it was through writing, or through researching *La Lune et les sabots* that—

HB: No. No, no, I did it completely afterward.

JB: Yes, but did the idea come to you...?

HB: No, I don't think that was so either.

JB: It was later?

HB: Yes, I think so, yes.

JB: So, then, you don't see any connection between—

HB: I don't, myself. Except that...the connection is only that...the *George Sand* had been very well received, and the editors asked me right away, "Couldn't you do another?" And it seemed to me that this subject came to me very easily. But otherwise there isn't a connection, no. Of course, you are free to establish one.

JB: Yes...

HB: But I didn't see a connection myself.

JB: Because what struck me is that the George Sand that you paint—and others have done so as well—is above all a maternal figure, for reasons that are evident [in your book]. That's why I wondered.

HB: Yes...she appears to be a maternal figure in the book?

JB: Yes. Yes, I believe so. Maternal for her lovers, maternal for—

HB: Yes, that's true. It was always an element of her relationship with her lovers.

JB: And particularly because she is seventeen...when you begin the book. So she is never very much a daughter in relation to her mother. It's true that there are flashbacks...

HB: It's true that...she had her two mothers, her mother and her grandmother, who competed for her affection, and who were divided about everything that concerned her, who each tried to tear her away from the other, but she herself...she herself did say that she had two mothers, after all, her grandmother and her mother, and she measures one against the other, and she shows how they were both important in her development.

JB: Yes, absolutely. But it's interesting that we each read in our own way, that is, we hear different resonances, and [in reading about Sand's life] I was struck by the little girl bereft of her mother and so…I believe I read *La Lune et les sabots* right after my first reading of *Histoire de ma vie.* And so this suggested a somewhat different approach to me.

HB: Well, yes, very different. Because *Histoire de ma vie* doesn't leave much room for her life as an adult woman; she speaks of her ancestors, and then of her childhood, and very little…her adult life is really reduced in the process.

JB: That's right.…[I]t can be dangerous to…to try to find or unbury or even, in a sense, to *save* the lives of these women—lives lost to us. My fear is that if we seek this illustrious woman—this omnipotent mother—then the woman who is our own mother, our immediate precursor, could never measure up, could never turn out to be as good…

HB: Yes, exactly. It's rather amusing, because I started to tell you the reflection my mother laughingly made to me—because she laughed a lot, she was rather droll, she loved to laugh—and she said right away when I told her, "You know, I want to write something about you.…" "Ah," she said to me, "after George Sand, me—it's not the same thing." And it's funny, because really, from time to time people ask me, "But you have—you admire George Sand—is she a model for you?" Never, ever, for me George Sand is not at all a role model. Nor is my mother, for that matter, because in a way I refused in my life to be what she was. But I wouldn't myself have had the idea to compare the two projects. You see…I mean, when I wrote about my mother it wasn't at all the same thing. I was speaking about myself when I wrote about my mother. When I wrote about George Sand, I was trying to do the most objective book possible about what this figure was all about.

JB: Yes. But what I like so much in *Rose Noël* is that you show the ambiguities, the ambivalences in the mother-daughter relationship.

HB: Yes, maybe, yes.

JB: Yes...So this book was commissioned in the sense that you were asked to do a book in the series? Or—

HB: Well, the one on George Sand, yes, that's right. Yes, I had written a novel, and I was at one point on television to present this novel. There were several authors; it was on...a segment of *Apostrophes* and I was part of it. And Françoise Giroud, who had just written *Alma Mahler* in that series, was there too. So I was with her on the show and I said to myself, "It would really interest me to write in this series, which is not a biography of the academic sort, but rather the portrait of a woman; it would really interest me to write something." I suggested it to the editor of the collection, Marie-Josèphe Guers, and I told her, "I would like to write a book in your collection." And then we talked about what work, what author, what figure, and I proposed—I would really have liked to write something about Violette le Duc. I would really have liked to write about Violette le Duc, and I proposed it to her. But the publisher, Robert Laffont, and Marie-Josèphe Guers eventually said, "We don't think she is sufficiently known for..." Basically this series was aimed at a general audience, not necessarily an audience...not a scholarly audience, not a very highbrow audience. It was a series that sought a varied readership, that tried to draw readers from different socioeconomic milieux. And so we looked around some more, and then Marie-Josèphe Guers, the editor of the series, said to me one day, "I could really see you writing on George Sand." Then I said to her...I was both kind of impressed and also not very excited. Because...George Sand struck me as a rather chatty character, rather...

JB: Yes!

HB: [laughter]...rather literary. And so—I should say that I didn't know her well, I knew what I had read when I was in school—

JB: François le champi...

HB: [nodding]...*La Mare au diable, La Petite Fadette,* that kind of thing, then...the rustic novel, I'm not all that crazy about them, but at the same time I was flattered that the subject was proposed to me, because George Sand is after all a monument in France. And so in the end I agreed. But I accepted because I didn't suspect the size of the task. If I had known that there were eighty volumes of correspondence, and everything else, I think I would really have hesitated. And so I accepted, and I did the work. But it wasn't completely a commission, because I'm the one who proposed to write a book, but it was a kind of compromise between the editor and me.

JB: I see. I see. I understand...the massiveness, but also the complexity.

HB: Yes. And if you have also studied her relationship with her own children, it is very, very complicated.

JB: Yes...

[bibliographical digression]

JB: But the book series ["Elle était une fois"] seems to have stopped.... The last one was published in '93, I believe.

HB: Yes, that's right, the last must have been six years ago...

JB: Is it because...the historic moment had passed?

HB: No, I don't think it was the historic moment; I think there must have been...you know, in the politics of these series, the publishers judge that at a certain point there is no longer sufficient interest....Robert Laffont was taken over by another publisher, by Fixot, so it's possible they simply did not choose to continue this line, without having...it might have continued, but it could simply have been for reasons of marketing politics that it stopped.

JB: There were at least twenty, maybe thirty...

HB: At least.

JB: The idea behind the series is what interests me, that is, the idea of "mirror biography," to quote [the publicity blurb on many of the covers: "C'est une collection de biographies-miroirs où deux femmes se reflètent, se font écho, se répondent"]....

HB: What she [Guers] was trying to do was to have a book written about a woman—since it's a collection devoted to women—a book about a woman by a woman with whom she felt there was some affinity, some identification, really. And—but that wasn't always the case. Because, for example, I know that Françoise Giroud told me that...she didn't like Alma Mahler and that she hadn't enjoyed doing that [book].

JB: Ah...

HB: On the other hand, I think Sagan—Françoise Sagan—had a lot of fun writing the Sarah Bernhardt book. Here it was also...[inaudible] the author's choice....But it was really important to Marie-Josèphe Guers that there not be in this collection any biographies of the, let us say, the usual kind. I just wrote a biography of Agatha Christie. And I published this biography of Agatha Christie with Flammarion, in a collection called "Great Biographies," and in that collection, they publish the kind of biography that is...

JB: Distanced?

HB: Yes, like...

JB: Objective?

HB: Yes, exactly. And she, on the contrary, was trying to find a somewhat more original angle....I just went to...two weeks ago there was a book fair on biography in Oxford. And of course...there were authors who write enormous, minutely documented biographies. And some of these biographies are of course truly remarkable. But personally, I continue to be a little nostalgic for those modest books that tried to paint a portrait....I prefer to write portraits rather than biographies....[B]iography is infinite; one can never say everything about a figure, really. And then it isn't always interesting to tell everything. On the other hand, to have a personal point of view—that can be very interesting.

JB: And so...one last question: What was your mother's reaction [to your memoir]? Did she read it?

HB: Yes. She read it. Yes, she was still alive...and...she told me...yes, she...she wept a bit, and then she...yes, it gave her great pleasure, she really did like it, I think.

JB: It's a really fine book.

HB: She...yes, she appreciated it for what it was, that is, it was a gift for her. And it's funny because I have five brothers and sisters, and my brothers and sisters said to me, a year or two later, "After all, you wrote about our mother, you should write a book about our father." [laughter] And [laughter] I, well, I set it to it. But with enormous difficulty— *enormous,* and it bears no resemblance to the one about my mother. I set it up as an investigation, because for me my father was...half unknown. There was a whole—there were entire stretches of his life that I didn't know about, if only because he had love affairs with women other than my mother. And in this regard one of my sisters said to me, "But maybe Maman too..." And we know nothing about this, it's inconceivable.... For me, Maman was...she was...it was as if she were transparent. Oh yes...I'm sure I'm deceiving myself, because... Yet I have always lived with this impression, that she belonged to us, to us children, that she was there only for us, and that she had no other existence than the one we were familiar with. While where my father was concerned, I took off from the principle that he had another existence. Both at work, because he lived...largely outside the house because he worked, and then also, I knew he had had other romantic relationships, that he divorced because of that, very late in life, and so I knew that he...that he had another existence, and I had the sense of doing detective work, trying to uncover who he was. Although I had a lot of affection for him, and...but—it didn't matter, it was...

JB: But it isn't the same thing.

HB: Not at all, not at all.

Commentary, June 2006

I.

I walked into my meeting with Huguette Bouchardeau with a series of convictions about the pairing of her Sand and her mother books— convictions that I wore like a second skin. Though in retrospect such interpretive certitude sounds alternately hubristic and naïve, I had lived with these books and the effort to articulate their relationship for such a long time that I hardly thought of my ideas as beliefs anymore: they simply formed an integral part of my sense of reality.

In this context the questions I put to Bouchardeau were evidently loaded (as, I imagine, questions are in most interview situations). I was seeking confirmation for my reading, perhaps amplification and expansion, and I hoped for some pithy citations. Beyond these expectations (and more open-mindedly), I was eager to learn more about the history of the "Elle était une fois" series in which the George Sand book had appeared, and which I had written about previously, and I wanted to engage one of its authors in a dialogue that might lead in new directions.

The conversation began as if I had scripted it. Bouchardeau's answer to my question about the close timing of *George Sand: La Lune et les sabots* and *Rose Noël* initially appeared to feed right into my argument: "When I finished the writing of *George Sand,...*I had a great desire to write—I don't know why—but I had a great desire to write a book about my mother."[2] Clearly the foremother biography had provoked a turn to the mother; the motivation was clinched by the unconscious voicing its occulted place: *"I don't know why."* The "Ah..." of complicity and gratification that Bouchardeau's response initially elicited from her interviewer, however, soon gave way to some consternation as she went on to explain the path from one book to the other as contingent and external (the idea for the second book had come later, on its own; public acclaim and editorial solicitation had played a role). From the author's perspective, the writing processes had not only *not* been continuous or interdependent but had even been oppositional: the Sand book was laborious while the mother book flowed; the Sand book had required intensive research and was objectively derived, while the other book had required only a flat surface to write on, and came from the self: "I was speaking about myself when I wrote about my mother."

In rereading the transcript of the interview, I catch myself fishing for answers that weren't immediately forthcoming:

JB: But it was through writing, or through researching *La Lune et les sabots* that [the plan for *Rose Noël* emerged]?

---

[2] Huguette Bouchardeau, *George Sand: La Lune et les sabots* (Paris: Laffont, 1990); *Rose Noël* (Paris: Seghers, 1990). References to these books are provided in the text.

> *HB:* No. No, no, I did it completely afterward.
> *JB:* Yes, but did the idea come to you [from the experience of writing *La Lune et les sabots*]?

Continuing to reread the interview transcript, I hear my incredulity emerge in a few questions that might rightly be called "leading the interviewee":

> *JB:* It was later?
> *HB:* Yes, I think so, yes.
> *JB:* So, then, you don't see any connection between [the two books]?
> *HB:* I don't, myself....Of course, you are free to establish one.

I recall that Bouchardeau's negative response was, at the moment of interviewing, a disappointment not much alleviated by her gracious reminder that other interpretations were possible. Expecting a confirmation that would have authenticated what I had previously written, I confess to not immediately receiving her generous encouragement to disagree, with the enthusiasm it might otherwise have merited. Her words and mine lived in contradiction in my mind.

2.

As memory initially replayed the interview, my dismay in the face of Bouchardeau's vigorous rejection of a significant connection between the Sand book and the mother book gave way to a fascination with her very insistent articulation of this rejection. Bouchardeau seemed to protest too much the possibility of a motivating link between the Sand book and the mother book. Were not the vehemence of her denial and her repeated insistence on differentiating and distancing the two projects in fact an asseveration of a deeply buried connection between them? Transcribing and translating the tape reinforced my interpretation of an overly zealous denial—indeed, in psychoanalytic terms, one might say a denegation—of a link between foremother and mother biography. In fact, at every step of the interview Bouchardeau

had focused on differentiating: first, the two stories and their subjects, from her mother's perspective; then, from her own, the writing processes; later, the motivations for the two projects. Everywhere
I heard the repudiation of an interrelated genesis of the two books. The
transcript reiterated the interview for me in a language of difference.

Bouchardeau began to relate the genesis-in-antithesis of *Rose Noël*
by quoting her mother's reaction to the passage from *George Sand* to
this new book about her: "You know, it isn't at all the same story,"
and again, "after George Sand, me—it's not the same thing." And
she went on to affirm and to elaborate on the dissimilarity, from a
writing point of view: "It was very different....I was leaving a work
where I had explored a lot of documentary material...and...this
book about my mother came to me with great facility....[I]t was really a completely different kind of writing." By the time she explicitly repudiated a connection between the two books, she had already
differentiated them on several counts: one was heavily researched,
the other written from the heart; one was a semi-commissioned
book, the other a labor of love; one strove for objectivity, the other
was baldly subjective; one was about a monumental figure, the other
an ordinary mortal; one had been generated in libraries and archives,
while the freefloating other had been written nomadically and
fragmentarily—on planes, on trains—in passing and in pieces.

In spite of the avowed distinction—indeed, in part *because of
it*—I persisted in my sense of Bouchardeau's overlapping relationships with George Sand and Rose Noël. The dual kinship emerged,
I thought, in her conjoined refusal to look to either one as a role
model: "For me George Sand is not at all a role model. Nor is my
mother, for that matter, because in a way I refused in my life to be
what she was. But I wouldn't myself have had the idea to compare the
two projects. You see...when I wrote about my mother it wasn't at
all the same thing." I began to scaffold an argument that would support my continued belief in a dual mother project, even in the face
of Bouchardeau's denial and my own responding fissures of doubt,
building on her resistance, her double refusal of a maternal ideal, and
certain inconsistencies I found in her oppositional discourse. Specifically, although Bouchardeau apposed the biographies of Sand and
Rose Noël on the basis of objectivity and subjectivity, respectively,
she later contrasted the books in Guers's "Elle était une fois" collection (in which her Sand book appeared) with traditional, documentary

biography ("enormous, minutely documented biographies"), favoring the more impressionistic and identificatory "portrait biographies" that Guers had all her authors strive for. She expressed a wistful preference for these books and defended the interests of personal perspective in biography. Didn't this plea for writing from an individual point of view reassign the Sand biography to the camp of subjectivity after all, despite the explicit opposition of the Sand and mother biographies on the respective lines of objectivity and subjectivity? This paradoxical return of the Sand book to subjectivity confirmed my sense of the author's affective investment in it and of its underlying connection to the mother book.

The intellectual argument was ready to be made, but I found myself unable to put it into writing. In the interim I had begun to replay the tape with some frequency after a lapse of time in order to tease out some barely audible words so as to finish transcribing the interview. These listening sessions began to erode my conviction or, more precisely, my sense of agency and legitimacy. The repeated avowals of difference, the denegations, the inconsistencies were all there as noted. The problem was not one of logic or argumentation. It had little to do with words. I was stopped by the voice on the tape.

3.

> Listening brings two subjects into relation.... The injunction
> to listen is the total interpellation of one subject by another;
> it places above everything else the quasi-physical contact
> of these subjects (by voice and ear): it creates transference:
> *"listen to me"* means *touch me, know that I exist.*[3]
> ROLAND BARTHES

When I add to these wonderfully astute words from Barthes the observation that the French *écouter*, "to listen," is derived from the verb *auscultare* in Latin, I may begin to suggest how listening to

---

[3] "L'écoute met en relation deux sujets.... L'injonction d'écouter est l'inter-pellation totale d'un sujet à un autre: elle place au-dessus de tout le contact quasi physique de ces deux sujets (par la voix et l'oreille): elle crée le transfert:' *écoutez-moi'* veut dire: *touchez-moi, sachez que j'existe."* Roland Barthes, "Écoute," in *L'Obvie et l'obtus* (Paris: Seuil, 1982), 222–23; in English, "Listening," in *The Responsibility of Forms*, trans. Richard Howard (New York: Hill and Wang, 1985), 251. Subsequent references are provided in the text.

Bouchardeau's voice transformed my sense of her words—and my own—on the page. From the Latin *auscultare* come the French *ausculter* and the English *to auscultate,* "to listen to sounds within the body," to which I join the example given by the *Petit Robert* dictionary: "to auscultate the bronchia, the heart" ["ausculter les bronches, le cœur"].[4] Listen to the air I take into my lungs, listen to the beating of my heart. By restoring a trace of physicality to the mundane injunction "listen to me," Barthes invests these words with the plea for recognition that founds the psychoanalytic transference (and all human bonds): "*listen to me* means *touch me, know that I exist.*"

By bringing Barthes's words to bear on Bouchardeau's voice on the tape, I do not mean to imply that she is asking to be recognized by me. I mean rather that her voice as it confronts my ear on the tape breathes out a tangible warmth and distinctiveness, which is to say, an individuality, a vulnerability that compels recognition, calls out to be known in its manifestation of otherness, as the spirit of an other physical being. To put it most succinctly: *she* is not *me,* and I want to listen to what she has said instead of appropriating her words in confirmation or contradiction of my own.

Briefly and simplistically stated, my thinking during and following the interview passed through two stages: (1) I was wrong (Bouchardeau disagrees with my analysis, I should burn the chapter); (2) I was right (Bouchardeau disagrees on a conscious level, but I will deconstruct her words to show that her unconscious supports my argument). There was a prelude to these monologic stages: I had a theory that Bouchardeau was writing her own mother story through George Sand's, in the larger context of exploring the search for feminine literary lineage that is the subject of my book, and I wanted at all cost to appropriate Bouchardeau's interview words in the service of this theory. My initial position was, I believe, a revisionist attempt to avoid the normative, traditional critical position—call it colonialist or patriarchal—to which I will come in a moment: instead I was yielding to a prior force, fusing with a point of view I did not want to fight. The second, stubborn position to which I reverted is a common critical stance with which some readers may be familiar: I was

---

[4] Definitions from *The Random House College Dictionary* and *Le Petit Robert.*

thinking as a literary critic, as "one presumed to know" about the object of critical inquiry, and one presumed to know where to find the blind spots that elude this object's consciousness. I was adapting male models, like Jane Gallop, who tells of bending Harold Bloom's "masculinist model" of the anxiety of influence to fit her own "maternal" stakes in the "aggressive...one-upping" of Barthes as precursor critic. (But here I was taking the stance of rebellious daughter.)[5] Or I was taking refuge in critical conquest, acting like Ruth Behar's archetypical anthropologist, anchored in a "legacy born of the European colonial impulse to know others in order to lambast them, better manage them, or exalt them."[6]

Now I was being moved by the voice on the tape into a third stage that might logically seem to announce itself as synthesis but was not. I wanted to listen to the sounds of difference without quite understanding how to proceed or what this would entail. I turned back to Barthes for help. He reminded me that listening is risky business that cannot be carried out behind a shield of theory: "The analysand is not a scientific object from whom the analyst, deep in his armchair, can project himself with objectivity. The psychoanalytic relation is effected between two subjects.... To recognize [the other's desire] implies that one enters it, tumbles into it, ultimately finding oneself there" (256).[7] Here as so often elsewhere, the context of the psychoanalytic dialogue can be clearly analogized to the relationship between a literary analyst and her subject. By way of Blanchot's rendition of the myth of Ulysses and the Sirens, Barthes goes on to evoke the imperatives and the dangers of listening: "The psychoanalyst cannot, like Ulysses bound to his mast, 'enjoy the spectacle of the sirens without risks and without accepting its consequences...There was something marvelous in that song...a song from the abyss which, once heard, opened an abyss in each word and lured one to vanish into it'" (256).[8]

---

5   Jane Gallop, "Precursor Critics and the Anxiety of Influence," in *Profession*, ed. Rosemary G. Feal (New York: MLA of America, 2003), 105–9.
6   Ruth Behar, *The Vulnerable Observer* (Boston: Beacon Press, 1996), 4.
7   "L'analysant n'est pas un object scientifique vis-à-vis duquel l'analyste, du haut de son fauteuil, peut se prémunir d'objectivité. La relation psychanalytique se noue entre deux sujets.... Reconnaître [le désir de l'autre] implique qu'on y entre, qu'on y bascule, qu'on finisse par s'y trouver" (227).
8   "Le psychanalyste ne peut, tel Ulysse attaché à son mât, 'jouir du spectacle des sirènes sans risques et sans en accepter les conséquences...Il y avait quelque chose de merveilleux dans ce chant...chant de l'abîme qui, une fois entendu, ouvrait

Neither Barthes nor Blanchot explains how to be a good listener; in fact Barthes specifically notes that the myth of the Sirens doesn't give instructions for good listening. It can be constituted, however, as a negativity, situated "between the reefs the navigator-psychoanalyst must avoid at all costs: plugging one's ears like the men of the crew, employing deception and giving evidence of cowardice like Ulysses, or answering the sirens' invitation and vanishing" (257).[9]

I recognized myself in Barthes's analyst, navigating among the fatal reefs of bad listening: I had begun by answering the siren song, and risked disappearing into its abyss. (This was my first stage of absorbing the interview: "I am wrong; I will yield to her voice.") Later, in a second stage, I had alternately closed my ears (denial) and shown my weakness by using cunning to deconstruct her words, binding myself in theory as Ulysses had bound himself to the mast in order to hear but not succumb.

Barthes, with Blanchot, suggests that steering clear of the rocks might mean a less immediate listening to a less immediate song, one that would be deferred, distanced, delayed: carried by narration and mediated by telling. For Freud, this secondary listening took the form of writing case histories. For myself, secondary listening takes this form right here: that is, recounting the interview, after seven years' delay, and through writing. Mediated in this way, the interview has become the story of my listening to a different voice, and of the difference this listening makes to the story of my own voice.

4.

Rereading, relistening, rethinking, listening to the breathing voice and beating heart of the words on tape and on paper, in transcript and in translation, I hear a language of difference. I sense that *distinguishing* and *differentiating* the two biographies was so much the subtext of Bouchardeau's conversation—the texture of her words—that what

---

dans chaque parole un abîme et invitait fortement à y disparaître.'" This is Barthes ("Écoute," 227) quoting Maurice Blanchot, *Le Livre à venir* (1959).
[9] "Entre les écueils que doit à tout prix éviter le navigateur-psychanalyste: se boucher les oreilles comme les hommes d'équipage, user d'une ruse et faire épreuve de lâcheté comme Ulysse, ou répondre à l'invite des sirènes et disparaître" (227).

is being differentiated is less important than the idea of *difference.* On tape and in print, the voicing of specific differences fades into reiterations and reverberations of conceptual difference. Where I once understood a particular message of disagreement or disclaimer of similarity, I now discern a pattern of differentiation and distinction. In fact Bouchardeau took pains not just to make a distinction between the book about Sand and the book about Rose Noël, and between the lives of the two women, but also ardently to mark her own distance from both: "George Sand is not at all a role model. Nor is my mother...because...I refused in my life to be what she was."

Later in the interview Bouchardeau spoke passionately of the dissimilarity between *Rose Noël* and the book she had gone on to write about her father, *Les Roches rouges,* in language echoing her opening remarks contrasting *Rose Noël* and *George Sand:*

> It bears no resemblance to the one about my mother....I have always lived with this impression, that she belonged to us, to us children, that she was there only for us, and that she had no other existence than the one we were familiar with. While where my father was concerned, I took off from the principle that he had another existence....I had the sense of doing detective work, trying to uncover who he was....I had a lot of affection for him,...but it didn't matter.

And to my suggestion that "it isn't the same thing," she emphatically added, "Not at all, not at all," summarizing the portrait of paternal alterity she had evoked piecemeal in our conversation.

In *Les Roches rouges: Portrait d'un père* Bouchardeau had established her father's anchorage in the outside world and his affinities with the unknown, in opposition to her mother's domesticity: "Maman...kept us warm, she took care of us, she fed us, she kept us wrapped in a cocoon. Papa brought with him a great breath of air from the outside world. With him, we went outside."[10] This man she

---

[10] "Maman...tenait chaud, elle soignait, elle nourrissait, elle nous gardait au cocon. Papa apportait avec lui le grand air du monde extérieur. Avec lui, on sortait." Huguette Bouchardeau, *Les Roches rouges: Portrait d'un père* (Paris: Écriture, 1996), 59; subsequent references are given in the text.

consistently refers to in his role of "Papa" rather than identifying with a distinguishing name is nonetheless defined by his marginality to familial and even familiar terms of definition: "Papa was more than a family man.... [H]e was 'elsewhere,' outside of routine daily life" (26).[11] He is identified by his very indecipherability: "as if all the secret crosscurrents that families have to reckon with were concentrated on him alone" (81).[12] In short, recounts this daughter, "on the paternal side, all was mystery" (89).[13] The man whose racial tolerance is emblematically ascribed by his daughter to "this capacity to welcome difference" (94)[14] embraces and embodies difference. The father who emerged from our conversation as the mother's Other, the family stranger, unknown and indecipherable, becomes in the paternal memoir the very figure of difference.

Bouchardeau summarizes her contrasting parentage in an elegant formulation: "Maman was made of milk, he was made of spice" (69).[15] The comparison evokes phenomenological oppositions (the bland and the pungent, the wet and the dry) and also strings of cultural associations (the domestic, the family, home, nature, limpidity, apposed to the exotic, the foreign, travel, culture, mystery). It also implies familiar roles in the signifying process as it is figured in gendered terms. Milk and spice: oceanic expansion and separation into discrete parts: matter and punctuation. But somehow, in her reiteration of differentiation and distinction, Bouchardeau aligns herself—against all the obvious paradigms (male is to female as foreign is to domestic, exotic to homelike, unknown to known, cutting to encompassing)— with the paternal principle. As she made abundantly clear in the interview, she too is a differentiator—"she who separates," to bend Foucault's classic definition of the father as "he who separates."[16] Crossing paradigms, she creates herself as a being of spice.[17]

---

[11]   "Papa était 'autre chose' que le père de famille.... [I]l était 'ailleurs' que dans la vie quotidienne."
[12]   "comme si se concentraient sur lui seul toutes les énigmes croisées que compte généralement une famille."
[13]   "Du côté paternel, tout était mystère."
[14]   "cette capacité à accueillir la différence."
[15]   "Maman était de lait, il était d'épices."
[16]   "celui qui sépare." Michel Foucault, "Le 'Non' du père," *Critique* 18, no. 178 (March 1962), 205.
[17]   A being of spice: surely to be understood in contrast to the being of milk to which she compared her mother in *Rose Noël:* "dwelling, fountain, cradle[,]...blanket

And Bouchardeau continues to undermine established binary categories by questioning her own unthinking construction of maternal difference, recognizing as an illusion the assumption that her mother's life is transparent and her father's opaque: "For me, Maman was...it was as if she were transparent....I'm sure I am deceiving myself, yet I have always lived with this impression." Hard-and-fast categories of opposition end up being other than what they had seemed; the idea of difference begins to differ from itself. Nor can I remain unchanged outside this spinning play of difference. Barbara Johnson was right: "Difference is a form of *work* to the extent that it *plays* beyond the control of any subject."[18] Tracking an author-daughter in the act of reconstructing a literary mother in tandem with a material mother, I have been drawn into the game: the critic of salvation biography falls prey to the same kind of reconstructive identifications and projections as the alleged salvation biographer herself, who is the object of these projections. My position diverges from the one I thought I held, in its very similarity to the object of my story. My differences with Bouchardeau as they arose in the interview stem from my similarity to the author-daughter I expected her to be (and from which she too diverges).

I have deliberately focused my interview commentary on the interpretative discord because it represents a *mise en abyme* of the very core of (fore)mother biography that I was hoping to explore and to mine—albeit from an external position—in my discussion with Bouchardeau. That is, I expected to engage Bouchardeau in a conversation about her personal experience of reconstructing a mother's life through the lens of a foremother's life; I was not prepared to hear the "song from the abyss" that engaged me personally and intellectually in this conversation about identity and relationship, through the bonds of critical affiliation and differentiation. As I worked—years after the fact—to reconstruct Bouchardeau's story through the testimony of our conversation, I found myself reliving, *en abyme*, the dynamics of identification, of influence, of reflexivity, of recognition that I was more generally exploring in the larger process of the

---

and nourishment...submersion...warm...white...bland" ["habitacle, fontaine, berceau...enveloppe et nourriture...submer[sion]...tiède...blanc...fade" (14)].
[18] Barbara Johnson, *The Critical Difference* (Baltimore: Johns Hopkins University Press, 1980), xi.

book. That is why I chose to tell the story of our interview *en abyme;* that is why I (re)write Bouchardeau's story now looking out from the abyss—which is perhaps to say, turning sound into image, through the looking glass. *Through the looking glass*—which is most vehemently not to say *in the mirror.*

I'm as skeptical about mirror critics as I am about mirror biographers, mirror mothers, and mirror stages that at once bestow too much power and too little recognition. It is all too evident in the best-intended mirror biographies, in which "two women mirror each other, echo each other, respond to each other," that the daughter is mother to the text, with the play of mastery, of projection, of monovision, and of monologism that inevitably results. And so I close on a note of intentional discord, neither retracting my understanding of Bouchardeau's twinned books nor undoing her denial of this relationship, leaving my reading with hers, like our crossed words in the interview exchange, suspended in dialogue. And the last word? Let it go to neither one of us but instead to Huguette Bouchardeau's mother, Rose Noël: "Oh, but that isn't...you know, it isn't at all the same story."

5

ONE'S OWN

*Reflections on Motherhood,
Owning, and Adoption*

Love is a rose but you better not pick it
Only grows when it's on the vine
Handful of thorns and you'll know you've missed it
Lose your love when you say the word mine.

NEIL YOUNG, "LOVE IS A ROSE,"
AS PERFORMED BY LINDA RONSTADT

Owning: The Story behind the Essay

First, a confession about how I came (almost not) to write this essay. When Holly Laird broached the idea of contributing to a forum on adoption, I initially recoiled in horror.[1] "Forum" and "adoption" struck me as antithetical and entirely incompatible notions, the one connoting the public and the political, and the other the private and the domestic. I wanted neither to transgress against my daughter by uncovering her (yet unwritten) story, nor to cross the lines so clearly drawn between my professional and personal life by theorizing my family and familiarizing theory.

This essay is dedicated to my extended adoptive family network in Charlottesville.

[1] Holly Laird was the editor of *Tulsa Studies in Women's Literature*, which under her leadership published, in fall 2002, "The Adoption Issue" (21, no. 2); its contributors were asked to consider, from a potentially autobiographical perspective, "the impact adoption has had on your thinking as a scholar, feminist, and/or theorist, and vice versa" (preface, 231).

The vehemence of my initial reaction was shadowed by a faint yet perceptible flicker of something else that I can vaguely call curiosity, provocation, or lure—something that I did not understand but that kept me from outright refusal. This nagging ambivalence gave me pause for thought in the weeks that followed—weeks that perhaps significantly coincided with a change in university affiliation and a geographical and cultural transmutation. In jolts and flashes no doubt induced by the physical and psychical gymnastics of moving, shards of past conversations and events resurfaced over the course of the intervening weeks. In dismayed fascination I beheld the barbed kindness of strangers and the unwitting cruelty of friends coinciding in a barrage of recollections whose most unrelenting theme was the surgically precise verbal triage of children into two camps clearly labeled "adopted" and "own."

The admiring unabashment of the stranger's flitting stare in the supermarket or on the bus is legend among adoptive parents. The subsequent well-meant if intrusive query, as the other's glance travels from child's to parent's face and back before asking, "Is she yours?" is a platitude in adoptive parents' circles—a platitude, to be sure, that is discussed, bemoaned, and mock-answered in order to be philosophized, neutralized, and dismissed until the next occasion arises, but a platitude nonetheless. Banal, too, is the approbation of acquaintances who praise adoption in such hierarchized terms as "We think adoption is a wonderful idea. In fact, *we* might adopt one day if we can't have our own"—or, as a common variant has it, "We're thinking of adopting after we have a few of our own."

Less frequently discussed, perhaps because at once more intimate, more painful, more confusing, and more corrosive, are comments similarly implying diminished connection made by close friends who have supported, nurtured, and embraced our adoptive children from the time they were mere decisions by their parents-to-be. How much more difficult it is to retort to a friend's cry "We want one of our *own*!" when we are privy to the context of newly discovered infertility—but also how much more tender the wound inflicted. How very complicated it is to find an adequate response to a friend's exulting in "my own flesh and blood!" when we are sharing the elation of new parenthood—and how much more lacerating the revelation of genetic privileging that has slipped from the cultural to the personal unconscious.

Such was the substance of the memories unleashed by Holly's invitation to write about adoption. The strength of their assault provoked me to think more about the boundary that, like a natural monument, like an ocean or a mountain range, had until then absolutely separated the familial and the scholarly for me, so that no passage between the two was conceivable. At the same time, my apparent inability simply to say no to Holly's proposal suggested how much my repugnance was tinged with something akin to desire. The surge tide of memories opened my eyes to the possibility that the natural boundary was an internalization of a much more complex cultural divide. Might the election of privacy be the negative imprint of a cultural hierarchization of family connectedness that places birth before adoption, genealogy before affiliation—a hierarchy emblematically institutionalized by the policies of my former university, which had denied me maternity leave on the grounds that adoption was not a qualifying event? What if the natural divide between the personal and the professional was in fact a cultural rift driven into what might otherwise have been conceived as continuous experience? What if the choice of privacy was at least potentially a retreat, an unwitting concession to the social marginalization of the adoption experience?

And so, despite misgivings, and for reasons that are obviously overdetermined, I decided to write this essay. I came to write this piece because I was surprised by the virulence of my ambivalence about doing so. (Even now as I draft it, I am struck by the hesitation between private and public, emotion and theory that shadows my text from its opening split between an academic and theoretical title and a popular and sentimental epigraph.) I write to explore this ambivalence, to experience and to theorize it as both a personal phenomenon and a social reflection. I write to tease out the meanings and implications of *owning* that awakened my intellectual and emotional curiosity. I write because Holly's invitation and my hesitation to respond together opened questions whose reverberations touch me as a mother and a writer, my daughter as an adoptive child, adoption as a source of family formation, and, not least, my friends as fellow travelers—both those already within adoption circles and those who were not, but who became part of the experience along the way. Finally, it is because I hold sacred certain relations of affiliation—which I take in this context to mean vital, evolving, unblooded connections with friends as well as with children—that I decided to write across and against my silence and to experiment with owning my unspoken reservations about what it means to have a child of one's own.

Owning: A Speculative Inventory

I want to ponder the pervasive equation of adoption with "not-own" by considering more generally how cultural discourse deploys notions of owning, ownership, and (one's) own in their various verbal, substantive, and adjectival manifestations. Both "ownership" and its verbal form, "to own," call up primary associations with property, proprietorship, possession. One owns, for example, real estate (a house, a store, a hotel), goods (a car, a VCR, a home gym, a coffee grinder), livestock, or pets—but rarely anymore people. The *OED* links ownership to "legal right of possession...property, proprietorship, dominion." If owning and ownership denote title and possession, they connote permanence, inalienability, mastery, and control.

The *OED* adds a potential puzzle in the form of an obsolete meaning of the verb *to own*, specifically, a sense of owning as process or becoming rather than as fact or state: "to make (a thing) one's own, appropriate, take possession of, seize, win, gain, adopt as one's own." This archaic definition of owning is difficult to distinguish from adopting, even before the term appears in the final clause. In fact, using very similar phrasing, the *OED* gives as one of its definitions of the verb *to adopt* "to take as one's own."

The literal uses of owning and ownership are extended, in current parlance, to more abstract territory. We counsel another: "own your space," "own your life," or "own your [life] story," with implications of taking control of, giving direction to, possessing with an air of entitlement, confidence, and autonomy. "Owning one's story," however, can also mean telling it: "to own" or "to own up," as the opening to this essay attests, can mean to bear witness, to give testimony, to confide or to confess—and thereby to assume, to appropriate, to authorize, or to legitimate. Paradoxically, though, this sense of owning comes almost to coincide with its opposite, for one owns up, or owns a story (or an experience or a thought or a fantasy), by giving it away: by sharing it, by surrendering sole proprietary rights, by making the private public. Curiously, even when confession is not at issue—that is, when the story being told is the story of an other—the telling seems still to invoke questions of ownership and concerns about dispossession.

Diane Wood Middlebrook, a great teller of lives, has gone on record as stating that death terminates self-possession: "All records left by the dead...are...'cultural property.'"[2] Janet Malcolm radically foreshortens the time of our self-possession, explaining that "as everyone knows who has ever heard a piece of gossip, we do not 'own' the facts of our lives at all. *This ownership passes out of our hands at birth,* at the moment we are first observed."[3] She goes on to compare biography to "a book that has been scribbled in by an alien"—that is, a kind of illicit ghostwriting—and to an act of burglary (184, 9). As Barbara Johnson observes, however, "the biographer does indeed steal, but what is stolen is something not owned. That is perhaps why there is so much struggle around it."[4] Johnson's astute sense of a quandary of ownership pervading biography cuts to the heart of a conceptual problem: Is "a life" a human existence or the narrative rendition of it? If a life is inseparable from its telling, then who has rights to it? Is telling a story—one's own or the story of another's life—necessarily a proprietary act?

When, following the tragedies of September 11, the *New York Times* sought to commemorate the victims, it instituted a daily series of capsule biographies that came to be known as "Portraits of Grief." Public reception was uneven: if on the one hand it was impossible to skip these pages, difficult not to grieve vicariously in a daily ritual of reading, it was painful to realize, as the portraits continued daily for a period of months, that we had all become "voyeurs in suffering," to use a phrase coined by the cultural historian Neal Gabler in 1996.[5] Indeed these portraits, each situated somewhere between a life sketch and an obituary, introduced a person's life to a public of strangers by affixing it to a few details, fixing it in place, freezing

---

[2] Diane Wood Middlebrook, "Telling Secrets," in *The Seductions of Biography,* ed. Mary Rhiel and David Suchoff (New York: Routledge, 1996), 128.

[3] Janet Malcolm, *The Silent Woman: Sylvia Plath and Ted Hughes* (New York: Knopf, 1994), 8, emphasis added; subsequent references are provided in the text.

[4] Barbara Johnson, intro. to Part 4, "Whose Life Is It, Anyway?" in Rhiel and Suchoff, *The Seductions of Biography,* 120.

[5] Neal Gabler, quoted by Michiko Kakutani, "Rituals for Grieving Extend Past Tradition into Public Displays," *New York Times,* September 18, 2001.

it in time, like a death mask, and effectively closing it down by the very gesture of preserving it. Anecdotes abound of grief-stricken relatives who resisted the journalistic burial of their dead. One reporter, peeved by the withholding of family memories, went so far as to etch a portrait manqué that replaced the untold personal details with an account of being packed off by the anguished widow.

The most eloquent response to the *New York Times*'s commemorative undertaking came obliquely, in a chilling article about retrieval or identification of remains. While notification brought many families relief and allowed them to move toward burial, David Egan, who lost two daughters in the towers' fall, drew no comfort from recovery: "He had never liked the term 'closure,' he said, and he likes it less now. If a simple notification is enough to close a chapter that had been open a lifetime, he said, 'Maybe there wasn't much pith to that chapter to begin with.'"[6] Egan's lucid resistance to closure, strategically if coincidentally placed on the facing page to an early October page of portraits, articulates the stance of families who refused to sit for portraits of grief, illuminating such studies as closural gestures, tributary encapsulations that symbolically entomb the dead.

It may well be that any time we own a story or appropriate a life by attempting to give it a definitive form, we are effectively packaging it, wrapping it up, enshrouding it, and committing it to the grave.[7] Can we conceive of a mode of storytelling, a practice of life writing, that would split off telling from owning? Is there a way out of the discourse of ownership?

To compound the ambiguities of owning, we note that the verb "to own" derives from the Old Teutonic substantive *aigin*, "property," and the past participle of the verb *aigan*, "to possess"; so too,

[6]   Amy Waldman, "A Knock at the Door, with the Message of Death," *New York Times*, October 5, 2001.
[7]   In much the same way certain religions and societies place a taboo on photographic images, whose fixity represents a closure evocative of death. See, too, Leo Bersani's comments in "Mallarmé in Mourning," review of *A Tomb for Anatole* by Stéphane Mallarmé, trans. Paul Auster, *New York Times Book Review*, January 15, 1984, on Mallarmé's abandoned project for a literary work monumentalizing his dead child. Bersani remarks, "For Mallarmé and Proust, to remember is, profoundly if secretly, not to preserve the past, but to erase it.... this means that the father actually replicates the work of death in the very act of his immortalizing Anatole" (10).

however, is the modern English verb "to owe" derived. Does the evolution of owning and owing from a common etymological heritage not imply a troubled semantic kinship and a resulting challenge to the possibility of pure, clear, untrammeled ownership?

When we turn to the dictionary's display of the adjective "own," we find an initial analogy with the primary meanings of the verb and noun: the adjective *own* has as its primary sense "possessed, owned (property), belonging to oneself, proper"; similarly, it serves to emphasize the possessive. With a view toward extricating the underpinnings of the own/adoptive dichotomy, it is worth digressing to note two ancillary meanings of "own," one expressing "tenderness or affection" and another (marked as "rare") implying "literal" kinship, that is, "own" in reference to relationship: "an own brother (as opposed to a figurative brother, a half brother, a brother-in-law)." This last usage of "own" suggests that a relative of one's own must be, in the dictionary's words, "opposed to a figurative [one]," that is, must be a blood relation. Yet the "tender or affectionate" subdefinition raises further questions for the distinction between "figurative" and "literal" kinship—that is, for a cultural severing of adoptive from own (as performed by a colleague's recent reply to my query about how many children an acquaintance has: "She has two of her own and one adopted from India").

The dictionary, as my reading suggests, is open to constant interpretation, emendation, and elaboration. In particular, it does not take us into a realm of "one's own" that is nonetheless inevitable and inescapable in contemporary feminist academic circles. I venture there in what follows.

Woolf's Legacy: A [   ] of One's Own

"Owning" arguably has a special, often defiant sense for women living under patriarchy. Virginia Woolf famously claimed the need for "a room of one's own" and thereby generated a seemingly endless succession of other wishful appropriations of objects and privileges traditionally denied to women in real time and space. "A room of one's own" has in fact become the model rallying cry of a generation of feminists seeking to appropriate not only independent quarters but also a sovereign literature, leisure, law, and life; an autonomous mind, voice, and faith; self-sufficient travel and work; and separate plots and time (to allude to a representative selection of book and article titles among the hundreds if not thousands published in the past thirty-odd years).[8]

Feeling not only oppressed by the banalization of Woolf's much-imitated feminized possessive but also wary of an indiscriminate rush to appropriate the so-called privileges of patriarchy that might otherwise be seen as its liabilities, I turned back to Woolf's text to review the founding territorial gesture of contemporary feminism, curious to see what the unfortunately expansive notion of having a room "of one's own" might have meant originally in her specific context. *A Room of One's Own* closes with the now aphoristic formula that "if we live another century or so...and have five hundred a year each of us and rooms of our own...then the opportunity will come and the dead poet who was Shakespeare's sister will put on the body

---

[8] See, for example, Elaine Showalter, *A Literature of Their Own: British Women Novelists from Brontë to Lessing* (Princeton: Princeton University Press, 1977); Karla A. Henderson, *A Leisure of One's Own: A Feminist Perspective on Women's Leisure* (State College, Pa.: Venture Publishing, 1989); Caroline A. Forell and Donna M. Matthews, *A Law of Her Own: The Reasonable Woman as a Measure of Man* (New York: New York University Press, 2000); Joan Dash, *A Life of One's Own: Three Gifted Women and the Men They Married* (New York: Harper and Row, 1973); Louise M. Antony and Charlotte Witt, eds., *A Mind of One's Own: Feminist Essays on Reason and Objectivity* (Boulder: Westview, 1993); Mickey Pearlman and Katherine Usher Henderson, *A Voice of One's Own: Conversations with America's Writing Women* (Boston: Houghton Mifflin, 1990); Barbara Zanotti, ed., *A Faith of One's Own: Explorations by Catholic Lesbians* (Trumansburg, N.Y.: Crossing Press, 1986); Thalia Zepatos, *A Journey of One's Own: Uncommon Advice for the Independent Woman Traveler* (Portland, Ore.: Eighth Mountain Press, 1992); Susan Wittig Albert, *Work of Her Own: How Women Create Success and Fulfillment Off the Traditional Career Track* (New York: G. P. Putman's Sons, 1992); Pru Goward, *A Business of Your Own: How Women Succeed in Business* (Crows Nest, New South Wales: Allen and Unwin, 2001); Ann Stokes, *A Studio of One's Own* (Tallahassee: Naiad Press, 1985), a title reinvented for the Boston Museum of Fine Arts exhibit and catalogue curated by Erica E. Hirshler, *A Studio of Her Own: Women Artists in Boston, 1870–1940* (Boston: MFA Publications, 2001); Sona Stephan Hoisington, *A Plot of Her Own: The Female Protagonist in Russian Literature* (Evanston: Northwestern University Press, 1995); Jeanne Stevenson Moessner, ed., *In Her Own Time: Women and Developmental Issues in Pastoral Care* (Minneapolis: Fortress Press, 2000); and, not least, Judith S. Modell, "A Child of One's Own: Being an Adoptive Parent," in *Kinship with Strangers: Adoption and Interpretations of Kinship in American Culture* (Berkeley: University of California Press, 1994), chap. 9.

which she has so often laid down."[9] But the summary association of feminine creative productivity with money and property—the material tools of patriarchy—is complicated earlier in the text, where the necessity for feminine capital and real estate is nuanced by the context. Contrasting Shakespeare with his imagined talented sister, and the abundance of his literary oeuvre with the deficit of hers, Woolf's comparison takes the form of a musing on mobility: "Could she even seek her dinner in a tavern or roam the streets at midnight?....No girl could have walked to London and stood at a stage door" (50–51). Mobility, Woolf implies, is not only physical but also social and psychological: "To write a work of genius is almost always a feat of prodigious difficulty....Dogs will bark; people will interrupt....And so the writer...suffers...every form of distraction" (53–54).

Being a writer, Woolf suggests, depends on the ability to control one's mobility, to be master of one's travels through outer and inner space. It is within this context that her call for women's property and funding must be elucidated:

> To have a room of her own, let alone a quiet room or a sound-proof room, was out of the question....Since her pin money...was only enough to keep her clothed, she was debarred from such alleviations as came even to Keats or Tennyson or Carlyle, all poor men, from a walking tour, a little journey to France, from the separate lodging which...sheltered them from the claims and tyrannies of their families. (54)

Any residual question as to whether Woolf in the name of woman is revindicating property and empire for their own sake can, I think, be dispelled by her comments—immediately preceding the call for a private room—disparaging territoriality:

> Anonymity runs in [women's] blood....They are not even now as concerned about the health of their fame as men are, and, speaking generally, will pass a tombstone or a signpost without feeling an irresistible desire to cut their names on it, as Alf, Bert

[9] Virginia Woolf, *A Room of One's Own* (New York: Harcourt Brace Jovanovich, 1957), 117–18; subsequent references are provided in the text.

or Chas. must do in obedience to their instinct, which murmurs if it sees a fine woman go by, or even a dog, Ce chien est à moi. And, of course, it may not be a dog, I thought... it may be a piece of land. (52)

What would it take, I wonder, following the spirit rather than the letter of Woolf's text, to unhinge the stories women tell from a rhetoric of owning and an economics of possession? Is it too late for us to reconsider or even refuse the rush to appropriate the uncertain privileges of patriarchy?

Questions of Ownership: Model Answers

What, then, does it mean to "own" a child? Is a child of "one's own" any different from a child that "one owns"? Is an adopted child less, or more, "one's own" than a biological child? Can one own an adopted child? Or could the line of questioning be reversed? That is, how might the culture of adoptive families generate questions about assumptions of ownership pertaining to birth families?

Having explored and critiqued some general lexical and cultural uses of "owning," I now want to consider more closely its place in the discourse of family formation and, more pointedly, the potential unsettling of this place. My sources are both empirical and theoretical: I draw on experience and anecdotal evidence but also on anthropological analysis, contemporary journalism, and the growing body of popular and scholarly writing on adoption.

The central question with which I began this piece, "own or adopted?" poses the basic binary model at the core of traditional discourse about parental-filial kinship. As I have anecdotally suggested, it is the case here as with most binary models that the apparently counterbalanced terms are neither equal nor neutral: binarization, as Hélène Cixous has brilliantly demonstrated, tends to imply dominance and subordination.[10] Yet I have observed a myriad of responses

---

[10] Hélène Cixous, "Sorties," in Cixous and Catherine Clément, *La Jeune Née* (Paris: 10/18, 1975), 115–20.

that refuse to take the binary question at its bipolar value and therefore work to destabilize the implied hierarchy.

The graying blond mother of a dark-haired baby born in Bolivia offered a group of us at a meeting of a local adoptive parents' support group her exasperated reply to the inevitable supermarket question: "I change his diapers, I feed him, I sit up with him at night when he's sick; *of course* he's my own." What I will call her "nurture response" ostensibly unsettles the privileging of biological parenting implicit in the own/adopted question, switching the slash to an ampersand. To invoke the concept of nurturing, however, in answer to the question of what makes a child "one's own" is also inevitably to evoke the "nature/nurture" debate central to child development theory and, in these terms, once more to polarize the question of family connectedness along the simplistic axes of nature and culture.[11]

Yet most theorists echo the binary terms of this anecdote, opting for either nature or nurture—or sometimes both—in the determination of "whose own" a child is. Elizabeth Bartholet, a law professor and mother to both adopted and biological children, comes down clearly on the side of nurturance: "I discovered that the thing I know as parental love grows out of the experience of nurturing, and that adoptive parenting is in fundamental ways identical to biological parenting."[12] She goes on more iconoclastically to refute the significance of genetic legacy: "You do not in fact live on just because your egg or sperm has contributed to another life.... The sense of immortality that many seek in parenting seems to me to have more to do with the kind of identification that comes from our relationship with

---

[11] In the nature/nurture controversy, nature of course is equated with birth, though as Barthes suggested many years ago, such "natural" events as birth and death could not be more culturally determined. See Roland Barthes, "La Grande Famille des hommes," *Mythologies* (Paris: Seuil, 1957), 161–64, and also the work of Emily Martin, *The Woman in the Body: A Cultural Analysis of Reproduction* (Boston: Beacon Press, 1987), and "The Egg and the Sperm: How Science Has Constructed a Romance Based on Stereotypical Male-Female Roles," *Signs* 16, no. 3 (1991): 485–501, for perceptions about how to reinterpret the culture of nature. The nature of nature is in fact an increasingly complex concept for determinations of maternity. See, for example, the question of maternity posed to a judge by the noncorrespondence of genetic mother and birth mother in Kathleen Burge, "SJC Quandary: What Determines Motherhood," *Boston Globe*, August 29, 2001.

[12] Elizabeth Bartholet, *Family Bonds: Adoption and the Politics of Parenting* (Boston: Houghton Mifflin, 1993), xvii; subsequent references are provided in the text.

our children, and with the ways in which that relationship helps shape their being" (xviii).

In a similar move, Adam Pertman replaces genetic predestination with a kind of social/emotional destiny, remarking that "we [adoptive parents] inevitably come to believe we were destined to have the children we do. That adoptive parents bond with their children as securely as any others is itself a reality."[13] Pertman's claim is large: he argues not only for the commensurability of social and biological bonding but also, from his title onward (*Adoption Nation: How the Adoption Revolution Is Transforming America*), for the radical transformation of the nature and shape of the American family through the powers of adoption. It is hard to resist the optimism that proclaims the advent and even the fashionability of an "adoption nation": "Stunningly, marvelously, for the first time in its history, adoption has come into vogue" (5). At the same time I find myself at a loss to reconcile Pertman's image of an iconoclastic family order washing over America with my sense of a genealogical backwash sweeping the land.

In a fascinating and disturbing piece called "The Tree of Me," John Seabrook reports on a parallel revolution in process in the field of genealogy, made possible by advances in DNA testing.[14] Family history, we learn, is currently the second-most-popular hobby in the United States (gardening is first), and genealogy follows only pornography as the most searched-for subject on the Web. At a time when, in Seabrook's words, "the controlling structure for the family seems to be evolving from a tree into something more like a root system, hairy with adoptive parents, two-mommy families, sperm-bank daddies, and other kinds of family appendages that don't fit onto trunks and branches" (58)—a time hailed by Pertman as the "adoption revolution"—why has ancestry become a cultural obsession? Seabrook's hypothesis that the vogue of genealogy coincides with the desolation of planned obsolescence ("in the United States, everything gets thrown out or torn down too fast, until all we've got left is

---

[13] Adam Pertman, *Adoption Nation: How the Adoption Revolution Is Transforming America* (New York: Basic Books, 2000), 132; subsequent references are provided in the text.

[14] John Seabrook, "The Tree of Me," *New Yorker*, March 26, 2001, 58–71; subsequent references are provided in the text.

our genes" [69]) seems a bit too easy, yet his linking of genealogical passion with a lust for land and the cult of capital is worth pursuing. Could it be that genealogy, "a way to find the ancestors we feel we deserve" (59), in Seabrook's words—or what we might call a genetic "heritage of our own"—continues to be modeled on notions of ownership and that even contemporary American ideas of family are inextricably bound to ostensibly outmoded aristocratic notions of property and wealth, that is, to a creed of economic entitlement bequeathed by blood?[15] Could it not also be that it is precisely the threat of a rampant (r)evolution of the traditional family tree "into something more like a root system, hairy with adoptive parents" (58), that feeds the contemporary American hunger for genealogy? In other words, Pertman and Seabrook may both be right: that is, adoption and genealogy may be equally trendy but in ways that need to be considered together if the interconnected ideologies of adoption and genealogy are to be unpacked rather than overloaded.

If there is a tendency among many contemporary proponents and/ or theorists of adoption both to spurn the discourse of having one's "own" child and, somewhat inconsistently, to relocate the concept of one's "own" to a nurturing source rather than to a gene pool, there is an equally powerful move to readmit biology, genealogy, and genetics into the adoption picture. Far from being suspended, the question "whose own?" now receives two answers. Betty Jean Lifton, herself an adopted daughter, affirms that "adoptees have two real mothers."[16] There is "the one who got up in the middle of the night" and the one who "went through nine months of sculpting the child

---

[15] I paraphrase here Seabrook's description of the British aristocracy, a model that I want to suggest continues to play itself out in Britain's former colony. The economic model again raises its suggestive head in Seabrook's conclusion, in which, using his own case as example (he has launched a quest for other Seabrooks and indeed found one), he finds paper and property to be more significant than relation and connectedness: "If the point of this ancestor-hunting was to get more connected, then shouldn't finding a living relative matter more than finding a paper ancestor? But now that I had found a new cousin and he was right across town, I felt more wary than curious" (71). Scholars of adoption also point to property and money as the testing ground for society's thinking about adoption; inheritance laws are the sticking point in social acceptance of adoption. See Modell, *Kinship with Strangers*, 24–26; subsequent references are provided in the text.

[16] Betty Jean Lifton, *Journey of the Adopted Self: A Quest for Wholeness* (New York: Basic Books, 1994), 18; subsequent references are provided in the text.

within her body" (17); yet she reserves the term "own mother" for the woman who gave birth to the adopted child (13). Lifton, like Pertman and many others, is an advocate for open adoption, the evolving system that recognizes the inter-involvement of a triad comprised of the child, birth parents, and adoptive parents, that supports the right of the birth mother to choose her child's adoptive parents, and that champions the end of secrecy and the unsealing of records pertaining to a child's birth and adoption.

Pertman, whose strong stance on adoptive family destiny we have seen, explicitly defines his adoptive children's "'real' parents" as "the people who hug them, help them with their homework, tuck them into bed" (138). Yet he advocates sustained personal contact, communication, and interaction between adoptive and birth parents, not least for the genetically related information that potentially can be received and shared with adoptive children (137). But Pertman's most significant claim for biological entitlement is much less a product of advocacy than a perhaps unwitting byproduct of autobiography: his book, shot through with brave personal allusions to belated procreative attempts, missed fertility, infertility treatments, and the substitution of adoption for conception, plays out in a minor key a dirge for fertility even as it celebrates adoption.

In her study of adoption and the reinterpretations of kinship that it negotiates in American culture, Judith Modell, an anthropologist and adoptive mother, argues that adoption "in a culture in which parenthood is created by birth—a biological fact—" is a fiction made in the image of biological kinship: "A made relationship, American law claims, can be exactly like a natural relationship: the child is *as-if-begotten*, the parent *as-if-genealogical.*"[17] In Modell's "as-if" construct of adoption, an anemic replica of the genealogical archetype, "blood is the model for conduct and for emotion, representing the unconditional love and enduring solidarity of a parent-child relationship. As a model, too, blood transforms the contracted into a seemingly reproductive link; the child is as if a product of the parents' union" (226). If for Modell blood provides the sustaining symbolism for adoption,

---

[17] Modell, "Kinship with Strangers," 2; subsequent references are provided in the text. In *Journey of the Adopted Self*, Lifton similarly speaks of giving an adoptive family "the aura of a blood-related one" (4).

it also introduces "a fatal flaw—an inevitable comparison with 'real' blood ties...a reminder that adoption is a *paper* kinship" (226).

The way out of the closed circuit, the self-replicating genealogical kinship system based on blood, for Modell, is open adoption: "More radical than it looks...it contains the seeds of a thorough upheaval....[O]pen adoption is more subversive than even its opponents claim, constituting an 'unselfconscious resistance' to ideologies of the family" (234–35). Her point, more specifically, is that the "sharing" of a child by otherwise unrelated people (and, in particular, by two mothers) subverts entrenched beliefs "about the inevitability, the *imperative*, of parenthood" (236). She elaborates: "If 'mother' includes the woman who bears but does not raise a child and, with equal significance, the woman who raises but has no birth tie to the child, then 'mother' is no longer absolute—or absolutely linked with nature" (236). To disassociate "mother" from "nature" successfully would indeed be to subvert the reigning ideology of the family, if Modell is correctly interpreting her data to suggest that "the legal transfer does not erode the claims of nature" for adoptive parents and others (28). The evidence of Modell's adoptive parent informants creates a record that is poignant and arresting—an account of parents "haunted by the fact that they had 'someone else's child'" (201) and pervaded by a sense of illegitimacy touching on theft: "I felt as if I had kidnapped a child" (28), an adoptive mother confided, and another admitted, "I really felt that I had kidnapped a baby" (202).

Unowning

What precedes, then, is a brief but representative review of some paradigmatic responses to proprietary parenthood. Even as I present them, I find myself increasingly impatient: alienated and perturbed by the lack of inclusiveness of these paradigms, which read to me like other people's models. (It strikes me that if the political is usually personal in most fields, this may hold true even more often in the field of adoption literature, which people tend to enter because of a vested interest.) And so, without being a strong fan of competitive identity politics, I add my voice and my stance to the fray, with a firm conviction that my marginal place in an already expatriate scene creates a space from which to draft new models or at least to designate the site of their lack. Or better yet, a space from which to generate new stories, for no paradigm can fill in the gaps or show the significant variation of individual narratives.

I am the mother of a daughter I adopted in China. Through a combination of chance and circumstance and perversity and conviction, I did not confront infertility on the way to maternity. *I chose adoption.* I chose to love and to raise, to hold and to cherish, a child who did not emerge from my body and did not share my genes, sensing that the holding and the bathing and the feeding and the changing and the grooming of a child beside and outside my body was a feasible way to ground a physical and psychical mother-child intimacy. I chose foreign adoption, knowing but not caring that I would see no medical records and would know no genetic history. I chose to adopt a child from China, with full knowledge that my daughter's birth parents would almost definitely remain unknown for a host of political, social, and logistical reasons. Like thousands of other American adoptive parents of Chinese-born children for whom open adoption is an impossibility, I grapple with grief and hope to give my daughter her mother tongue and her birth culture in symbolic stead of an unreachable face and scene of origin.

Although infertility often breeds conversions to profound faith in adoption and fosters recognition, in Pertman's honest words, that "the mistake...is concluding that second choice means second best" (35), it is not the only adoption scenario. Many of us who opt for "kinship with strangers"—and, at the extreme, kinship with strangers from foreign lands and different races—do so not as a fallback but as a predilection. The decision to adopt often represents a *choice* of otherness and difference and the unknown.

Without wishing to vie for seditious credit, I would argue that transracial family structures, along with chosen single-parent family configurations, are as potentially subversive of traditional American kinship patterns as are open adoptions. All of these patterns are iconoclastic in the sense that they make visible the irrelevance of consanguinity to family bonds and the reality of alternatives to conventional family structures.

Finally, I must add that my sense of my child and my construct of our family relationship is not "as if" but "as is." We construct and reinvent family life every day as a family of two bound irrevocably by choice, and not by blood.

What response does my "as is" paradigm give to the binary question at the core of this essay? Where does "as is" fit into or modify the available slots of the "own or adopted" alternative? The most obvious solution is to change the terms by depolarizing them. But if we dissolve the dichotomy, rewriting it as "own *and* adopted," we risk falling into the "as if" model. For "own," when opposed to adoption in the binary question, clearly works as a screen for "genetic," "biological," "birth," or "blood"—with all the attendant assumptions of ownership, predictability, and control. I would like instead to propose "unowning" children: that is, first and cosmetically, as others have proposed, systematically replacing the "own" word by the less charged term "biological"—but then, more substantively, using the adoption model to divest biological kinship relationships of their baggage of ownership. A utopian project, perhaps, but one useful to think and to theorize with.

Ellen Goodman, not an adoptive parent herself but a clever observer of the adopted children of others, perceives as an advantage the fact that adoptive parenting "come[s] without a full genetic set of assumptions" and suggests that this inherent characteristic of adoption could be beneficially acquired by biological parents, who "give [their] genes as well as [their] love to children [and] set out to reproduce...[them]selves." The lesson of adoption, in Goodman's words, is that "our children may be our own, but we can't claim ownership. What I have learned is that...we must learn to share children. We share them with the world. But most particularly, we learn to share them with themselves."[18]

Experience has confirmed Goodman's words for me. Like most parents I know, I am utterly possessed by my child. When I am away overnight, my body is as disoriented as if it had lost a limb. When my daughter performs at school, I feel a burst of recognition and a reflective glow. But I continue to be surprised and full of wonder as her unanticipated talents and skills unfold, often in (welcome) contradiction of established family traits. I cannot walk on ice or rocky terrain without

[18] Ellen Goodman, "What We Discover as We Get to Know Our Children," *Boston Globe*, August 29, 1993.

stumbling; she can dangle from trees by her toes. I cannot carry a tune; she can imitate any succession of notes on first hearing. I agonize over every alternative; she leaps spontaneously toward each decision. I turn in circles without a map; she backseat-drives with glee and flawless spatial precision. And yet, like me, my daughter likes cooking, cuddling, puzzles, red, and irony. Coincidence? Parallel genetic construction? Environment? Nurture? Chance? Magic? Does it matter?[19]

Kinship systems in other parts of the world are not all based on blood relationships. In Pacific Island societies, adoption is a sanctioned and venerated family configuration (Bartholet, 169–70). In fact Robert Levy speculates that in Polynesian and Micronesian cultures, adoption may even be the most privileged mode of family formation, and the societal ideal, to build "between parents and natural children relationships which coincide as nearly as possible with those between parents and adopted children."[20] Levy also reads in Polynesian and Micronesian adoption the broader message that "there is no relationship which is *not* conditional" (86). Might we imagine, building on Levy's and Goodman's perceptions, a utopian kind of "as if" construct, which would have a biological relationship made in the image of an adoptive one: the child, freed from the onerous expectations of ownership, would be *as-if-adopted*, the parent *as-if-adoptive*. Which is to say, in terms at once simpler and more radical, "as is."

Owning Up: Leaving China

We left for the United States in an oversold jumbo jet without a single empty seat. The airline provided my daughter, six months and

---

[19]   The Jungian analyst James Hillman, not an adoption theorist, offers a theory of destiny and character that aims to transcend the nature/nurture paradigm. While I find Hillman's work problematic in its reliance on a phallic metaphorics and its potential grounding of an ethic of irresponsibility, it is worth reading for its refutation of deterministic theories based on either genetics or environment, nature or nurture. Hillman explores a determinism associated with soul, fate, imagination, and the unknown. See James Hillman, *The Soul's Code: In Search of Character and Calling* (New York: Random House, 1996).

[20]   See Robert I. Levy, "Tahitian Adoption as a Psychological Message," in *Adoption in Eastern Oceania*, ed. Vern Carroll (Honolulu: University of Hawaii Press, 1970), 83; subsequent references are given in the text.

eleven pounds, with a euphemistically named "floor cradle," which in fact was a kind of vinyl sport bag that could be unzipped, opened, and furnished with a blanket to soften the ride. Flushed, congested, and feverish on the day of her expatriation, she manifestly did not feel very cradled in her gym bag at my feet and spent most of the trip with wide startled eyes awake in my arms.

When we took off from Hong Kong for the transpacific flight after a very short hop from Guangzhou, the plane made a sharp ascent, rising almost vertically from the airport surrounded by mountains. Reliving this moment as I have many times since, my heart dives in memory as I see the mountain looming directly before us as the plane hurtles toward it. Reliving this moment anachronistically since September 11—following an emotional chronology I do not completely understand—I relive a superimposed moment of terrified knowledge that our flight is hurtling into the tower looming directly and unavoidably before us. Then we inexplicably surge upward and above and emerge over an unending expanse of ocean, and I know even as I am flooded with relief and elation that I have moved this tiny child permanently and irrevocably into a danger zone.

In the long ensuing hours of flight filled with no scene but blinding sunlight reflected by the sea, I vow to learn the only language my daughter would have heard before I came, a mute and token gesture to express my blind recognition of the unknown world no longer on the horizon, the kingdom from which she is now forever removed.

Reviewing this scene today, a scene of origin for me, in the light of the matter of this essay, I cannot claim to understand much with precision, but I understand in shadow more than I did before. I mean most crucially, and utterly unfacetiously, that I am overwhelmed by the realization that the essence of the unconscious is to be precisely inaccessible to consciousness, and that this unconscious is minutely structured by culture. From here I am led to suspect that although we may tell and retell our stories, along with the ones we appropriate, we own none of them, in any conventional sense of the verb: it is they that own us.

And yet I continue to believe that we might resist becoming marionettes in the tales that are culturally available to us. What does it take to withstand being told by our stories? The simple answer—that we must ceaselessly work to invent and to circulate new ones—may be a little too glib, if it is true that we can tell only the stories we already know how to tell.[21]

The field of adoption writing is too young and as yet too pragmatically driven to have its literary theoreticians, but it can profitably borrow from other theoretically more seasoned fields to articulate its latent underpinnings. Shoshana Felman's work on reading women's autobiographies as missing is particularly useful in its refusal to assume that these lost life stories can be found and put in place.[22]

If we posit the analogy that women's autobiography is to men's as adoptive family stories are to biological life stories (the first term on each side of the equation covering the unwritten, subordinate, "as if" side of the binary couple), we can then work from Felman's thinking about how to tell the unknown stories without having them take the place, voice, or shape of the dominant narratives. For Felman, the idea that women do not *own* their stories, that they are dispossessed of their lifelines, is not reducible to a lack of powerful model narratives.[23] Much more important than maintaining a balance sheet of narrative haves and have-nots are recognizing that we do not know to

---

[21]   As Carolyn Heilbrun puts it, "One cannot make up stories; one can only retell in new ways the stories one has already heard.... We cannot yet make wholly new fictions; we can only transform old tales." Carolyn G. Heilbrun, "What Was Penelope Unweaving?" in *Hamlet's Mother and Other Women* (New York: Columbia University Press, 1990), 109; subsequent references are provided in the text.

[22]   Shoshana Felman makes clear that the reason why women's autobiographies are not available to them is that "we cannot simply *substitute ourselves as center* without regard to the *decentering* effects of language and of the unconscious, without acute awareness of the fact that our own relation to a linguistic frame of reference is never self-transparent. We can neither simply 'write' our stories nor decide to write 'new' stories, because we *do not know* our stories, and because the decision to 'rewrite' them is not simply external to the language that unwittingly writes us." Shoshana Felman, *What Does a Woman Want? Reading and Sexual Difference* (Baltimore: Johns Hopkins University Press, 1993), 156–57n17; subsequent references are provided in the text.

[23]   The coinciding rejection of ownership in Felman's perception of women's narratives and my discussion of adoption narratives suggests an opening onto a series of potential theoretical intersections. I cannot here pursue these crossways but want in passing to mention a divergence, namely that for Felman, ownership is impossible (and perhaps implicitly unwanted), while for me, ownership is undesirable (and perhaps secondarily infeasible). I believe that the difference, at least initially, is one of emphasis.

whom we speak and seeking to understand our unknown "structures of address" (124). Felman asks:

> Whom do we *write for*? Whom do we *wish* to be *read by*? Whom are we *afraid* to be read by? Whom do we *trust* to know how to read our writing? Whom do we need in order to *help us grasp the truth* that lies in wait (for us, for others) in our story but that alone we do not have the strength to grasp? Who can help us, or *enable us*, to *survive our story*? Who is our *internal witness*? Who is our *external witness*? Who is our *voluntary* witness? Who is our *inadvertent* witness? (130–31)

Felman's questions uncannily frame my initial internal debate about whether this essay could be written. "Who will be reading this issue?" I asked Holly. For whom would I be writing? Who would be listening? Who would be hearing, and who would mis-hear my sense? Which truth, and how much of it, could I tell? How could I write, or even think, what I lacked the words to say, and what I didn't more than hazily understand? Would I be addressing people like my adoption friends and colleagues, who share my knowledge of family issues but might be bored by my musings in narrative theory? Would I be addressing my academic colleagues and friends, who read critical theory fluently but could not be expected to intuit or even wholly understand the intimate—and core—family issues? There was the divide. How could I bridge it? How could I possibly talk across it? And yet I could not think on one side alone.

This essay is the record in time of a halting, hopping, cobbled journey of discovery across the endlessly infinitesimal space of an internal cleft. I have come to see, following no small effort, that its contradictions, hesitations, repetitions, and inconsistencies cannot be smoothed without erasing my text. In fact its central concerns cannot be separated from its style, from its groping attempts to move forward into the gaps it finds. This may well be the only way to invent and to circulate new stories without falling prisoner to the old. That is, we have to do piecework, improvising, weaving our differences bit by bit in the gaps and tangles of stories we already know, and ever unweaving the wholes. Though I have in mind Carolyn Heilbrun's image of Penelope unweaving in order to avoid being caught in another's myth, I want to part ways on the ultimate design. For if Penelope's triumph, as Heilbrun observes, was "to stop unweaving *and* to invent a new story" (111), victory here would mean instead perpetual snagging, constant reworking: to *keep* unweaving *and* to invent a new story.

To unweave: that is, to undo the text of "one's own" assumptions and presuppositions along with the old other stories. To imagine one's ideal readers and one's illegitimate eavesdroppers, and to ask why. To question oneself, to search for unacknowledged forces of address, to refuse to speak "as if" in borrowed tongues. Yet such a textual unraveling would be not a mark of deficiency but the sign of a common human narrative consciousness heightened by struggling to grasp all that "as is" might be.

Thinking back, I realize that my peculiar impulse to write a dedication before I finished my first page was the key that unlocked this text (see the headnote). That is, by identifying those I most wanted to address, those I best imagined listening, I was able to begin to write. I understand today, when I reread the dedication and the tension of my opening pages one year later, that if I wanted to speak to those who had told me their adoption stories, or who had such stories waiting to tell, I propped this desire on the inevitable knowledge that when you have a story to tell, as Balzac put it, "there are always people listening in."[24]

September 11, 2002

---

[24] This knowledge of an audience wider than one consciously intends is at once pragmatic and hopeful and, my darker voices tell me, many other things besides, among them, reproachful, monitory, confrontational, even perhaps vengeful. But this is the start of another essay. The translation of Balzac's words is mine. He wrote, "Il y a toujours du monde à côté." See Honoré de Balzac, *La Maison Nucingen*, in *La Comédie humaine*, vol. 6 (Paris: Gallimard [Pléiade], 1977), 392.

6

MOTHERS AND LOVERS, OR THE GREAT BANALITIES OF EXISTENCE

Colette's La Naissance du jour

A tender snapshot from that vacation captures the parents and [five-year old] child embracing on a parterre at the castle, but thirty years later, a grown-up Bel-Gazou would share a more somber memory with a journalist. She and her mother, she recalled, had been waiting anxiously for Henry to arrive, and she had been dressed up to greet her father. While running down a flight of stone steps, she tripped, took a bad fall, headfirst, and scraped her face. Colette rushed over, but not to offer comfort. "Her irritation expressed itself with a pair of slaps and this sentence: 'I'll teach you to ruin what I've made!'"

JUDITH THURMAN

Exergue

To open a literary reading of *La Naissance du jour* with a biographical anecdote is to flout my best critical sensibilities and intents, but to do so with a sense of necessary perversity. The illegitimacy of the enterprise is compounded by the triple embedding of the epigraph, four times removed from Colette and unrelated to her writing: operating as a literary critic, I borrow from a biographer a journalist's recounting of a childhood memory of maternal handling related by Colette's adult daughter.[1] I mean in this way to emblematize the challenges and risks

---

[1] Judith Thurman, *Secrets of the Flesh: A Life of Colette* (New York: Knopf, 1999), 274. Thurman gives as archival source BN 18718 (Archives of the Bibliothèque Nationale, Paris).

of reading (for) the mother in any of Colette's three mother-centered novels, which have traditionally been assimilated by critics and biographers to Colette's own life story. Fiction and autobiography, biography and correspondence, indiscriminately bundled for decades by Colette's biographers and critics, have become virtually indistinguishable in the secondary work. If the establishment of such a continuum between the books and the life was encouraged and ostensibly even launched by the efforts of her first husband and most zealous publicist, Willy, producer of a large-scale Colette industry,[2] this was due less to any innovative genius on his part than to his extraordinary talents as reader of cultural mythology, including, in particular, an intuitive grasp of the cultural feminization of women's books,[3] a convention that Colette herself would refer to as "the fatally autobiographical writings of woman" ["les œuvres, fatalement autobiographiques, de la femme"].[4]

Like Colette, I would like to resist this life/work stew. I would prefer to remove from my reading of *La Naissance du jour* the insights, however startling or illuminating, that come from interviews, correspondences, and biographies, to exclude them as lateral rather than background information, extraliterary, beside the textual point, in order to read Colette as I do the work of other writers: as a fine and precious artifact, apart. I say Colette: I mean the writer, the writing, the text. But before I know it, I find myself caught up with the remains of the woman, the living, the life—particularly when reading *La Naissance du jour*, whose wily snares wind us in novelistic filaments that defy an untangling of fictional from autobiographical and biographical threads.[5]

---

[2]   Colette acted the character who dominated her early work, Claudine, on stage and in town; she was (often by design) confused with her character, which led to the marketing of a panoply of signature objects: Claudine dresses and hats, *glace* Claudine, *gâteau* Claudine, *cigarettes* Claudine, and so on. See Elaine Marks, *Colette* (New Brunswick, N.J.: Rutgers University Press, 1960), 73.

[3]   Lynne Huffer rightly applies to Colette Mary Ellman's observation that "books by women are treated as though they themselves were women" (*Another Colette: The Question of Gendered Writing* [Ann Arbor: University of Michigan Press, 1992], 4).

[4]   Colette, *La Naissance du jour*, in *Œuvres*, vol. 3, ed. Claude Pichois (Paris: Gallimard [Pléiade], 1991), 316. All references are to this edition and are provided in the text. Translations, which I have modified when necessary, are from Colette, *Break of Day*, trans. Enid McLeod (New York: Farrar, Straus and Giroux, 1961). In this case, McLeod's translation, "women's writings [which] can't help being autobiographical," does not do justice to Colette (63).

[5]   Colette herself referred to *La Naissance du jour* as a novel in her correspondence. See Jerry Aline Flieger, *Colette and the Phantom Subject of Autobiography* (Ithaca: Cornell University Press, 1992), 24.

Questions about how art and life relate to each other, which are intrinsic to all literature, are intensified in Colette's text by her self-conscious play with them. Like all of Colette's critics, like Colette in her flirtation with them, I am not always able to keep her life and art pure. That is why, perhaps again like Colette, I play with the conventions that confuse the two. And that is why I choose to feature in my epigraph—or, more pointedly stated, why I put *en exergue*—everything that I would like to banish from my own reading of Colette, everything I would like to cast out from my own text.

OED, Exergue: prob. intended as a quasi-Gr. rendering of Fr. *hors-d'œuvre,* something lying outside the work.

Petit Robert, Exergue: lat. mod. *exergum* "espace hors d'œuvre," gr. *ergon* "œuvre."

Mettre en exergue: that is, to place outside my work, as if by ritual purging, by an abjection of what threatens to contaminate it. I put *en exergue* all that I would prefer not to consider, all that I want to exorcise from my text. I concentrate it, encapsulate it, cordon it off in that space *hors-d'œuvre.* But that outlying region is also a primary space, a privileged place that comes ahead of the rest of the text: the first place my reader will see, the inscription she or he will read before anything else except the chapter title. An *hors-d'œuvre* with all the attendant ambiguity of that phrase: a deportation, a place of exile, an outer darkness—but also an *amuse-gueule,* an appetizer, a seductive foretaste of what is to come. What is outside the work also precedes the work; what is rejected is potentially the most influential part, by its position of primacy. The *hors-d'œuvre* then comes to coincide in meaning with the *chef-d'œuvre:* etymologically, the work that is at the head of what follows, the leading work.

By the classic logic that underlies hierarchical thinking, what I marginalize spatially in my approach to Colette cannot effectively be excluded from it, because it is in fact symbolically central to my thinking about her.[6] A pattern of conflictual representation of Colette

---

[6] See Peter Stallybrass and Allon White's analysis, via Hegel's *Phenomenology,* of symbolic extremities of high and low in European cultures, in *The Politics and Poetics of Transgression* (Ithaca: Cornell University Press, 1986), especially 5–6.

dominates contemporary literary-critical and biographical accounts, following her own ambiguous self-presentation, and—try as I might to deny it—scars my own thinking as well: that is, her life is ostensibly subordinated to her work, distinct from it, suppressed by it, only to reemerge within it, in unexpected forms and spaces. Since I cannot avoid in some way replicating this pattern, I lead with it, seeking secondarily to understand the antagonistic relationship between her work and life as I engage in my primary search for the place of the mother in the work. Let us then pluck from the daughter's memory of her mother, Colette, as represented in my *exergue,* some threads to lead into the text of *La Naissance du jour*—and let us simultaneously raise the questions of legitimacy and authenticity posed by letting auto/biography intrude, in just such a way, into fiction's text.

Before anything else, I want simply to acknowledge the shock value of the anecdote. It provokes a visceral reaction on the part of the reader, eliciting sympathy for the doubly wounded child and horror for the mother's aggression.[7] It is helpful here to step back and think about just what cultural notions of the mother, the maternal, and mother love are implicitly invoked as they are radically subverted to the point of engaging our emotions. What sort of mother would rush to her hurt child's side to offer reprimand and punishment instead of consolation and comfort? What mother would make of her child a means by which to woo her man rather than an end in its own fledgling self? What mother would treat a child's injury as a blow to her own narcissism and a threat to her own integrity? And

---

[7] I should make clear that since we are always situated as readers, I am speaking first of—and as—the contemporary American reader, operating within a child-centered culture, and with all the cultural assumptions that position entails, and which no doubt intensify the perturbing effect of the story. See Raymonde Carroll, *Cultural Misunderstandings: The French-American Experience,* trans. Carol Volk (Chicago: University of Chicago Press, 1988). As Anne de Jouvenel also reminds us in her preface to Colette, *Lettres à sa fille 1916–1953* (Paris: Gallimard, 2003), "children's education was different at the time—children had no rights—except those of being quiet, obeying, and honoring the family" ["À cette époque l'éducation des enfants était différente....Les enfants n'avaient aucun droit, sauf celui de se taire et d'obéir...faire honneur à sa famille" (8)]. On contemporary cultural expectations of mothers, see, for example (among the rash of recent books on the topic), Judith Warner, *Perfect Madness: Motherhood in the Age of Anxiety* (New York: Penguin [Riverhead], 2005); Ann Crittenden, *The Price of Motherhood* (New York: Henry Holt, 2001); Sharon Hays, *The Cultural Contradictions of Motherhood* (New Haven: Yale University Press, 1996).

for what kind of mother is a child's subjectivity reconfigured as an objet d'art? Cultural expectations would, of course, have the "good mother" steadily at her child's side, offering encouragement and succor.[8] A "good mother" keeps the erotic and the maternal distinct. A "good mother" is instinctively aware of a child's needs, and places them before her own. A "good mother" is not constantly away while her child is raised by a governess and by consignment to friends. A "good mother" is, of course, rarely also a "good writer," if we take that to mean a reputed author with a strong publication record.

Is Colette then the proverbial "bad mother"?[9] Why should such a question be raised in the context of a literary discussion, and how does it matter for our reading of her work? Author of maternal odes

---

[8] In interviews a grown-up Bel-Gazou reflects variously on the ways in which her mother did not correspond to the cultural norms of the maternal. For example, as Anne de Jouvenel relates: "She [Colette de Jouvenel] was often asked what kind of mother Colette was. She answered: 'If I were to say that Colette was a maternal mother, in the ordinary sense of the term, that wouldn't be correct. A *maternal* mother is supposed to spend her life huddled over her child, the child being the center of everything, sometimes to excess. No, my mother wasn't like that'" ["On lui demandait souvent quelle sorte de mère était Colette, elle répondait: 'Si je devais dire que Colette était une mère maternelle, au sens où on entend cela ordinairement, ce ne serait pas exact. Une mère *maternelle* est censée vivre penchée sur son enfant. L'enfant étant le centre de tout, et parfois peut-être jusqu'à l'excès. Non, ma mère n'était pas cela'"] (preface to Colette, *Lettres à sa fille*, 18). Colette was intensely aware of the tension she would call, in *L'Étoile vesper*, "the contest between book and childbirth" ["la compétition, livre contre enfantement"] (in *Œuvres*, vol. 4, ed. Claude Pichois and Alain Brunet [Paris: Gallimard (Pléiade), 2001], 876; all references are to this edition. Translations, with my modifications, are from Colette, *The Evening Star*, in *Recollections*, trans. David Le Vay [New York: Macmillan, 1972]). Her daughter in turn reflected on it from her own perspective: "A child doesn't easily agree to share her mother.... I had to learn to share her with a 'work.' A work....Could she be expected—could I expect her—to possess every virtue? Those of a writer who wrote sixty volumes, and those of a mother hen devoting to me her clearest and most enthusiastic hours?" ["Un enfant accepte mal de partager sa mère....[I]l me fallait apprendre à partager avec une 'œuvre.' Une œuvre....Pouvait-on, pouvais-je lui demander d'avoir toutes les vertus? Celles d'un écrivain qui composera soixante volumes et celles de la mère poule qui m'aurait dédié le plus clair et le plus chaud de son temps?"]. Cited by Claude Pichois and Alain Brunet in *Colette* (Paris: Éditions de Fallois, 1999), 346–47.

[9] Speculations about Colette's failings as a mother are legion in the biographies and literary criticism. Some commentators link her maternal shortcomings directly to her success as a writer, as if one were a consequence of the other. Michel Del Castillo distinguishes himself from most critics by separating the women from the opus. See Michel Del Castillo, *Colette, une certaine France* (Paris: Stock, 1999).

and author-to-be of a "Supplément" au *Traité de l'éducation des filles, de Fénelon* (which, however, never materialized),[10] Colette might be likened to Rousseau, author of a similar treatise on education, the *Émile,* and far from a model father. And yet I wonder if Colette's maternal shortcomings are not somehow more consequential to the reception of her work as a writer than the analogous paternal failings of Rousseau are to his.[11]

I am not alone in the temptation to include, in my reading of Colette, elements usually considered to be bad form in literary criticism: loss of critical distance, interference of life in art, gossip, emotional investment, and identification. Colette's writing elicits very personal, idiosyncratic, dialogic, relational readings, especially (but not exclusively) from her female critics.[12] Nicole Ward Jouve begins an excellent and enlightening study with some confessional remarks that constitute her personal manifesto for reading Colette: "It was my own dialogue with Colette I wanted to recount.... Immersed for months in Colette studies, and in Colette's own works, I had so wanted to yield, be taken over.... To have any chance of saying anything relevant about Colette, I must face up to her as I am, for what I am worth. Thus I start from what I can deduce from my experience of Colette."[13] Ward Jouve's words are representative of many women's responses to Colette, including my own. Colette's writing resists me but won't let me go. Her sentences elude me and dare me to pursue. Her poetics of self and other challenges me to participate in an analogous poetics

[10]   Announced by the Éditions du Trianon in 1927. See Pichois and Brunet, *Colette,* 349.
[11]   For the narrative about Rousseau's abandonment of his five children, see, for example, the editors' notes in Jean-Jacques Rousseau, *Œuvres complètes,* ed. Bertrand Gagnebin and Marcel Raymond (Paris: Gallimard [Pléiade], 1959), or Leo Damrosch's account in his *Jean-Jacques Rousseau: Restless Genius* (New York: Houghton Mifflin, 2005). At the risk of generalizing, I'll suggest that commentary on Rousseau's abandonment of his children and what we might call Colette's emotional abandonment of her daughter differs in nature. For Rousseau, critics and biographers tend to place the abandonment in historical-psychological context and to make psychoanalytic-formal links with his development as a writer. For Colette, the mode tends to be rather uncomplicated reproach.
[12]   See Del Castillo, *Colette, une certaine France,* for a personally invested account on the part of a man (who was a friend of Colette de Jouvenel). An unexamined world exists in the interstices between Colette's texts and her readers. There is a reading of readings of Colette (and especially of *La Naissance du jour,* with its embedded reader, Vial) to be done that would help enormously to elucidate her work.
[13]   Nicole Ward Jouve, *Colette* (Bloomington: Indiana University Press, 1987), 4–6.

and politics of reading, to reexamine my critical voice and my critical stance, and to take the measure of my distance from her text. The aesthetic questions raised by reading Colette are entangled with ethical questions. What is at stake for women reading Colette? What do women want from Colette? How can women's reading desire legitimate Colette and be, in turn, legitimated, without violating the integrity of her writing and living self?

The problem of subjectivity and relation raised by my reading of the biographical exergue recurs on the level of reader response to *La Naissance du jour* as we seek Colette (the writer, the woman) among her constructs, and ourselves among her embedded readers. Which Colette are we reading? Which reader are we? These questions are uncannily shadowed within the novel, which is a meditation on recognition and identification. A host of related puzzles ricochet in the space between biography and literary text, and are worth signaling from the start.

Colette is the mother reconstructed by Bel-Gazou's reminiscence in the exergue; Sido is the recreated mother in *La Naissance du jour.* As we consider one or the other, our attention refocuses. The ambiguous identity of the mother not only shifts our perspective away from the particular toward an abstracted, depersonalized contemplation of the maternal but also limns a maternal chain that will figure in the novel.

Judith Thurman's juxtaposition of a photograph of tender familial embrace with a memory of brutal maternal rebuke usefully opens the question of where the mother is to be found, and how the maternal might be defined. Both location and recognition are recurrent concerns of Colette's *Naissance* text in its quest for a maternal representation that transcends banality.

Bel-Gazou bedecked in her finery for Henry, torn and undone like a gift whose wrapping has been ripped before ever reaching its recipient, spoils the surprise, shames the giver, shifts the reader's interpretation from a maternal to an erotic register. The scene has literary and biographical counterparts. It anticipates a similar scene from *Sido* (to which we shall return), in which the child Minet-Chéri is wrapped in blue and tied with a ribbon, then sent with an ornament of flowers to Sido's best friend, the seductive Adrienne, as emissary, though one might also say as offering or gift: a message of love. Minet-Chéri, herself seduced by Adrienne's wild charms, lingers, arouses Sido's jealousy: extends the mother's message, rewrites her text. Minet-Chéri, like Bel-Gazou, dispatched as a love letter, becomes a text that overflows its borders, a Frankensteinian creation, Colette's monster: a Galatea that begins to breathe on her own. This scene in turn evokes another from the life narrative. Colette's stepson by Henry de Jouvenel, Bertrand, who was her young lover in the early 1920s, was originally sent as an emissary by his cunning mother, Claire Boas, who sought to use her charming sixteen-year-old son to persuade her ex-husband, through Colette, to allow her to continue to carry his name. Bel-Gazou finely wrapped by Colette for Henry, Minet-Chéri beautifully adorned by Sido for Adrienne, Bertrand in his stunning nubility dispatched by his mother to Colette, who is charmed more than was perhaps intended[14]: here are the same criss-crossed threads of nurturance and seduction that structure *La Naissance du jour.*

The lines of mother love and erotic love that weave between text and life also solder text to life. My child, my gift; my child, my text: "I'll teach you to ruin what I've made!" My daughter as opus, punished for aesthetic flaw. In fact Sido speaks of Colette in her letters as her work of art, an image her daughter repeats and embroiders upon in *Sido* and elsewhere. If Colette's own daughter represents herself to interviewers as a failed masterpiece, a lesser work, in her mother's eyes, Colette's letters let us understand just why Bel-Gazou might have had this impression, for we shall see that she often addresses her daughter there as a creation who did not live up to her creators' inspiration, an unfinished work unworthy of her makers.

After having resolved to exclude all biographical information from my critical text, I found the *hors-texte* already within. In parallel fashion, I discovered (and will show) that *La Naissance du jour* is a work that endlessly recontains its own outer bounds in Borgesian or Escheresque fashion, evacuating and then reabsorbing its apparent other. Have I then come full circle at the point of entry into the

---

[14] More than one commentator, however, has suggested that Claire Boas knew exactly what she was doing (unconsciously or lucidly) when she asked Bertrand to intercede on her behalf, and that the Colette-Bertrand affair was engineered to take revenge on her ex-husband, Bertrand's father and Colette's current husband. See Julia Kristeva, *Le Génie féminin: Colette* (Paris: Fayard, 2002), 77; Thurman, *Secrets of the Flesh,* 291; Pichois and Brunet, *Colette,* 330n55.

literary text? Does art always mirror life? Does life necessarily produce art's legend? But wait: I do not want even to imply that Colette's fiction is autobiographical. On the contrary; I propose that all her life's a book, and that life is her most extravagant text.

Where Are the Mothers?

The first of Colette's three mother-centered books, *La Maison de Claudine*, famously opens with the daughter's memory of the mother's habitual cry for her noiselessly straying offspring: "Where are the children?"[15] Sido's refrain, her routine rallying call, has traditionally been read as a rememoration of childhood: Colette's madeleine, a key to retrieving lost childhood paradises. The question, though put in a mother's mouth, is taken from a child's perspective, albeit a child now grown up; this is, after all, a daughter's memoir. But here one must pause to wonder which daughter, which Colette? Are we listening to Colette, née Sidonie-Gabrielle Colette, formerly Minet-Chéri or Gabri, daughter of Adèle-Eugénie-Sidonie Landoy Colette, or to Colette, narrator-protagonist daughter of the textual mother Sido, also former child Minet-Chéri recreated as such in Colette's autofictions, and therefore a creature shared by the realms of life and art? Does the second cancel the first?[16] Or are they the same?[17]

Looking back, the daughter, remembering, reconstitutes what it was like to live under the regime of childhood. "Where are the children?" or its allegorically slipped form, "Where is childhood?" is the

---

[15] "Où sont les enfants?" is the title of the first chapter as well as the reiterated cry that punctuates the opening pages of Colette, *La Maison de Claudine*, in *Œuvres*, vol. 2, ed. *Claude Pichois* (Paris: Gallimard [Pléiade], 1986), 967–71; subsequent references are to this edition and are provided in the text. Translations are my modifications of Colette, *My Mother's House*, trans. Una Vicenzo Troubridge and Enid McLeod, in *My Mother's House and Sido* (New York: Farrar Straus and Giroux, 1995), 5–10.

[16] So Claude Pichois claimed, speaking of Sido in his introduction to the second volume of Colette's works: "Prompted by the need to both narrate and dominate, by creating Sido, she annihilated Sidonie, the real-life mother" ["Animée du besoin à la fois de raconter et de dominer, en créant Sido, elle abolit Sidonie, la vraie mère"]. See preface to Colette, *Œuvres*, 2:lii.

[17] In recognition of the problem of distinguishing art and life, some critics choose to use quotation marks to signal the textual Colette or Sido. This practice, however, assumes that it is possible to tell the difference.

query that opens the first book, the portal of the three books that seek the whereabouts of the mothers[18]—a quest I pluralize, because Sido has many faces that emerge from many sources, and the mother, multiple incarnations beyond Sido. Sido encompasses the cruel child who tortuously reshapes her infant half-sister's fingers, the survivor of domestic violence in the house of her first husband, the earth mother who forages for mushrooms and knows the ways of all plants, the iconoclast who reads Racine in church and supports the unwed mother who works for her, the possessive controller who writes to her daughter, "Moi, c'est toi,"[19] and the wise, unorthodox ghost of *La Naissance du jour*. Colette's other maternal incarnations include Adrienne, her mother's best friend who nursed her one day when the two friends exchanged infants (*Sido*); Mélie, maid to Colette's alter ego Claudine (*Claudine à Paris*) and wet nurse to the infant and child who would become Colette ("Puérilité"); and the mother who unwittingly kills her daughter while aborting her grandchild (*Gribiche*).[20] The list could continue, moving away from manifest mothers and mother surrogates to include (among others) the dead mother of the Claudine novels and the aging courtisane Léa, lover-protectress of the child-man Chéri (*Chéri, La Fin de Chéri*).

But I catch myself on the other side of a Möbius strip, having slipped inadvertently out of autobiographical narrative into life and letters and on into fiction. I don't believe that the legitimacy of such a continuum can be assumed, and I don't know which was the first false step, or even if I am responsible for taking it. Mélie's crossing from the novel *Claudine à Paris* to the autobiographical essay "Puérilité" makes her one of a number of commuting characters in Colette's works, characters who wind their way between fiction and autobiography. Sido and Colette are two others. And the case of *La Naissance du jour* is even more complicated: historical figures such as the artists André Dunoyer de Segonzac and Luc-Albert Moreau sit down to dinner with Colette and her creatures of fiction Vial and

---

[18]   *La Maison de Claudine* (1922); *La Naissance du jour* (1928); *Sido* (1930).
[19]   Cited by Michel Del Castillo in *Colette, une certaine France*, 97.
[20]   Colette, we should recall, contemplated writing a story about infanticide in *La Naissance du jour:* "I've sometimes wanted to write a story about offspring devoured, bones and all, by their parents" (40) ["J'ai parfois voulu écrire l'histoire d'une progéniture dévorée, jusqu'aux os, par ses géniteurs" (*Naissance*, 300)].

Hélène, while her mother's ghost hovers nearby and her real-life letters—rewritten—collaborate with Colette's text.[21] So we follow a sinuous trail that leads to questions at every bend. If we're reading Colette's memoirs and autobiographical novels for the mother's traces, can we legitimately seek supporting evidence in, for example, the Claudine novels, which are widely accepted as thinly disguised (if salaciously embroidered) autobiographical accounts of Colette's adolescence and young womanhood? If not, how about *La Maison de Claudine*, a series of autobiographical vignettes that significantly are not, however, called *La Maison de Colette*? Does the name of Claudine in the title (strictly irrelevant to the content of the text) serve to fictionalize the memoir-like character of the text? Or to remind us that life transferred to writing can at best lie within a genre fluctuating between biography and fiction?[22] Or is the *Claudine* title a strictly commercial gesture, a marketing tactic with no effect on textual essence? What about the fictions? Can we reconstruct the mother using details from the novels—and if not narrative details, what about scenarios of desire and loss continuous with what we read in the memoirs and the letters?[23]

If the question recalled by the now adult child narrating *La Maison de Claudine*, "Where are the children?" screens another, "Where is the mother seeking the child that I was?" it is, in either case, one we understand in context to be rhetorical, a query into the nature of time past and memory fading. I mean, though, to pose the question of the mother's whereabouts otherwise as well, and

[21] I will have more to say later about these letters, written by Sido but rewritten by Colette.
[22] Eight decades later, the questions Colette's text raises about how to classify works that fall between the lines of fiction and nonfiction, (auto)biography and novel, are very familiar ones frequently raised by the books we read—though we are no more ready to supply easy answers. For a summary that expertly maps the rise of relevant intergenres (auto/biography, autogynography, autobifiction-alography, autographics, autofiction, biomythography, and so on) and discusses the web of concepts that have come with them (truthiness, emotional truth, autobiographical as opposed to confessional narrative, biologized versus anti-identitarian histories, relational narrative), see Nancy K. Miller, "The Entangled Self: Genre Bondage in the Age of the Memoir," *PMLA* 122, no. 2 (March 2007): 537–48. See, too, an issue of *Magazine littéraire* titled "Les Écritures du moi: De L'Autobiographie à l'autofiction," no. 409 (May 2002).
[23] Flieger calls such continuities "a phantasmal network," something like "an obsessional myth in Mauron's sense of the term" (*Phantom Subject*, 20).

to look elsewhere for an answer; which is to say that the mother's location becomes quite literally a question of direction—*sens,* in French: an inquiry into not only her place and her trajectory but her signification as well. For *La Naissance du jour,* the novel written under the mother's ostensible aegis, punctuated by the mother's letters, haunted by the mother's return, is strangely devoid of a certain maternal presence. Writing her mid-life reckoning fifteen years after her mother's death—which is to say, some fifteen years after her daughter's birth as well, since this child was conceived in the month following her grandmother's death—Colette writes the novel much more as her mother's daughter than as her daughter's mother. She begins the narrative with a filial affirmation that reverberates throughout its first pages:

> *I am the daughter of* the woman who wrote that letter.... *I am the daughter of* a woman who, in a mean, close-fisted, confined little place, opened her village home to stray cats, tramps, and pregnant servant-girls. *I am the daughter of* a woman who many a time, when she was in despair at not having enough money for others, ran through the wind-whipped snow to cry from door to door, at the houses of the rich.... Let me not forget that *I am the daughter of* a woman who bent her head, trembling, between the blades of a cactus, her wrinkled face full of ecstasy over the promise of a flower. (5–6)

> [*Je suis la fille de* celle qui écrivit cette lettre.... *Je suis la fille d'*une femme qui, dans un petit pays honteux, avare et resserré, ouvrit sa maison villageoise aux chats errants, aux chemineaux et aux servantes enceintes. *Je suis la fille d'*une femme qui, vingt fois désespérée de manquer d'argent pour autrui, courut sous la neige fouettée de vent crier de porte en porte, chez des riches.... Puissé-je n'oublier jamais que *je suis la fille d'*une telle femme qui penchait, tremblante, toutes ses rides éblouies entre les sabres d'un cactus sur une promesse de fleur. (*Naissance,* 277–78; emphasis added)]

Proclaiming herself four times the daughter of her mother, Colette opens a book that will leave largely unvoiced her own maternal subjectivity. As in her two other mother books, it is a daughter's subjectivity that explicitly reigns.[24]

If *La Naissance* is about Sido, it is especially preoccupied with Colette's similarities to and differences from her, with the ways in which she identifies with and distinguishes herself from her mother. In the space opened by this paradox (which might be paraphrased, "I speak as a daughter of the ways I am like my mother"), I want to resist reading only for the conspicuous filial perspective in order to tease out whatever traces of a maternal subjectivity or texture might also inhabit these pages. I suspect that Colette could not have articulated a sense of her mother without having first acceded to a maternal subjecthood that enabled identification with and dissociation from her mother.[25]

Colette invokes her daughter and her own motherhood explicitly in only one passage of *La Naissance*. At the end of a long excursus on her preference for animals to humans, Colette explains that she is moving toward what we might call a discretionary position on them: a silencing of her former expansiveness on the subject of creatures, which she extends to include her daughter:

> For if I see no objection to putting into the hands of the public, in print, rearranged fragments of my emotional life, it's understandable that I should tie up tight in the same sack, strictly private, all that concerns a *preference* for animals and—it's a question of partiality too—the child whom I brought into the world. How charming she is, that child, when she scratches, in a thoughtful, friendly way, the granular head of a huge toad.... Ssh! Once upon a time I took upon myself to make a girl

---

[24] In *La Maison de Claudine* there are a few anecdotes related from a mother's perspective, though the daughter's point of view dominates; *Sido* is once again under the daughter's empire, although the daughter's perspective there includes the father as well as the mother. For some excellent pages on the mother's perspective through sewing metaphors in *La Maison de Claudine*, see Huffer, *Another Colette*, 111–29.

[25] See Thurman, *Secrets of the Flesh*, 307, and Ward Jouve, *Colette*, 114–15, 129, for the theory that it was not Colette's biological motherhood but rather her accession to motherhood through her position as lover to her stepson, Bertrand, who traveled back with her both literally and figuratively to her childhood home, that initiated the works on her mother.

of fourteen or fifteen the heroine of a novel. May I be forgiven, for I did not then know what I was doing. (45)

[Car, si je ne vois aucun inconvénient à mettre, imprimés, entre les mains du public, des fragments déformés de ma vie sentimentale, on voudra bien que je noue, secrets, bien serrés dans le même sac, tout ce qui concerne une *préférence* pour les bêtes, et—c'est aussi une question de prédilection—l'enfant que j'ai mise au monde. Qu'elle est charmante, celle-ci, quand elle gratte, réfléchie et amicale, la tête grumeleuse d'une vaste crapaude.... Chut! Autrefois, je me suis mêlée de camper, au premier plan d'un roman, une héroïne de quatorze à quinze ans.... Que l'on m'excuse, je ne savais pas, alors, ce que c'était. (303–4)]

It is tempting to read this passage as an articulation of a certain aesthetics of writing, and even of life. On the one hand—in deference to writing—we might understand that one never writes well of what one loves, to paraphrase Roland Barthes;[26] that silence is often the best and most legitimate describer of the sacred. On the other hand—in deference to life—we might see that certain subjects, even for Colette, are taboo. There is an unexpected but steady cult of silence in Colette, a faith in the power of blanks and ellipses to convey a weight of meaning that language cannot fully bear.[27] The relegation

[26] Roland Barthes, "On échoue toujours à parler de ce qu'on aime," in *Le Bruissement de la langue* (Paris: Seuil, 1984), 333–42.

[27] A few examples of Colette's omnipresent valorization of the incorporeal and the unverbalized: in *Le Pur et l'impur* there is a chapter devoted to the Ladies of Llangollen, an eighteenth-century English couple who essentially eloped and shared a life together in Wales. The narrator compares the older woman's diary to the unwritten diary of the younger, clearly implying that the phantasmatic journal is the authoritative one, by virtue of its nonexistence (*Le Pur et l'impur*, in *Œuvres*, 3:625). In *La Vagabonde*, the actress-writer Renée Néré remembers the "dropped stitch" ["la petite faute inaperçue, la maille tombée, ce qu'à l'école on appelait 'une manque'"] she was made to retrieve as a child learning to knit, and revalorizes it as a positive writing aesthetic, the hole or snag in the pattern that quickens the text (*La Vagabonde*, in *Œuvres*, vol. 1, ed. Claude Pichois [Paris: Gallimard (Pléiade), 1984], 1225; in English, Colette, *The Vagabond*, trans. Enid McLeod [London: Penguin, 1954], 183; all references are to these editions and are provided in the text). And in *Sido*, the blank volumes left as her father's legacy, described by his writer daughter as "this immaterial legacy" ["cet héritage immatériel"] constitute a phantasmatic palimpsest, an invisible text that underwrites Colette's writing. Colette, *Sido*, in *Oeuvres*, vol. 3, ed. Claude Pichois (Paris: Gallimard [Pléiade], 1991), 532; translations are my modifications of Colette, *Sido*,

of Bel-Gazou, with Colette's other preferred beasts, to the hushed undertones and secret pockets of writing would appear to conform to this veneration of the unspoken that transcends a banal fear of publicity and exposure: a veritable ethos of silence. Yet the possibility remains that ethos may be reducible to alibi. Bel-Gazou, grown up into the adult Colette de Jouvenel, commenting on her childhood and Colette's motherhood, borrows but demystifies a similar discourse of mothers and animals: "[Colette] is like the mother cat who, at a certain point, tells her kitten to manage on its own" ["[Colette] est comme la chatte qui, au bout d'un certain temps, dit à son petit de se débrouiller seul"].[28] Is it possible to dismiss from perceptions of the text of her life what one knows about this life from other people's texts? Is there a way to construe Colette's muting of her daughter and reticence about her motherworld in *La Naissance* as respectful tact, as treading softly on hallowed ground? Or is discretion not better read here as distraction, as repression and neglect? As a continuation of the doubting silence in which Colette experienced the gestation of this child: "I remember welcoming the certainty of this late child— I was forty—with a considered mistrust, and keeping quiet about it. It was myself that I mistrusted. ... I was worried about my maturity, my possible inaptitude for loving, understanding, absorption" ["L'enfant tardif—j'avais quarante ans—je me souviens d'avoir accueilli la certitude de sa présence avec une méfiance réfléchie, en la taisant. C'est de moi-même que je me méfiais. ... Je craignais ma maturité, ma possible inaptitude à aimer, à comprendre, à m'imprégner"].[29]

According to most accounts, Colette was less than a devoted mother. Her intense absorption in her work and life seemed to preclude the assimilation of a child's world into her own, and she quickly consigned her daughter's care to a governess. Colette, who spoke lucidly of the incompatibility of maternity and authorhood, regarded herself as essentially an author and accidentally a mother.[30] Late in her life

---

trans. Una Vicenzo Troubridge and Enid McLeod, in *My Mother's House and Sido*, 197; subsequent references are provided in the text.

[28] Quoted by André Parinaud in *Colette, mes vérités: Entretiens avec André Parinaud* (Paris: Éditions Écriture, 1996), 46.

[29] Colette, *Evening Star*, 275–76; *L'Étoile vesper*, 871.

[30] "If, exceptionally, when I was young I busied myself with some needlework, Sido would shake her divinatory brow: 'You'll never look like anything but a boy sewing.' Had she not said to me: 'You'll never be more than a writer who has

she would acknowledge her bias in a letter to her daughter that she began to close with these words: "Was there ever such an unmaternal mother? I am your old scribbler, who was too often preoccupied with material concerns" ["Y eut-il jamais mère si peu maternelle? Je suis ton vieux gratte-papier, qui fut trop souvent obsédé de soucis matériels"].[31] The words play on a material split, the maternal ceding to the materiality of writing. The adult Bel-Gazou spoke often and plaintively of her mother's dual loyalties: "No, one doesn't interrupt a mother who is working, with questions. I held back. And this was the hardest part....What I couldn't have guessed is that she was in fact busy writing the answers to all my unformulated questions. Not for my own benefit, for the benefit of many people" ["Non, on ne pose pas de questions à une mère qui travaille. Je me retenais. Et c'était le plus dur....Ce que je ne devinais pas, c'est que la plupart des réponses à toutes mes questions informulées, elle était occupée à les écrire. Non pour mon seul profit, pour le profit de beaucoup de gens"].[32] The daughter's jealousy of the mother's books culminates in her sense of their mutual exclusivity: "Could one ask this woman who went into labor every day, to give birth every morning to twins: her work and her child?" ["Elle qui chaque jour enfantait, pouvait-on demander qu'elle mît au monde chaque matin des jumeaux: son travail et son enfant?"].[33] This rivalry is the counterpart of the conflict Colette later referred to as "the contest between book and childbirth" ["la compétition, livre contre enfantement"].[34] Colette, whose favorite work of

---

produced a child'? She, at any rate, would not have been unaware of the fortuitous nature of my maternity" (Colette, *Evening Star*, 282) ["Quand j'étais jeune, si je m'occupais, par exception, à un ouvrage d'aiguille, Sido hochait son front divinateur: 'Tu n'auras jamais l'air que d'un garçon qui coud.' Ne m'eût-elle pas dit: 'Tu ne seras jamais qu'un écrivain qui a fait un enfant.' Elle n'aurait pas ignoré, elle, le caractère accidentel de ma maternité" (*L'Étoile vesper*, 876)].

[31] Letter of October 27, 1952, in Colette, *Lettres à sa fille*, 514.
[32] Ibid., 18–19.
[33] Ibid., 19.
[34] *Colette, Evening Star*, 281; *L'Étoile vesper*, 876. In the extended citation it becomes clear that one must choose between mediocre writing and mediocre mothering: "My strain of virility saved me from the danger which threatens the writer, elevated to a happy and tender parent, of becoming a mediocre author, of preferring henceforward the advantages conferred by a visible and material growth: the worship of children, of plants, of breeding in its various forms" (281–81) ["Mon brin de virilité me sauva du danger qui expose l'écrivain, promu parent heureux et tendre, à tourner auteur médiocre, à préférer désormais ce que récompense une

fiction was Balzac's *Le Chef-d'œuvre inconnu,* surely knew—in art and life—the precarious equilibrium, if not to say the radical incompatibility, of art and life.[35]

Colette seems to have resolved the problem of incompatibility, rhetorically at least, by assimilating her daughter to her work: my daughter, my text, the work of art I have made. The filial opus wrapped for Henry and then ruined reappears in other circumstances as aggressive: "I always seem angry with you when you're sick....I worry when you don't look well, and that makes me...a little grouchy. When you're sick, it's as if you'd hurt me" ["J'ai toujours l'air fâchée contre toi quand tu es malade....Je me tourmente quand tu perds ta bonne mine, et cela me rend...un peu méchante. Quand tu es malade, c'est comme si tu m'avais fait quelque chose de mal"].[36] Small wonder if Colette expressed her daughter's shortcomings in terms of wounding imperfection and failed art, for she would always represent herself in Sido's words as prized product, opus, masterpiece. Her own daughter then becomes an *œuvre manquée* for reasons that Colette charges to a lack of originality or uniqueness: "Chattering, laughing...these are banal activities. An undisciplined student is a student who is like a hundred—no, a thousand—other students. You don't stand out....On the contrary, you become what I have always despised: an *ordinary* person" ["Bavarder, rire...ce sont des choses banales. Une élève dissipée est une élève qui ressemble à cent, mille autres élèves. Tu ne te singularises pas....Au contraire, tu deviens ce que j'ai toujours dédaigné: quelqu'un d'*ordinaire*"].[37] Repeatedly, Colette deems her daughter a trivial creation that shames her makers: "We didn't bring you forth for this. Your father and I have the right to require that our daughter...be *someone*" ["Nous ne t'avons pas mise au monde pour cela. Ton père et moi nous sommes en droit d'exiger que notre fille...soit *quelqu'un*"]. And similarly,

---

visible et matérielle croissance: le culte des enfants, des plantes, des élevages sous leurs formes diverses" (876)].

[35] During the time when Colette and her stepson-lover Bertrand de Jouvenel revisited her childhood haunts, which led to the writing of her first mother book, *La Maison de Claudine,* they were reading *Le Chef-d'œuvre inconnu.* See Kristeva, *Le Génie féminin,* 481; Bernard de Jouvenel, *Un Voyageur dans le siècle* (Paris: Laffont, 1979), 57.

[36] Letter of March 1922, in Colette, *Lettres à sa fille,* 44.

[37] Letter from 1923, ibid., 59.

"What do you expect me to recognize in you? Neither me nor your father....I ask myself, 'Where in her is my daughter and the daughter of Henry de Jouvenel? I can't find her anywhere'" ["Que veux-tu que je reconnaisse en toi? Ni moi, ni ton père....Je me dis 'Où est, la-dedans, ma fille et celle d'Henry de Jouvenel? Je ne la trouve nulle part'"].[38] The adjective Colette regularly applies in her letters to this daughter who is failing to bring justly deserved glory to her creators is "quelconque": commonplace, ordinary, lacking in distinction. Yet a comment in a letter to her friend Germaine Patat suggests a more nuanced, if fleeting, understanding of the ordinary and the banal as they operate in her family's rather extraordinary psychosocial universe: "What a lousy situation to be the daughter of two somebodies. My daughter would be a hell of a lot better off if her name were Durand [i.e., Jones]" ["Quelle fichue situation d'être la fille de deux quelqu'un. Elle a un sacré besoin de s'appeler Durand, ma fille"].[39] Striving, in response to her mother's criticism, to distinguish herself, to transcend her relegation to the ordinary, the child attempts to write pithy, remarkable letters worthy of Colette, only to feel herself inevitably backsliding into banality: "It's your birthday today, right, *Maman*? I wish you a very happy birthday....I would have liked to write you a spectacular letter for today, but wanting to do that is enough to make me come up with a banality that doesn't translate my feelings" ["C'est aujourd'hui...ton anniversaire n'est-ce pas, maman? Je te souhaite un très heureux anniversaire....J'aurais voulu t'écrire une lettre sensationnelle pour ce jour, mais il suffit que je veuille pour immédiatement pondre une banalité qui...ne traduit pas mes sentiments"].[40]

The concept of banality, like others in Colette's world (the "pure" and the "impure" are other important examples),[41] needs unpacking, for it circulates widely and does not correspond exactly to mundane

---

[38]   Ibid.; letter from 1927, ibid., 123.

[39]   Ibid., 13.

[40]   Letter of January 26, 1928, ibid., 140–41. See Michel Del Castillo's commentary on the fate of Colette de Jouvenel's writing, "suffocated" by her mother. In her preface to Colette, *Lettres à sa fille*, Anne de Jouvenel notes that when Colette de Jouvenel (her aunt) abandoned journalism and became an antiques dealer, her address was "Impasse de l'écritoire" (Writing Case Impasse), 17.

[41]   See Marks, *Colette*, 219, for an astute analysis of the pure and the impure in Colette. Marks understands the concept of the pure, for Colette, to correspond to

usage. For Colette as for Sido, the routine, the common—the *doxa*—is
to be eschewed.[42] Sido's letters routinely praise singularity, and disparage banality often. In the novels, Colette's Sido follows suit, if
with greater irony and literary flair.[43] But the category of the banal
as it gathers heft across Colette's work is more layered and complex;
to begin, it means more than the mere ordinary, which, for Colette,
often is a cover for the extraordinary. An exploration of the banal
is especially critical to a reading of *La Naissance du jour* because
it negatively structures Colette's (re)writing of the maternal as she
writes it against the mothers of convention.

On Banality

> Une des grandes banalités de l'existence, l'amour, se retire
> de la mienne. L'instinct maternel est une autre grande ba-
> nalité. Sortis de là, nous nous apercevons que tout le reste
> est gai, varié, nombreux. Mais on ne sort pas de là quand,
> ni comme on veut.
> COLETTE, *LA NAISSANCE DU JOUR*

As an author, Colette is renowned for tales of passion, and for reconstructions of her mother. As a woman, Colette is best known for
her amorous adventures, and for an idyllic childhood spent under
the wing of a charmingly eccentric mother. Yet in *La Naissance du
jour*, the first-person essayistic novel featuring the odd coupling of
a mother's ghost and a young man foreshadowed as lover, Colette
yokes maternal instinct and erotic passion together in the inflexible
service of banality. Can a text about the maternal and the erotic survive its own consigning of maternal instinct and erotic desire to banality? Must it turn upon itself, self-deconstruct in writhing throes
of irony? Or might it blaze a trail out?

---

what is concentrated, unadulterated, and characterized by complete, undistracted
devotion.

[42] Marie-Françoise Berthu-Courtivron refers to "the requirement of uniqueness"
["l'exigence d'unicité"] as Sido's example and expectation (*Mère et fille: L'Enjeu du pouvoir, Essai sur les écrits autobiographiques de Colette* [Geneva: Droz, 1993], 229).
[43] So, for example, Colette has Sido congratulate her childhood self in *Sido* with
the words, "You're a prodigy of sweetness and insipidity!" (170) ["Tu es un miracle
de gentillesse et de fadeur" (512)].

Somewhere, outside the banal, suggests Colette, skies are new. Outside banality is "all the rest": a cornucopia of happy surprises. But the extra-banal, like other utopian realms, allows difficult if not only virtual access. It poses an implicit topical problem: a question of semantic location or definition as well. Beyond banality: a new order of experience? Or a new category of expression? Are sexual impulse and maternal instinct condemned to be always already trite in the living, or is it the telling that banalizes by putting them into discourse as fixed categories of experience?

In the pages of her novel Colette repudiates an achingly nubile paramour and reproduces a dying mother's epistolary renunciation of a visit with her faraway daughter in order to await a cactus flower's rare bloom. Meanwhile, however, in the wings of her writing, in the space biographers call "life," Colette had recently taken a new young lover whom she would embrace until her death,[44] and had rediscovered a letter announcing her mother's decision to forgo the cactus blossom for the rare chance to see her daughter. By staging a retreat from eros and by contradicting what is known as maternal instinct, Colette rewrites life's traces in perversely original scenarios of paradox and self-love. But it would be a gross binary simplification to align banality with life and originality with art. Elsewhere in the novel the narrator's would-be lover, mundanely seductive, is identified with the cactus flower she has her mother iconoclastically choose: "Flee, my favorite! Don't reappear until you have become unrecognizable. Jump through the window and, as you touch the ground, change, blossom, fly, resound.... When you return to me I must be able to give you, as my mother did, your name of 'pink cactus'" (140) ["Fuis, mon favori! Ne reparais que méconnaissable. Saute la fenêtre, et en touchant le sol change, fleuris, vole, résonne.... Lorsque tu me reviendras, il faut que je puisse te donner, à l'exemple de ma mère, ton nom de 'Cactus rose'" (369)]. Cast from her life, the poor rejected suitor, this most explicitly common of mortals ("ce garçon ordinaire" [363]) who plays the most hackneyed of roles, leaps toward metamorphosis, well on the way to becoming that most extraordinary cactus plant, the unorthodox flower of maternal embrace

---

[44] Maurice Goudeket, who would become her third husband.

that, in passing, inhabits the skin of a mere paramour.[45] The banal and the exceptional come together, enjoy a delicious flirtation, exchange places and change form.

The banal is not a static category for Colette, and the exceptional can be found in the everyday. Banality is roughly coextensive with discourse (in a Foucauldian sense) in Colette's text: it is a mechanism of power that defines and limits what can be said within the normative structures of language and plot. As such, it anticipates as well Hannah Arendt's sense of the term as encompassing everything that is naturalized and therefore taken for granted.[46] This is perhaps why the most dominant technique Colette wields in *La Naissance du jour* is paradox, which functions as a form of passive resistance against the *doxa*, and it is also one of the reasons why the novel goads the reader, demanding and resisting interpretation in general, and synopsis in particular.

Instead of synopsis, I can offer only an inventory of items placed in commerce by this book that circulates paradoxes of self, other, mother, lover, life, art, autobiography, fiction, death, birth, originality, and banality. Colette's *Naissance* arguably initiates a genre we might call the midlife novel—despite its title, whose incongruous reference to birth compounds the factor of paradox. It is a kind of manual for women's midlife living. The narrator suggests at one point that she may be in the process of writing a book that tells men and women how to coexist.[47] I would add that it ponders how to do

---

[45] As Berthu-Courtivron has remarked, speaking of *La Naissance du jour* and of *La Vagabonde*: "In both cases, it isn't surprising that the lover to be ousted had already been devalued for a common reason: his all-embracing mediocrity....Being among the most common of mortals is a disqualifying factor for the lover who therefore stands no chance of belonging to the elite" ["Dans les deux cas, il n'est pas étonnant que l'amant à exclure ait été préalablement dévalorisé sur un thème commun: sa médiocrité universelle....Le fait d'appartenir au commun des mortels est rédhibitoire à l'amant qui n'a donc jamais accès à l'élitisme"] (*Mère et fille*, 268n1).

[46] Hannah Arendt, *Eichmann in Jerusalem: A Report on the Banality of Evil* (New York: Penguin, 1964). I do not want to imply, however, that Colette's use of banality bears any conventionally political connotations.

[47] "One of my husbands used to suggest to me: 'When you're about fifty you ought to write a sort of handbook to teach women how to live in peace with the man they love, a code for life as a couple.' Perhaps I am writing it now" (22) ["Un de mes maris me conseillait: 'Tu devrais bien, vers cinquante ans, écrire une sorte de manuel qui apprendrait aux femmes à vivre en paix avec l'homme qu'elles aiment, un code de la vie à deux....' Je suis peut-être en train de l'écrire" (288)].

many other things besides—all of which individually or collectively thicken the weave of paradox:

1. how to write a midlife novel about beginnings
2. how to leave a lover
3. how to meet a mother's ghost
4. how to take on a mother's life and death
5. how to survive a mother's life and death
6. how to conceal the self in an autobiographical novel
7. how to use lies to tell necessary truths of self-discovery
8 how to milk death to nourish life
9. how to milk death to feed writing
10. how to write the banal without writing banally
11. how to live deeply in what have banally been called life's "passages" without living a banal life
12. how to distinguish banality in life and art
13. how to defy critics and biographers to write anything not banal about you—and so on.

When Colette consigned erotic and maternal instincts to banality in the early pages of *La Naissance du jour* but went on to write this novel about mothers and other lovers, she opened a space for rereading mothers, maternity, lovers, banality, and the writing that represents them. This is the space of paradox, by which I mean not only this particular series of examples but also paradox as process, as a means of disarming banality. "Banality," the dictionary tells us, is derived from the noun "ban": a public proclamation or edict, as in the banns—the notice of an intended marriage, thrice repeated in the parish church of each of the betrothed—or the feudal summoning of a sovereign's vassals for military service, or the feudal requirement that tenants' corn be ground at a certain mill and baked in a certain oven for the lord's benefit.[48] Having to do in each case with community regulation of eroticism, family, aggression, and sustenance, or, in other words, with socially sanctioned love, reproduction, work, and war, the banal might be understood at root as institutional

---

[48]   *Random House College Dictionary, OED, Petit Robert.*

decree, social ruling, and sovereign law (that is, not only as the law of the sovereign but also as the sovereignty of community and communality): the reign of the commonplace, of received ideas or social discourse. "Paradox" is defined in corresponding terms. Derived from the Greek *para doxos*, the paradoxical runs contrary to received opinion or common wisdom; it goes beyond or against social expectations or beliefs; it exhibits contradiction with known laws, runs contrary to what is theoretically reasonable, and deviates from the normal.[49]

Colette speaks under the regime of paradox when she maintains the possibility of escaping from banality even while recognizing its hold: "Once we've left these behind, we find that all the rest is gay and varied, and plentiful. But one doesn't leave all that behind when or as one pleases" (18) ["Sortis de là, nous nous apercevons que tout le reste est gai, varié, nombreux. Mais on ne sort pas de là quand, ni comme on veut" (285)]. While her narrator survives a mother's death and dismisses a lover, her narrative makes its home between mother and lover. What does it take to live with hackneyed subjects but to transcend banality? How might love be rewritten outside banality? And, most critically for setting up parameters of reflection here, how does one write a mother's book differently? How can one think maternity without writing it into the rut of maternal instinct?

Colette's book about rewriting mothers and revising love is perhaps most crucially about reinventing the novel, and about the necessary interconnectedness of the three projects. Like Flaubert, for whom expression habitually consigns lived experience to communality—but, more exceptionally, raises it to the stars—Colette uses writing to flee banality, extracting the extraordinary from the everyday, transforming it with words. Rewriting the very ordinary renounced lover as a quite extraordinary phenomenon of metamorphosis, the narrator revises the conventional love plot as she closes her novel alone in her house writing: "The ambiguous friend who leapt through the window is still wandering about. He did not put off his shape as he touched the ground....But I only have to help him and lo! He will turn into thickets, sea spray, meteors, unbounded open book, cluster of grapes, ship, oasis" (143) ["L'ami ambigu qui sauta la fenêtre erre

---

[49]   See the sources cited in note 48.

encore. Il n'a pas, en touchant le sol, abdiqué sa forme....Mais que je l'assiste seulement et le voici halliers, embruns, météores, livre sans bornes ouvert, grappe, navire, oasis" (371)]. She revises maternal instinct when she reinvents Sido's letter so that it gives precedence to plant life before family life. She alters the notion of maternal instinct by defying it, within and without *La Naissance du jour*.

In *L'Étoile vesper*, as we have seen, she reminisces frankly about her skepticism anticipating motherhood, during pregnancy. In the essay "Maternité" (in *Paysages et portraits*), the new mother (called only "elle" in the third-person narrative voice), awakening after giving birth, awaits meeting her daughter with trepidation about producing the expected emotions: "My God, my God, she prayed to herself, here comes the terrible moment. I have only apprehension and fear, and I should be mad with joy, filled with a normal *maternal* hunger. How can I simulate it, how can I not tremble in shame?" ["Mon Dieu, mon Dieu, supplie-t-elle en elle-même, voilà l'instant terrible. Je n'ai que de l'appréhension, que de la peur, et je devrais être folle d'une joie avide, normale, d'une joie *maternelle*...Comment la simuler, comment ne pas trembler de honte?"].[50] The narrative continues once the mother has seen her child: "Then she grows sad again because she didn't feel the 'great rush,' the famous surge everyone always talks about....Am I a monster? Am I a wicked mother?" ["Puis elle s'attriste de nouveau parce qu'elle n'a pas eu le 'grand élan,' le fameux élan dont on parle toujours....Suis-je un monstre? Suis-je une méchante mère?" (323)]. Finally comes the release into rapture...but contrary to conventional expectation, it is provoked by the imprint of the father in his child: "I'm being carried away, I'm leaping with joy—but toward him, only toward him, toward that part of him that is inscribed in this trembling little etching. The cry that just escaped me is still a lover's cry" ["Je m'élance, je bondis,—mais vers lui, vers lui seulement, vers ce qui s'inscrit de lui dans la petite esquisse tremblante. Ce cri qui vient de m'échapper, c'est encore un cri d'amoureuse" (324)].

---

[50]   Colette, "Maternité," in *Paysages et portraits*, in *Œuvres complètes*, 16 vols., ed. Claude Pichois (Paris: Club de l'Honnête Homme, 1973–1976), 13:322–23; subsequent references are provided in the text.

There as elsewhere Colette writes against conventions of what is commonly called "maternal instinct," and in daring to do so, anticipates by many years the more recent writing of maternal ambivalence by contemporary authors such as Adrienne Rich, Jane Lazarre, and Susan Suleiman.[51] When I suggest, however, that Colette writes the mother extra-banally, I do not primarily have in mind a thematic or anecdotal rewriting of family life or roles, such as the display of an iconoclastic mother in *La Maison de Claudine,* or the rendering of an eccentrically restructured family in *Sido,* or the haunting of an irreverent maternal ghost in *La Naissance du jour.* In fact I would argue that these thematic restructurings preserve relatively unshaken—despite introducing occasional fault lines—prevailing icons like the beneficent earth mother and the idyllic mother-daughter couple. To move instead somewhat closer to what Ward Jouve has called "something mythic and revolutionary in the way Colette rewrote the terms of domestic experience," we need to look beyond thematics, toward psychodynamic and textual processes.[52] We can turn first to Colette's variations on the psychodynamics of love and identity formation, which work quietly and effectively to subvert maternal instinct, romance, and the woman's novel generically charged with delivering both.

Recognitions

Another paradox: I said maternal subjectivity was lacking in *La Naissance,* and yet it is clear that Colette identifies with Sido as she ages; the novel records her increasingly mother-identified self. To see the mother mirrored in the self is not necessarily, however, to see the self mirrored as mother. Colette's growing awareness of Sido's ineradicable presence is based, it turns out, on identifications that have little to do with traditional idealizations of their mother-daughter couple.

---

[51] Jane Lazarre, *The Mother Knot* (New York: McGraw-Hill, 1976); Adrienne Rich, *Of Woman Born: Motherhood as Experience and Institution* (New York: Norton, 1976); Susan Suleiman, "Writing and Motherhood," in *Mother Reader: Essential Writings on Motherhood,* ed. Moyra Davey (New York: Seven Stories Press, 2001), 113–37.
[52] Ward Jouve, *Colette,* 18.

Nor is it physical resemblance that is the most compelling. Colette ends the first chapter of *Naissance* with the ironic observation that as her aging features grow increasingly to resemble those of her mother, she would likely be progressively *less* recognizable to her mother, *as her daughter*, were Sido to return from the dead—as if somehow the daughter had lost her filial identity and taken on the mother's identity as the generations turned. The point of recognition for Sido's ghost would, rather, be the dawn moment at which she would glimpse her daughter, awake before the rest of the world, as Sido often was, yet unlike Sido, not carrying pruning shears and a wooden bucket, and not wearing a blue apron with pockets full of chickenfeed. Colette, unlike the chaste Sido, would appear in a thin wrap thrown hastily over her naked and trembling body, and would be shielding the shadow of a man. And here, in the daughter's feverish pose and beating heart, in her outstretched hands and stifled cry, is the paradoxical kernel of identification, the unmistakable resemblance to the pure maternal ghost. Sido recognizes as her own, in the two figures passionately silhouetted on the doorstep, not only her daughter but also the unnamed man who is the object of her daughter's ardor, and the passion that draws them together:

> Why, isn't what you're embracing my pink cactus, that has survived me? How amazingly it's grown and changed! but now that I look into your face, my child, *I recognize it. I recognize it* by your agitation, by your air of waiting, by the devotion in your outspread hands, by the beating of your heart and your suppressed cry, by the growing daylight all about you, yes, *I recognize, I lay claim to all of that....* [F]or I see that he is in truth my pink cactus, that has at last consented to flower. (7)

> [Ah! N'est-ce pas mon cactus rose qui me survit, et que tu embrasses? Qu'il a singulièrement grandi et changé!...Mais, en interrogeant ton visage, ma fille, *je le reconnais. Je le reconnais* à ta fièvre, à ton attente, au dévouement de tes mains ouvertes, au battement de ton cœur et au cri que tu retiens, au jour levant qui t'entoure, *oui, je reconnais, je revendique tout cela....* [C]ar il est bien, en vérité, mon cactus rose, qui veut enfin fleurir. (278; emphasis added)]

The object of the daughter's desire, bearer of no human name, but not quite nameless, is given, in fact, a botanical name, for the mother perceives him as that rare specimen of her own desire, her infrequently flowering pink cactus. Colette wins a wager with the ridiculous here: by metamorphosing virile shadow into pink cactus, she both trivializes the lover and ennobles the cactus, suggesting that all passions are equal. *Reconnaître* paradoxically takes its sense here in the shadow of *méconnaître*—that is, from the assimilation of two very different objects that ought not to be thought together—suggesting that recognition bears some affinity to the work of metaphor.

Sido, assigned to the category of "great lovers...of our sort" (24) ["les 'grandes amoureuses'...de notre sorte" (290)] is assimilated to her daughter by her passions, despite her chastity. Colette explains the contradiction: "Serene and gay in the presence of her husband, she became disturbed, and distracted with an unexplained passion when she came in contact with someone who was passing through a sublime experience" (24) ["Sereine et gaie auprès de l'époux, elle devenait agitée, égarée de passion ignorante, à la rencontre des êtres qui traversent leur moment sublime" (290)]. The erotic vocabulary is unmistakable, unadulterated by its often unexpected contexts: "She trembled with longing in the presence of a closed calyx, a chrysalis still rolled in its varnished cocoon" (25) ["Elle trembla de désir autour d'un calice fermé, autour d'une chrysalide roulée encore dans sa coque vernissée" (290)]. Dragged incongruously beyond the ordinary, we glimpse a place over the horizon of banality where desire might survive love and maternal instinct in any number of joyful and changing forms.

To speak of Sido's recognition-in-passion of her daughter is to reverse Colette's projections of herself, to read, as if from the mother's point of view, the daughter's sense (or, more pointedly, the *writer's* sense) of self as identified with her mother. As *Naissance* advances, the narrator progressively appropriates the recognition process originally attributed to her mother, extending the initial grounds of identification to focus increasingly on a complicity in aging, that is to say, a shared predilection for life's forces in the face of death. Aging, for Colette writing and reflecting on her mother's example, comes to coincide with collecting, in fact, with hoarding. She invokes her mother: "Oh, you hoarder of treasure!...[A]n age comes for a woman when the only thing that is left for her is to enrich her own self. She hoards and reckons up everything, even to blows and scars—a scar being a mark which she did not carry at birth, an acquisition" (34) ["O thésauriseuse!...[U]n âge vient où il n'est plus donné à une femme que de s'enrichir. Elle entasse, elle recense jusqu'aux coups, jusqu'aux cicatrices—une cicatrice, c'est une marque qu'elle n'avait pas en naissant, une acquisition" (296–97)]. She explains that even the sufferings a man inflicts on a woman become, in her stockpile of memory, so many accumulations, so many gifts of experience. But who is the hoarder in the portrait: Sido, Colette, Everywoman—or all three? Having slipped from the second person (you, my mother) to the first (I, Colette) to the third (she, Woman), and from the particular to the general, in the course of this excursus on aging and avarice, Colette closes with an enigmatic question to the reader about the source of her reflection: "Is anyone imagining, while reading me, that I'm portraying myself? Have patience: this is merely my model" (35) ["Imagine-t-on, à me lire, que je fais mon portrait? Patience: c'est seulement mon modèle" (297)]. The disavowal is famously ambiguous. Does she mean that instead of a finished self-portrait, she is producing something provisional: a sketch, or a draft? Or does she speak of creating the portrait of another—mother or other—as model for the self?

In either case, the question of model and copy, origin and derivation, has a troubled path in *Naissance*, beginning with the epigraph, which reproduces verbatim the portrait/model quotation, excerpting it from its place deep within the text. That part of the text usually taken from outside, from an *other* body of writing, here emerges from inside, from the text itself, preceding or anticipating its own existence, in a sense. The epigraph is both copy and model: it reproduces another text, like a copy, but it comes first, at the point of origin, like a model. Colette coyly rephrases the problem of origin and copy as a question comparing her mother's writing and her own: "Between us two, which is the better writer, she or I? Does it not resound to high heaven that it is she?" (141) ["D'elle, de moi, qui donc est le meilleur écrivain? N'éclate-t-il pas que c'est elle?" (370)]. The explicit answer, her deferential "it is *she*," is a tease, because "she" is produced by "me": Sido is Colette's creation, and her writing, as represented in the letters "reproduced" in *Naissance*, is really reinvented by her daughter.[53] If Colette does not explicitly address the equivocal authorship of the letters, she does acknowledge the inaccurate citation of her mother's words: "When I try to invent what she would have said to me, there is always one place at which I falter. I lack the words. . . . Now they well up in what I write and sometimes they are thought beautiful. But I know well that, though *recognizable,* they are deformed by my personal notions" (27–28) ["Quand je tâche d'inventer ce qu'elle m'eût dit, il y a toujours un point de son discours où je suis défaillante. Il me manque les mots. . . . Ils resurgissent maintenant de moi, et quelquefois on les trouve beaux. Mais je sais bien que, *reconnaissables,* ils sont déformés selon mon code personnel" (292; emphasis added)].

How do you tell origin from copy? Author from text? Bearer from borne? They are in fact not always distinct, and rarely maintain constant positions. "I felt stirring at the root of my being she who now inhabits me, lighter on my heart than I was once in her womb" (93) ["Je sentis remuer au fond de moi celle qui maintenant m'habite, plus légère à mon cœur que je ne fus jadis à son flanc" (336)], writes Colette, gestating her mother's ghost. It becomes clear as she describes herself carrying the maternal legacy, lodging the maternal spirit, that Colette *becomes* her mother's house, or more accurately *la maison de Claudine:* which is to say, the house of writing. To read within the framework of this house is to take a step toward understanding why Colette's text is so disorienting, why so many of its representations turn out to be different than they initially appeared. When, for example, Colette opens *Naissance* by presenting herself four times in rapid succession as her mother's daughter ("je suis la fille de celle qui . . . je suis la fille d'une femme qui . . . je suis la fille d'une femme qui . . . je suis la fille d'une telle femme qui . . ." [277–78]), we have to shrug off the numbing weight of the repetition to remind ourselves of the full text of the first assertion: "I am the daughter *of the woman who*

---

[53] As Michel Mercier observes in the "Notice" to *Naissance:* "It has been established that the text of Sido's letters has been corrected, amended, distorted, indeed completely invented by Colette, and it is equally well established that the relationship between mother and daughter was not nearly as simple as the novel suggests" ["Or il est avéré que le texte des lettres de Sido a été corrigé, amendé, déformé, voire inventé de toutes pièces par Colette, et il est non moins avéré que les rapports de la mère et de la fille n'eurent pas la forte simplicité que suggère le roman" (1386)].

wrote that letter"(5) ["Je suis la fille *de celle qui écrivit cette lettre"* (277; emphasis added)]. Since Sido *did not* in fact write this letter but instead one that was very different in wording and in spirit, Colette in effect declares herself to be a self-creation, the daughter of her writing. One might even say that she kills Sidonie so that her mother can be reborn in writing, as writing, as the daughter of (her) writing.[54] Her youngest stepson, Renaud de Jouvenel, anticipated my point when he explained that he couldn't recognize himself as he appeared in Colette's letters: "She exaggerated...because she was carried away by fantasy, saw people through a glass that magnified and deformed them, and...she idealized things, swept away by her own fervor, by her need to transform everything into literature" ["Elle exagérait....[C]'est qu'elle débordait de fantaisie, voyait les êtres au travers d'une loupe grossissante et déformante et...idéalisait, emportée par la chaleur de son temperament, le besoin de tout transformer en matériau littéraire"].[55]

I don't believe it is entirely by chance that Colette was renovating La Treille Muscate, the house in St. Tropez to which she had recently moved, at the time she was writing and rewriting *La Naissance du jour*, her meditation on (mis)recognition, change, and lodging the midlife soul.[56] Her letters from the period are preoccupied with projects for adding a garage and two rooms to constitute a separate apartment, but meanwhile, while the renovations proceed, with finding a space in which to accommodate her visiting daughter. Constructing

---

[54]   I am embroidering on Pichois's earlier-cited words ("En créant Sido, elle abolit Sidonie"). Or, as Sylvie Tinter astutely observes: "The margin was indeed great between the real-life mother, Sidonie Landoy, and the literary myth, and if the aging Colette seems to bring to fruition the teachings of Sido, revealing herself worthy of being Sido's daughter, isn't that fundamentally because the literary Sido was the daughter of Colette's creative genius?" ["La marge en effet était grande entre la mère réelle, Sidonie Landoy, et le mythe littéraire, et si Colette vieillissante semble...tirer tous les fruits de l'enseignement de Sido, s'en révéler la digne fille, n'est-ce pas, fondamentalement, parce que la Sido littéraire était la fille du génie créateur de Colette?"] (*Colette et le temps surmonté* [Geneva: Slatkine, 1980], 78–9).

[55]   Renaud de Jouvenel, "Mon Enfance à l'ombre de Colette: Lettres de Colette à Renaud de Jouvenel," *La Revue de Paris* (December 1966): 5.

[56]   "Is this house going to be my last?" (*Break of Day*, 8) ["Est-ce ma dernière maison?"] (*Naissance*, 279), asks the narrator at one point of her extended musing on familiarity and change. For an analytic inventory of houses and domestic space in Colette's novels, see Marie-Françoise Berthu-Courtivron, *Espace, demeure, écriture: La Maison natale dans l'œuvre de Colette* (Paris: Nizet, 1992).

her daughter's house, she reconstructs herself as her mother's house, the dwelling place of "[the woman] who now inhabits me" (93) ["celle qui maintenant m'habite" (336)]. The house that Colette built: the house of writing. It is a *heimlich* place that draws one deeper and deeper inside until the familiar becomes unrecognizable—*unheimlich*—and recognition coincides with mistaken identity.[57]

Up to this point I have explicitly discussed recognition as identification, which emphasizes its assimilatory sense; yet it has become increasingly evident that folded within the idea of recognition as identity and similarity, in Colette's text, is a sense of difference and change as well. It is time to turn once more to the dictionary. A summary scan of the *OED* and the *Petit Robert* confirms that in English and in French the dominant thrust of the verb "to recognize," *reconnaître*, and the noun "recognition," *reconnaissance*, goes in the direction of identification, identity, assimilation. To recognize something or someone is to identify (it/her/him) as previously seen, known, or perceived; to perceive or to treat as true or valid; to acknowledge; to show appreciation of; to acknowledge as one's own. From here to the idea of appropriation is only a small step. Barbara Johnson goes so far as to claim that recognition is "a form of blindness, a form of violence to the otherness of the object."[58] From within the dictionary affirmations of sameness, however, comes a shift, which, despite its subtlety, splits the meaning of recognition in two. For if *to recognize* is "to know again; to perceive to be identical with something previously known," it is shadowed by a qualification: "to know by means of some distinctive feature." And if *to recognize* is "to know again or further," it is followed by a shade of difference: "to mark or to distinguish again."[59] The *Petit Robert* offers an illustrative citation from Bergson: "To recognize a man consists of *distinguishing him from other men,* but to recognize an animal is usually to take note of the species to which it belongs" ["Reconnaître un homme consiste à *le*

---

[57]   On the turn of the *Heimlich* into the *Unheimlich,* see Sigmund Freud, "The 'Uncanny,'" in *On Creativity and the Unconscious,* ed. and trans. Benjamin Nelson (New York: Harper and Row, 1958), 122–61.

[58]   Barbara Johnson, "The Frame of Reference: Poe, Lacan, Derrida," in *The Critical Difference: Essays in the Contemporary Rhetoric of Reading* (Baltimore: Johns Hopkins University Press, 1980), 137.

[59]   *OED.*

distinguer des autres hommes; mais reconnaître un animal est ordinairement se rendre compte de l'espèce à laquelle il appartient"]
(emphasis added). The meaning of recognition as assimilation and
legitimation then evolves to include as well an understanding of the
term as distinction, dissimilarity, and differentiation. The idea of recognition, like that of its analogue, the *Heimlich* (a concept embracing
all that is homey, familiar, known, reassuring), increases in intensity
until it reveals an internal rift by means of which it turns into its ostensible opposite. At the heart of identity is a dark chamber in whose
recesses lies divergence. This semantic division and transformation
has ramifications to which we shall return.

"How do you know me?" Or better phrased, "How do I know you?
Let me count the ways." The list of recognitions is long, and I have
touched only on fragments: recognition in writing, identification in
passion, shared lust for life, shared greed for experience, facial mirroring, twinned marital history: "each of us had two husbands" (28)
["nous eûmes, chacune, deux maris" (292)], notes Colette (though
she would go on to have three). But of all the forms to be inven-
toried in Colette's collected recognitions of her mother, the oddest
is a kind of goading, a taunting call to recognition, a dare to admit
complicity just where difference appears most extreme: in short, an
identification in incest. The incest, to be sure, is virtual, and Sido
may lie unstained in her grave. More curious than any potential sin
is the implicit malice of the charge, the glee with which Colette recognizes herself in a sister-in-sin who happens to be her oh-so-chaste
mother:

> *To bring my mother close to me again* I have to think back to
> those dramatic dreams she dreamt throughout the adolescence
> of her elder son, who was so beautiful and wild, full of false
> gaiety, given to maledictions, ordinary, plain-looking, and on
> the alert. Oh, if only I could see her again thus diminished, her
> cheeks flushed red with jealousy and rage! If only I might see
> her thus and *she might hear me, in order to recognize herself* in
> what she would most strongly have reproved! If only I, grown
> wise in my turn, could show her how much her own image,
> though coarsened and impure, survives in me, her faithful ser-
> vant, whose job is the menial tasks! She gave me life and the

mission to pursue those things which she, a poet, seized and cast aside. (25)

[Me voici contrainte, *pour la renouer à moi,* de rechercher le temps où ma mère rêvait dramatiquement au long de l'adolescence de son fils aîné, le très beau, le séducteur. En ce temps-là, je la devinai sauvage, pleine de fausse gaîté et de malédictions, ordinaire, enlaidie, aux aguets.... Ah! que je la revoie ainsi diminuée, la joue colorée d'un rouge qui lui venait de la jalousie et de la fureur! Que je la revoie ainsi et *qu'elle m'entende assez pour se reconnaître* dans ce qu'elle eût le plus fort réprouvé! Que je lui révèle, à mon tour savante, combien je suis son impure survivance, sa grossière image, sa servante fidèle chargée des basses besognes! Elle m'a donné le jour, et la mission de poursuivre ce qu'en poète elle saisit et abandonna. (290; emphasis added)]

We have two sorts of virtual incest here before us: if it is given to Colette to *live* the "dirty work" her mother *dreams* "en poète"— that is, to realize Sido's incestuous impulses—it is also Colette's lot to de-realize or to symbolize the family bonds that underlie Sido's desire for her son: family bonds symbolized by Colette-the-writer, in her narrator's relationship to the much younger Vial of *La Naissance du jour,* and by Colette-the-woman, in the recently ended affair with her adolescent stepson Bertrand de Jouvenel and the new liaison with the younger Maurice Goudeket, whom she would eventually marry. It is not clear which of these virtual mother-son relationships might correspond to the "mission" Colette received to enact the virtual sex practiced by her mother ("ce qu'...elle saisit et abandonna"). What is clear is that a three-dimensional triangle is implied: a structure of desire and jealousy suspended across the line that ostensibly separates life from text:

Poor over-loved sons! Preening under feminine glances, wantonly nuzzled by the female who carried you, favorites from the deep night of the womb, beautiful cherished young males, whatever you do you can't help betraying when you pass from one mother to another. You yourself, my very dear mother, whom

I liked to think untouched by my ordinary crimes, even in your correspondence I find, conveyed in a handwriting that strove in vain to hide the irregular pounding of your heart, these words: *"Yes, like you I've found Madame X very changed and sad. I know there is no mystery in her private life; so we can bet that big son of hers has his first mistress."* (32–33)

[Fils trop aimés! Lustrés de regards féminins, mordillés à plaisir par la femelle qui vous porta, préférés dès la profonde nuit des flancs, beaux jeunes mâles choyés, vous ne passez pas d'une mère à une autre sans trahir, malgré vous. Toi-même, ma très chère, toi que je voulais pure de mes crimes ordinaires, voilà que je trouve dans ta correspondance, déposés d'une écriture appliquée, en vain, à me cacher le tumulte saccadé du cœur, ces mots: *"Oui, j'ai trouvé comme toi Mme X bien changée et triste. Je sais que sa vie privée est sans mystère: parions donc que son grand fils a sa première maîtresse."* (295–96)]

Let us take just a brief look at a few possibilities raised by these two passages. The textual Sido is caught in a triangle that includes her unnamed eldest son and his mistress(es). In parallel fashion, by implication, the textual Colette (narrator and character of *Naissance*) takes Sido's place in a triangle that, in turn, includes Vial and the younger woman who wants him, Hélène. The excerpted letter in which Sido(nie) recognizes Madame X's jealousy of a son's mistress, however, has the effect of mixing life with the novel, so that we can at least somewhat legitimately fill in the son's name, now assuming a triangle that includes Sidonie, Achille, and his first known mistress.[60] From there the door opens wide to (auto)biography, and we might draw another triangle that includes Colette, Bertrand, and Marcelle Prat, the younger woman Bertrand eventually married, or, in her place, any of the other younger women his mother set in his path in an attempt to lure him away from Colette. Or, in another variation, we could redraw the triangle to include Bertrand's mother, Claire Boas, Bertrand, and Colette, with Colette this time in the position of mistress and rival to the mother.

[60] See *Naissance*, 1402n2, 1404n1.

Between the points of the explicit mother-son-mistress triangle, however, lie other lines of force that imply a variation on this triangulation. Colette's exultant memory of her mother's jealousy of her eldest son's powers of seduction ("if only I could see her again thus diminished" ["que je la revoie ainsi diminuée"]), and the sheer excess of her invocation of sons ("poor ever-loved sons!...favorites from the deep night of the womb" ["fils trop aimés!...préférés dès la profonde nuit des flancs"]), suggest a mother-son-daughter triangle that has been biographically represented by Judith Thurman, who speaks at length of Sido's "romance with Achille," and comments that "one of [Colette's] own first and formative passions was jealousy of her mother's jealousy of Achille."[61] That Thurman's documentation is as much literary—using evidence drawn from *Naissance*—as epistolary is evidence of the Möbius path we travel through this text, to life, and back. The difference, of course, in the Sido-Achille-Colette triangle is that lines of force connect the two women as much as the mother and son; the erotic and incestuous lines are doubled.

Alternatively, we could return to the twin triangles that configure Sido's and Colette's erotic domains along lines of force pitting mothers and sons against sons and mistresses, now picturing the double triangles superimposed in parallel planes, with the points occupied by Sido and Colette bound by lines of jealousy and desire that link the two triangles just as forcefully as the lines of each triangle link its internal points. In this schema, two triple-pointed configurations recreated in tandem connect two points. "If only I could *see* her thus and she might *hear* me, *in order to recognize herself*" (25; emphasis added) ["Que je la *revoie* ainsi et qu'elle m'*entende* assez *pour se reconnaître*" (290)], wills Colette, invoking the senses in the graver interests of the mind and the heart: To recognize, that is, paradoxically, to distinguish by identifying with, to know the other in the self, and the self in the other, through the self's perception of the other, and the other's perception of the self—a series of reverberating, ricocheting reflections. But also, to accept and to authorize the self through the other's self-reflecting existence. To have and to hold the

---

[61] Thurman, *Secrets of the Flesh*, 313, 54.

other, in the self. We must not imagine a traditional mirror image, but instead, a constantly revised and changing gaze: Proteus as the looking glass.

Mothers and Lovers

When, early in the novel, mothers and lovers are relegated as a pair (in their qualified forms of maternal instinct and erotic passion) to the devalued standard of banality, they are not just dismissed and abandoned. For the plotline (such as it is) of *La Naissance du jour* follows the narrator in her daily entanglement and evolving disentanglement with a budding lover, while its structural line depends on a spectral mother's imagined epistolary interventions. Reductively synopsized, the novel unfolds a double rejection of banality: at the beginning, the mother subordinates the daughter to an unusual flower, and at the end, the daughter renounces the lover. Pages turn: maternal instinct and erotic love yield to more exotic scenarios of language, without ceasing to dominate the novel's surface.

On the micro-level as well, lovers and mothers must be thought together in underlying patterns of analogy, association, and metaphor, woven with varying materials of the manifest text.[62] Colette, for example, tries to explain to Vial the astonishing phenomenon of transcending her reliance on love, being reborn on her own, with nothing but an occasional "love reflex," and she describes the novelty of this phenomenon by analogizing it to postpartum experience: "When a woman has just given birth to a child, a reflex action sometimes makes her cry out again on waking from her first sleep after deliverance. And I, you see, still have the reflex of love, I forget that I have put aside the fruit I once produced" (112) ["Quelquefois des accouchées, après leur premier sommeil de délivrance, s'éveillent en recommençant le réflexe du cri...J'ai encore, figure-toi, le réflexe de l'amour, j'oublie que j'ai rejeté mon fruit" (350)]. What Colette names the "love reflex" is analogously represented in the novel as the maternal

---

[62]   Whereas Lynne Huffer argues that mother and lover represent competing plots, I want to represent them as doubling each other. See Huffer, *Another Colette,* 29–44.

ghost: in each case it is a question of psychic remains, or a kind of involuntary illusion of presence in the place of real absence (whether the absence is figured by renunciation or by death). And in each case—being delivered of a child, of an embryonic ghost, or a lover—being reborn means recognizing one's solitude, one's identity, as separate: in Colette's words, "rejecting one's fruit." Elsewhere, loving—and, more significantly, having recovered from love—borrows the vocabulary of rebirth: "A woman lays claim to as many native lands as she has had happy loves. She is born, too, under every sky where she has recovered from the pain of loving" (13) ["Une femme se réclame d'autant de pays natals qu'elle a eu d'amours heureux. Elle naît aussi sous chaque ciel où elle guérit la douleur d'aimer" (282)].

Less abstractly, a letter attributed to Sido compares, with ostensible naïveté, her awe before a beautiful child to an erotic encounter: "There is about a very beautiful child something I can't define which makes me sad.... They say that great lovers feel like that before the object of their passion. Can it be then that, in my way, I am a great lover?" (23) ["Il y a dans un enfant très beau quelque chose que je ne puis définir et qui me rend triste.... On assure que les grands amoureux, devant l'objet de leur passion, sont ainsi. Je serais donc, à ma manière, une grande amoureuse?" (289)]. Colette, however, takes it upon herself to define the sadness of what remains indefinable for Sido, and to name the unnamed erotic impulse: "When she bent over a glorious childish creature she would tremble and sigh, seized with an anguish she could not explain, whose name is temptation. For it would never have occurred to her that from a youthful face there could emanate a perturbation, a mist like that which floats above grapes in their vat, nor that one could succumb to it" (23) ["Penchée sur une créature enfantine et magnifique, elle tremblait, soupirait d'une angoisse qu'elle ne savait nommer, et qui se nomme tentation. Mais elle n'aurait jamais imaginé que d'un puéril visage se lève un trouble, une vapeur comparable à ce qui flotte sur le raisin dans la cuve, ni qu'on puisse y succomber" (289)]. One is reminded here of the similarly unspoken desire circulating in the vignette called "L'Enlèvement" in *La Maison de Claudine*, in which Sido so fears the abduction of her adolescent daughter at the hands of a Gypsy, a rake, or a suitor that she bears the child off in her sleep, back to her childhood room. The young girl, waking in different surroundings, speaks the truth in the voice of her wise child's unconscious: "Mother! Come quick! I've been abducted!" (29) ["Maman! Viens vite! Je suis enlevée!" (984)]. Realizing her worst fears, Sido acts out her greatest desires as well, suggesting that the circular abduction corresponds to the circle in which fear and desire are continuous, and mother and lover coincide. Or similarly, in *Sido*, ambivalent mother-daughter identifications slide the story between abduction and seduction, jealousy and desire, when Sido delivers her daughter to the home of her alter ego, Adrienne, and the scene of what the adult daughter writing calls "a first seduction" (173) ["une première séduction" (515)]. The child, remembered to have been ten or eleven at the time, loses herself there in the seductive disorder of scattered books and wild strawberries, fossils and freshly picked mushrooms. Recalling how the artful indifference emanating from Adrienne and her lair both charmed and wounded her, the narrator tells the strange story of nursing babies exchanged at their mothers' breasts:

> Once when my mother and Adrienne were suckling their infants, a daughter and son respectively, they exchanged babies for fun. So occasionally Adrienne would laughingly challenge me with the words: "you whom I once fed with my own milk!" At that I would blush so madly that my mother frowned and scanned my face to find out what could have made me so red. How was I to conceal from that clear gaze of hers, blade-grey and threatening, the image that tormented me of Adrienne's swarthy breast and its hard, purple knob? (172)

> [Quand ma mère et Adrienne allaitaient, la première sa fille, la seconde son fils, elles échangèrent un jour, par jeu, leurs nourrissons. Parfois Adrienne m'interpellait en riant: "Toi que j'ai nourrie de mon lait!..." Je rougissais si follement que ma mère fronçait les sourcils, et cherchait sur mon visage la cause de ma rougeur. Comment dérober à ce lucide regard, gris de lame et menaçant, l'image qui me tourmentait: le sein brun d'Adrienne et sa cime violette et dure. (514)]

What Colette calls a "game of exchange" crystallizes an entire structure of exchange operating in this scene and beyond it. From the point of view of the babies (which is also the author's, some fifty years later), it is of course the breasts and not the babies that are exchanged. Sido's breast is replaced by Adrienne's, and, the trajectory of the passage implies, the maternal breast is exchanged for the erotic one. But once Sido and Adrienne are inserted into a structure of exchange, they become essentially fungible, so that the idea of eroticism and that of maternity circulate freely between them.[63]

In *La Naissance*, Sido's pink cactus, avatar of the two-headed abductor in *La Maison de Claudine*, presage of the split erotic/maternal identification in *Sido*—reincarnation of the mother's desire in both— marks another hybridization of lover and mother. "Isn't what you're embracing my pink cactus?...[Y]es, I recognize, I lay claim to all that....[H]e is in truth my pink cactus, that has at last consented to flower" (7) ["N'est-ce pas mon cactus rose...que tu embrasses?... [O]ui, je reconnais, je revendique tout cela....[I]l est bien, en vérité, mon cactus rose, qui veut enfin fleurir" (278)]. This manflower who is both recognized and claimed by Sido—I am tempted to say *owned* by her, in the double sense of possessed and confessed that I developed in chapter 5—in fact covers a lot of territory. The pink succulent, flower of the mother's desire, Colette's abstract lover, Passion by name, represents as well the becoming of her more tangible would-be lover, Vial, who, dismissed, might be readmitted in metamorphosed form: "Flee, my favorite! Don't reappear until you have become unrecognizable. Jump through the window and, as you touch the ground, change, blossom....When you return to me I must be able to give you, as my mother did, your name of 'pink cactus'" (140) ["Fuis, mon favori! Ne reparais que méconnaissable. Saute la fenêtre, et en touchant le sol change, fleuris....Lorsque tu me reviendras, il faut que je puisse te donner, à l'exemple de ma mère, ton nom de 'Cactus rose' ou de je ne sais quelle autre fleur en forme de flamme...ton nom futur de créature exorcisée" (369)]. But behind Vial there is an

---

[63] The confluence of the maternal and the erotic through the breast has, of course, been well theorized by Freud. As Marilyn Yalom remarks, "Whatever reservations we may have about Freudian breast theories, we must give them credit for uniting the two major strands of breast history into a powerful psychological paradigm: the maternal breast and the erotic breast have become one" (*A History of the Breast* [New York: Knopf, 1997], 153). Usually, though, this unifying effect takes place from a man's (son's) perspective. Colette's text is remarkable for its representation of a woman's (daughter's) experience of the maternal erotic breast.

allusion to Colette's eldest brother, Sido's cherished son, Achille, who leaps his way through the windows of *Sido*, ever on the alert for the need to escape the social amenities of everyday life.[64] Linked, then, to Achille by virtue of the unusual penchant for leaping out of windows, the metamorphosing Vial, on his way to becoming a pink cactus, would be doubly recognizable to Sido, doubly marked as her passionflower, her son.

Stories of the Breast

The scientific name of Sido's pink cactus was *mamillaire* ("nipple cactus," in its English translation), according to a passage in *En Pays connu*, where Colette describes it this way:

> Sido's "pink cactus" was a nipple cactus. I just finished a nee-
> dlepoint portrait of a nipple cactus. The somewhat thick stitch
> doesn't work to its advantage. Spherical to the extent permitted
> by its teats and its spiny, blue-green ribs, the nipple cactus is
> crowned by a flat little cap of pink flowers. The overall effect is
> difficult to describe.

> [Le "cactus rose" de Sido était une mamillaire. Je viens d'achever
> le portrait de la mamillaire au point de tapisserie. Le point un peu
> gros ne l'avantage pas. Sphérique autant que le lui permettent
> ses tétines et ses côtes épineuses d'un vert-bleu, la mamillaire
> est coiffée d'un petit chapeau plat de fleurs roses. Le tout est
> difficile à rendre.][65]

---

[64]   "I have seen him, that wise one, vault through a window on a hundred occasions, as though by a reflex action, every time there was a ring at the door which
he did not expect" (*Sido*, 219) ["Ce sage, je l'ai vu cent fois franchir la fenêtre,
d'un bond reflexe, à chaque coup de sonnette qu'il ne prévoyait pas" (*Sido*, 548)].
On the relationship between Sido and Achille, see Thurman, *Secrets of the Flesh*,
and also Sido's letters to Colette, in which she often plays her oldest, local child
against her far-off, inattentive daughter.

[65]   Colette, *En Pays connu*, in *Œuvres completes*, 11:376. Sido's *mamillaire*,
however, is called by a different name in the letter she sent to Colette's husband
weighing the relative merits of visiting her daughter or tending her plants (a letter
further complicated, we recall, by the fact that it is reversed by its textual "copy,"
which has Sido opt for the plants instead of the daughter (see 1396–97n1 in *Naissance*). Not only does Sido not speak of a nipple cactus in her letter; she doesn't

As an adjective, *mamillaire* technically refers to the anatomical point where the milk ducts discharge: a woman's nipple or, by analogy, anything that bears a similar form. Régine Detambel associates the prickly surfaces of the nipple cactus with the pungency of the wet nurse Mélie's breast when she slathered it with mustard, according to the text of "Puérilité," in order to wean the sixteen-month-old Gabri. Colette remembers the stinging of her nurse's mustard-coated breast doubled by the treacherous turn of profusion into deprivation.[66] We might think about the sharpness of this moment as compounding the effects of an initial weaning. (Sido nursed her daughter very briefly before hiring a wet nurse.) We might further speculate about the relationship of Sido's nipple cactus, her infant daughter's successive weanings, and this daughter's future oral adventures, including a well-known gourmandise that ranged from a taste for munching onions whole, like apples, to a passion for *fruits de mer.*[67] The temptation to read homonymously *fruits de mère*, literally "mother's fruit," instead of seafood is irresistible, all the more so because Sido and Colette play on the *mer/mère* homophony often in their writing. Sido's letters to her daughter abound in anxieties about potential seasickness and fears about the treachery of the sea. "Are you seasick?" and "You weren't seasick?" are typical queries ["As-tu le mal de mer?"; "Tu n'as pas eu le mal de mer?"].[68] She warns Colette (who was thirty-six at the time): "Beware of the sea, perfidious as the tide. It's true. If a wave picks you up and bears you off, there's no resisting it. The wave comes and goes, and takes you with it. I had this experience, and if my brother hadn't been with me, I'd be gone, and people wouldn't have been able to enjoy reading your books or contemplating nature's masterpiece" ["Méfie-toi de la mer; perfide comme l'onde. Vrai ça.

---

mention a cactus of any ilk, but instead speaks of the pull (which she resists) of her sedum and gloxinia.

[66] Régine Detambel, *Colette: Comme Une Flore comme un zoo* (Paris: Stock, 1997), 47. For Colette's account of the profound deceitfulness of her weaning, see "Puériculture," in *Prisons et paradis*, in *Œuvres complètes*, 7:212.

[67] For an exploration of Colette's gourmandise in its literary and mythic manifestations, see Brigitte Mahuzier, "Colette's 'Écriture gourmande,'" in *French Food*, ed. Lawrence R. Schehr and Allen S. Weiss (New York: Routledge, 2001), 99–113.

[68] *Colette, Sido: Lettres*, ed. Bertrand de Jouvenel, Jeannie Malige, and Michèle Sarde (Paris: des femmes, 1984), letters of March 15, 1911, 419; March 19, 1911, 425.

Si une vague te prend, et t'emmène, rien ne résiste à cela. La vague arrive, s'en va, et vous emmène. J'ai éprouvé la chose et si je n'avais pas eu mon frère auprès de moi, j'étais fichue, et...les populations n'auraient pu se délecter à la lecture de tes œuvres ni contempler le...chef-d'œuvre de la nature"].[69] What is at stake in her slip from a generality about the perfidious ocean to the memory of almost drowning in it while still a young girl turns out to be nothing less than her future as generatrix: in *la mer perfide* there lies implicitly the fate of *la mère.* As for Colette, the sea is a better mother: "I remember how I used to take a child every year to the sea, as to a maternal element better able than I to ripen, teach, and perfect the body and mind I had drafted" ["Je me souviens d'avoir mené un enfant chaque année à la mer, comme à un élément maternel capable mieux que moi de mûrir, d'instruire, de parfaire ce que j'avais, corps et esprit, ébauché"].[70]

If, however, we revisit the cactus that launched this excursus on the mother and the sea, we note that beyond the decidedly female name, *mamillaire*, that Colette attributes to the plant in *En Pays connu*, its gender attributes are mixed. Spherical and nippled, it is breastlike; spiny-ribbed and crowned, it is phallic. Colette's very pointed description of her needlepoint portrait ("au point de tapisserie") of this cactus points redundantly to the point ("le point un peu gros ne l'avantage pas")—but which point? The phallic images protruding from the mammary descriptions—applied, we remember, to a cactusman or a man-cactus—are startling. They remind us of the scene from *Sido* I discussed earlier, in which the adolescent Minet-Chéri, sent to Adrienne by her mother, is seduced by "memories" (or fantasies?)[71] of nursing at the "cime violette et dure" of Adrienne's breast (even more ambiguously rendered in the translation by Enid McCleod as "hard, purple knob").[72] Tiresias-like, the cactus-lover crosses gender

---

[69] Letter of August 10, 1909, ibid., 293.

[70] Colette, "Regarde...," in *Autres Bêtes*, in *Œuvres*, 2:195.

[71] Colette was weaned from the wet nurse (Émilie Fleury) at sixteen months of age but from Sido in the first months of life (Thurman dates the exchange of nurslings at four months [*Secrets of the Flesh*, 34n11]). There is, then, a strong possibility that Colette's "memories" should be read as fantasies.

[72] Colette, *Sido*, 514; *My Mother's House and Sido*, 172. Ward Jouve notes that "Colette" means "little hill," and goes on to free-associate to the name: "little hill, little mound, clitoris, Little Phallus" (36).

categories, becoming male or female as readily as he shifts between vegetable and animal. The possibility exists that Adrienne is Sido's cactus—or Colette's.

I am obviously wildly conflating auto/biographical fantasy, historical record, and literary imagination in these remarks. The fact that Adrienne's son confirmed a family legend of nurslings exchanged at the breast, years later in a letter to Colette, just adds more ingredients to a brew from which none can be singly distilled.[73] Reading for the breast across genres and especially over the art/life divide feels reckless and leads to no overarching interpretation. Yet lactating breasts dominate Colette's writing and life in patterns that cannot be ignored. A catalogue would be at once endless and ridiculous; some illustrations are obligatory.

Claudine's maid and former wet nurse Mélie in *Claudine à Paris* (who reappears as wet nurse in "Puérilité") has the strange habit of weighing and hoisting her breasts in her palms, constantly thrusting them in the eye of the beholder. She is the literalized emblem of her author, who makes similar textual displays before the eye of the reader. Claudine's exasperation with the unseemly gestures of this woman who parades through the novel "cupping her uncorseted breasts in the palms of her hands as if she were weighing them"; "twiddling her boobs"; "weighing her breasts" ["en soupesant dans ses paumes ses seins sans corset"; "tripot(ant) ses nénés"; "soupesant ses mamelles"][74] explodes in the alimentary rhetoric of the question "Have you finished weighing your breasts like melons? Which one's the ripest?"(315) ["As-tu fini de peser tes seins comme des melons? Lequel est le plus mûr?" (363)]. Claudine's father assures her that Mélie nursed her "with 'superb' milk" (193) ["avec un lait 'superbe'" (224)], and Claudine is revolted by this intimate connection to Mélie's overly present breasts: "I feel vaguely disgusted to think that I was suckled at them" (193) ["ça me dégoûte vaguement de songer que je les ai tétés" (224)]. Claudine's first lover (and eventual husband), Renaud, fondly watching her take in glass after glass of Asti,

---

[73]   See Pichois and Brunet, *Colette*, 19.
[74]   Colette, *Claudine à Paris*, in *Œuvres*, 1:224, 231, 341; translations, with my modifications, are from Colette, *Claudine in Paris*, in *The Claudine Novels*, trans. Antonia White (London: Penguin, 1963), 193, 199, 296.

remarks, "You drink like a baby nurses" (308) ["Vous buvez comme on tète" (356)]. When Renaud asks for Claudine's hand in marriage, her father gives his bewildered consent: he himself, he indicates, prefers women endowed like wet nurses.[75]

The textual exhibition of Mélie's, as of Adrienne's, endowments is oddly countered by the textual occultation of Sido's two mastectomies in the novel bearing her name. Here is the patch of text that performs the cover-up:

> She recovered, as she always did. But when they removed one of her breasts and, four years later, the other, my father became terribly mistrustful of her, even though each time she recovered again. When a fish-bone stuck in her throat, making her cough so violently that her face turned scarlet and her eyes filled with tears, my father brought his fist down on the table, shivering his plate to fragments and bellowing: "Are you finished?" (192)

> [Elle guérit,—elle guérissait toujours. Mais quand on lui enleva un sein, et quatre ans après, l'autre sein, mon père conçut d'elle une méfiance terrible, quoiqu'elle guérît encore, chaque fois. Pour une arête de poisson qui, restée au gosier de ma mère, l'obligeait à tousser violemment, les joues congestionnées et les yeux pleins de larmes, mon père, d'un coup de poing asséné sur la table, dispersa en éclats son assiette, et cria furieusement:—Ça va finir? (528)]

The interrogative is a bluff. It masks the cause of his jealous rage: the affirmative "you are finished" [*ça va finir*], the inevitability of the end. Colette's text more specifically masks the mother's amputations by presenting them wrapped in the attention-grabbing narration of more trivial ailments. Borrowing a dinner table technique familiar to us all, Colette uses a coughing fit to change the subject. Like the fish-bone caught in Sido's throat, the mention of her mastectomies gets caught in the narrator's craw. It is as if the text were choking on its

---

75 "'But personally, when it comes to marrying, she wouldn't be at all my type. I prefer women more...' And his hands sketched the outline of the breasts of a nursing mother" (326) ["'Mais moi, pour épouser, elle ne serait pas du tout mon type. Je préfère les femmes plus...' Et son geste dessine des appas de nourrice" (375)].

own words. Sputtered in a gasp between a longwinded account of a nonspecific illness and the noisy details of a choking attack followed by a fist blow to the table, a shattered plate, and a screaming Captain, the story of Sido's breast cancer is almost inaudible.

A few biographies of Colette confirm, without amplification, that Sido underwent two surgeries for breast cancer (though it was ultimately her heart that caused her death).[76] To my knowledge no more of the story is told elsewhere by Colette (who, here as more generally, doesn't write about death and mourning directly).[77] It seems particularly significant that the mother's mastectomies are articulated in oral terms of what the text cannot swallow, cannot incorporate, for this resonates with psychoanalytic models of mourning as a work of introjection (beginning with Freud and Melanie Klein).[78] According to such theories, the paradigmatic lost object is the breast at weaning.[79] Although nowhere in the text of *Sido* does the narrator

---

[76] See, for example, Claude Francis and Fernande Gontier, *Colette* (Paris: Perrin, 1997), 253; Thurman, *Secrets of the Flesh*, 234.

[77] Breast cancer was a taboo subject in France, as in much of the world, until recently (see Yalom, *A History of the Breast*). Given Colette's propensity, however, for writing about socially unacceptable subjects, even personal ones thinly transferred into fiction, I don't think societal interdictions are primarily responsible for her silence about her mother's mastectomies here. What I see as a refusal to mourn in Colette's work leads to a diffusion of mourning in a text that is rich in ghosts, spirits, and a past that will not rest. See Flieger, *Phantom Subject*, for a Freudian reading of Colette's phantoms.

[78] The psychoanalytic literature on the subject is of course vast. To begin, see the classic texts: Sigmund Freud, "Mourning and Melancholia," in *The Standard Edition of the Complete Psychological Works of Sigmund Freud*, vol. 14, ed. James Strachey et al. (London: Hogarth Press, 1957), 237–58; Melanie Klein, "Some Theoretical Conclusions Regarding the Emotional Life of the Infant," in *Developments in Psychoanalysis*, ed. Melanie Klein et al. (London: Hogarth Press, 1989), 198–236; and Melanie Klein, "Mourning and Its Relation to Manic-Depressive States," in *Love, Guilt, and Reparation and Other Works, 1921–1945* (London: Virago, 1988), 344–69.

[79] It is important to remember that for the nursing exchange to occur, there had to have been a disjoining. The child's removal from her mother to Adrienne—an initial *enlèvement*—prefigures definitive separation, or *sevrage:* weaning and also severing. But the separation cuts both ways. It is not just the mother who removes her child, passes her on, then replicates the violence through surgery and death. The daughter writing appropriates the separation, returns the violence as she substitutes Adrienne for Sido in the triple structure of nurturance/seduction/narration. In an ambiguous act that evokes ritualized mourning, mummification, and a violence that perpetuates mourning, Colette cuts up a blue linen dress her mother wore as a young woman, to bind the manuscript of *Sido*. She writes (with just a touch of defensiveness): "I'm not sorry I took the scissors to [the dress],

elaborate on the loss involved (for Sido or for herself) in the removal of her mother's breasts, she does earlier in that novel deliver a negative counterpart to the veiled story, in the form of the anecdote we have seen, exposing the breasts of her mother's friend Adrienne. If Sido and Adrienne mirror each other, perhaps the mastectomy and breast-feeding passages can be read as inverted images of each other, the double absence of the suppressed loss in the first case reflected in the double presence of the flaunted remembering in the second. Lack is reflected as excess, and mourning as desire.

Colette writes oddly intricate scenarios of nursing for the animals in her novels. In *Claudine à Paris* the cat Fanchette is pregnant; Claudine notes that her tiny teats are painfully swollen.[80] When she is left with only one of the three kittens originally in the litter (the others having been drowned by order of Mélie), Claudine assiduously cycles the remaining one from nipple to nipple, fearing that its preference for a particular one will deform the mother cat (344). In *La Maison de Claudine* there is a tri-generational nursing feast—"this chain of mutually suckling cats" (50) ["cette chaîne de chattes s'allaitant l'une à l'autre" (1000)]—when the cat Bijou produces a litter the very night after her mother, Nonoche, has done so. Minet-Chéri finds Bijou with a string of tiny kittens clinging to her teats, awkwardly sucking

---

because its soft blue with white flowers continues to dress, and will forever, as in the past, my cherished 'Sido'" ["Je ne me repens pas d'y avoir porté les ciseaux, puisque d'un bleu doux, et ramagée de blanc, elle habille comme par le passé, elle habille encore et toujours ma très chère 'Sido'"] (cited by Maurice Delcroix in his "Note sur le texte," in *Sido*, 1466). Remembering the idealized Sido, Colette dismembers the woman Sidonie—to echo Claude Pichois's observation (see note 16). Writing sometime in between Colette's evocation of the mother and the more recent search for foremothers, Adrienne Rich provides a means of assimilating the two by a model of split identification applicable synchronically in the first case and diachronically in the second: "Many women have been caught—have split themselves—between two mothers: one, usually the biological one, who represents the culture of domesticity, of male-centeredness, of conventional expectations, and another, perhaps a woman artist or teacher, who becomes the countervailing figure" (*Of Woman Born: Motherhood as Experience and Institution* [New York: Norton, 1976], 247). Rich explains the splitting of the self as a carving out of identity that can involve severing identification with the mother: "Our personalities seem dangerously to blur and to overlap with our mothers'; and in a desperate attempt to know where mother ends and daughter begins, we perform radical surgery" (236).

[80] Colette, *Claudine à Paris*, in *Oeuvres*, 1:306; subsequent references are provided in the text.

at her own mother with her oversized tongue, drinking the mother's milk meant for her newborn siblings—the kittens of Nonoche's new litter. This scene has a human cognate in *Claudine à Paris*, where Claudine describes to the infatuated Renaud a memory from her Montigny schoolgirl days: a fourteen-year-old classmate, Célénie Nauphely, announces that she must leave school early to go home to be breast-fed. Claudine explains that the girl's sister was weaning her baby; swollen with too much milk, she relied on Célénie to relieve her twice a day (295). A vignette included in *La Maison de Claudine* ("Les Deux Chattes") relates another tale of foster feeding. While the neighbor's cat is mourning the loss of her drowned kittens, she comes upon a newborn nursing kitten, whom she eyes suspiciously and then begins to court: "She came with a belly heavy with milk, her swollen teats bursting through her black fleece, making soft cooing sounds, mysterious nursing calls" ["Elle vint avec un ventre lourd de lait, des tétines tendues qui crevaient sa toison noire, des roucoulements assourdis, des invites mystérieuses de nourrice" (1068–69; my translation here and below)]. Following a brief rivalry between the two mother cats, the mourning cat triumphs, takes over as nursing mother, while the forsaken birth mother cat "lost her milk, gave up her roles of mother and nurse, and took on her melancholic roving" ["perdit son lait, résigna ses droits de mère et de nourrice, et contracta sa mélancolie errante" (1069)]. When the kitten approaches to play, the rejected mother "folded her paws under her dried up teats" ["replie ses pattes sous ses mamelles taries" (1069)].

In the memoir written when she was well into her seventies (*L'Étoile vesper*), Colette recounts the aftermath of her decision not to nurse her newborn daughter: "My little swaddled larva which had been put down for a moment on my bed...divined, scented, the presence of my forbidden milk, strove toward my stopped-up source. Never have I wept with so rebellious a heart. What is the suffering of asking in vain, compared with the pain of denial?"(280) ["Ma petite larve emmaillotée, que l'on avait posée un moment sur mon lit...devina, flaira la présence de mon lait interdit, s'efforça vers ma source aveuglée. Jamais je ne pleurai d'un cœur aussi révolté. Qu'est le mal de demander en vain, au prix de la douleur de se refuser?" (875)].

Strange coincidences related to wet-nursing punctuate Colette's life. Sido met her first husband, Jules Robineau, when she was briefly passing through Saint-Sauveur in order to visit her former wet nurse. Colette became engaged to Willy when he brought his illegitimate baby son Jacques to live with a wet nurse in Saint-Sauveur. She was the Colettes' next-door neighbor, and had been procured for Willy by Colette's parents when he asked them for help a few weeks after the baby's mother died.[81]

What connections might be drawn among the overflowing lactation scenarios of Colette's writing, her double weaning, her mother's two mastectomies (undergone in the years approaching her death in 1912, and Colette's own pregnancy that same year), and her own decision not to breast-feed? What speculations might be made about the transformations of a man into a cactus and a cactus into a breast—a breast that turns out to have phallic features? Beyond marveling at Colette's cornucopia of polymorphous sexuality with its casual continuities of male and female, maternal and erotic, novel and autobiography, I hesitate to proceed. At risk is my voice; that is, my literary-critical voice. With Colette as with no other writer, the validity and the value of every word I have to say is on the line. Reductiveness and redundancy loom large at the close of every sentence I write. I question my critical ethics, the critical ethos in which I was formed, and, more specifically, the position or place of criticism in relation to a literary text and its author: its *orientation*, in the full etymological sense of a relationship to the Orient, the east, the rising sun, the privileged source. If literature is that sun, am I not Icarus, if not Prometheus, flying too high, presuming too much, raiding the gods' own light? What, I ask, is criticism's appropriate stance, its place, its route, before or behind or intersecting the literary text? What is its geographical metaphor? How near to, how far from a literary text should a critic stand; how closely embrace, how distantly examine the writer?

The dialectic of distance and relation intrinsic to any epistemological undertaking in which a subject speaks of or for an object (a dialectic especially prominent in a narrative text) is exacerbated in Colette because of the whirling dynamic of self and other that she sets in play. As her would-be critic (in the sense of her commentator

---

[81] See Thurman, *Secrets of the Flesh.*

or interpreter), I am sensitive to the danger of becoming her effective critic (in the sense of her evaluator or judge), and I begin to worry about a potential "critical imperative" model. Must literary criticism work under a latent doctrine of "manifest destiny"? Does it share with other modern intellectual disciplines a colonizing birthright from which it borrows its textual authority?[82] Reading Colette makes me increasingly reluctant to follow these critical conventions (the conventions of patriarchal criticism that I discuss in chapter 4). I recognize in my work on Colette, with some uneasiness, a reactive (some might say feminist) intimacy with Colette. It is like Ward Jouve's desire "to yield, to be taken over" (by Colette's text), or like an extreme version of Ruth Behar's "vulnerable observer" adaptation of anthropology's "participant observer" model.[83] Even as I applaud the concept of vulnerable observer as antidote to cold, distracted, or rugged observation, to paraphrase Behar (3), I recognize the real potential for a vulnerable observer to slide into something like an "observant wound": a subjectivity that registers little but its own emotivity or affective complicity.

I want to speak of Colette with neither authority nor complicity. Her harsh narcissism, her familial and political agnosticism, her belief in no thing but writing confuse and repel me. The dark knot of her psyche—the psyche of her writing—intrigues me, draws me in. Yet I do not want to understand her too well. If I am too intimate with her psyche, I lose the relationship to the writer. But if I begin to think I know the writing, I erase it. Gilles Deleuze articulated a similar dilemma: "My ideal, when I write about an author, would be to write nothing that could cause her sadness, or if she is dead, that might make her weep in her grave. Think of the author you are writing about. Think of her so hard that she can no longer be an object, and equally so that you cannot identify with her. Avoid the double shame of the scholar and the familiar."[84] I am taking a few liberties with Deleuze. I have

---

[82] See Ruth Behar, *The Vulnerable Observer: Anthropology That Breaks Your Heart* (Boston: Beacon Press, 1996), 4; subsequent references are provided in the text.

[83] Ibid.; Ward Jouve, *Colette*, 4.

[84] Gilles Deleuze and Claire Parnet, *Dialogues*, trans. Hugh Tomlinson and Barbara Habberjam (New York: Columbia University Press, 1987), 119. I am grateful to Claire Lyu for the reference and the conversation.

feminized his author pronouns to suit my context here, and I also want to propose collapsing the "double shame" of which he speaks—that of the scholar and of the familiar—into a shame that, though double, is not necessarily partitioned in two: a shame that may well be the scholar's double burden. For the dual temptations of distance and of identification (attributes of the scholar and the familiar, respectively, for Deleuze) seem to me appropriately to describe the double specter today haunting my own approach to Colette (and no doubt ready to take up residence in other readable sites).

I fear knowing too much about Colette's childhood and I fear caring too much about her writing. Taking to heart Balzac's lesson of the scholar and the madman (*le fou et le savant*) standing before the abyss, I know it is equally foolhardy to take the measure of the abyss, and to fall in.[85] Yet neither do I want to stand open-mouthed in admiration and awe before her work. Such a reaction, like the tautology that inevitably expresses beauty for Barthes, can only hush what it would laud.[86] I'd like to stand safely between authority and intimacy, less concerned with a critical approach or method than with a critical stance or ethos. I seek a criticism that is a return to reading: reading that is at once an interrogation of the text *and of the self,* an engagement of the self in a dynamic bilateral process, a process of critical relationship.

Such a reading would involve a different kind of writing, one that would let a reader speak about a writer's work without needing to feel shame, without risking the violation of knowing the author's work or her person too well. A writing that would let a reader love a writer's work and yet speak words that would not eclipse the work and could not eclipse themselves. A writing that would not attempt to fill in ellipses more articulately left as blanks, that would not "see" where the author was prophetically blind, but that might instead register a process of change, *of being oneself changed by* the reading process. A writing that would neither make a dead author "weep in her grave" nor, in the more likely Colettian scenario, let her have the last underground laugh.

---

[85]   Honoré Balzac, *Théorie de la démarche,* in *La Comédie humaine,* vol. 12, ed. Pierre-Georges Castex (Paris: Gallimard [Pléiade], 1976–1981), 259–302.
[86]   Roland Barthes, *S/Z* (Paris: Seuil, 1970), 40–41.

Reading for the breast in Colette risks either engaging the reader/ critic in a dialectic of fusion and separation with the (literary) mother (to use the thematically appropriate object relations model) or engaging her in a typically masculine "fatally autobiographical" reading (to paraphrase Colette)—which, I would add, risks producing fatally trapped criticism.[87]

Fatal Autobiography

"Man, my friend, you willingly mock the fatally autobiographical writing of women" (*Break of Day*, 63) ["Homme, mon ami," warns Colette, "tu plaisantes volontiers les œuvres, fatalement autobiographiques, de la femme" (*Naissance*, 316)]. Addressing herself here to a particular kind of reader she earmarks as a man and a (would-be) fellow writer[88]—and so, might we presume, the antithesis of the ideal reader for Colette—she plays with conventions that assume any writing by a woman to be transparent, true, and autobiographically correct. Colette's phrase "les œuvres, fatalement autobiographiques, de la femme"—only half-rendered in the McCleod translation as "women's writings [which] can't help being autobiographical"[89]—owes its force to its ambiguity. To call women's works "fatally autobiographical" means, on the one hand, that they are doomed to be autobiographical—but does "being autobiographical" mean that they are *written* or *read* autobiographically? And it means, on the other hand, that they are fatal *because* autobiographical. Lethal writing. Who, or what, is the victim? As in the expression *la femme fatale*, which lends its force along with its potential reversibility to the notion of fatal feminine autobiography, the ostensible purveyor of death (the woman writer, her text) may well be the victim instead. Certainly

---

[87]   As I mentioned earlier, Colette introduces, in *Naissance*, the idea of "woman's fatally autobiographical works" (63) ["les œuvres, fatalement autobiographiques, de la femme" (316)]; see my commentary in the next section.

[88]   "Why do men—writers or so-called writers—still show surprise that a woman should so easily reveal to the public love-secrets and amorous lies and half-truths?" (*Break of Day*, 62) ["Comment les hommes—les hommes écrivains, ou soi-disant tels—s'étonnent-ils encore qu'une femme livre si aisément au public des confidences d'amour...?" (*Naissance*, 315)].

[89]   Colette, *Break of Day*, 63.

Colette felt misread, attacked in her status of author when the journal *Femina* represented her essay "Maternité" as a woman's autobiographical text, changing her title to "A Mother's Impressions: The First Hours" ["Impressions de maman. Les premières heures"].[90] Here is the text of the letter she wrote to the editor in angry dismay:

> My Dear Pierre Lafitte,
>
> I would like to make clear what belongs to *Femina* and what belongs to me. I wrote an article for *Femina*. You added illustrations that did it honor, and a title that does me none. It is obvious that the illustrations are not by me. One might, however, attribute the title to me. You can imagine that this is not what I want. That I am a mother is not the reader's business. I give the reader a work that I hope is literary; it's *the author* who appears before him, and not the woman, and if it is his right to judge me as a writer, his right stops there. Yet the editors of *Femina* seem to offer him another right, by titling the article "Impressions of a Young Mother." There's a nuance of difference there—in fact a little bit more than a nuance. You are too astute, my dear friend, not to have noticed this.
>
> Very sincerely yours,
> Colette

[90]   The title given on the cover, as in Colette's letter, was "Impressions of a Young Mother" ["Impressions d'une jeune maman"]. *Femina* also added this introductory caption to Colette's text: "*Femina* is happy to notify its readers of the beginning of its collaboration with Colette, the eminent author whose profoundly human novels and articles, marked by a highly sensitive nature coupled with supreme gifts of style, are unanimously admired. The fine page we are publishing is a true ode to maternity; only a woman's pen would be capable of such an accurate description and analysis, relating with such delicacy the moving awakening of a young mother, who, leaving a heavy induced sleep, comes at last to contemplate the dear little unknown face of the newborn child; we are sure that our female readers will understand the pure beauty of these remarkable lines. N.D.L.R." ["*Femina* est heureuse de signaler à ses lectrices le début de la collaboration de Colette, l'éminent écrivain dont les romans et les articles, profondément humains et qui révèlent une sensibilité si aiguë jointe aux plus précieux dons du style, sont unaniment admirés. La belle page que nous publions est un véritable poème de la maternité; seule une plume féminine était capable d'une description et d'une analyse aussi justes, relatant avec autant de délicatesse le réveil émouvant de la jeune mère qui, au sortir du lourd sommeil artificiel, va contempler enfin le cher petit visage inconnu de l'enfant nouveau-né; nous sommes certains que nos lectrices comprendront toute la pure beauté de ces lignes remarquables. N.D.L.R"]. My source for this information as well as for Colette's letter is Pichois and Brunet, *Colette*, 260–61.

[Mon cher Pierre Lafitte,

Je voudrais bien qu'il fût rendu à *Femina* ce qui est à *Femina*, et à moi ce qui est à moi. J'ai écrit pour *Femina* un article. Vous y avez ajouté des illustrations qui lui font beaucoup d'honneur, et un titre qui m'en fait moins. Les illustrations, on peut être sûr qu'elles ne sont pas de moi. Le titre on pourrait me l'attribuer. Imaginez-vous que je n'y tiens pas. Que je sois mère, cela ne regarde pas le lecteur. Je lui donne une œuvre que je souhaite littéraire, c'est *l'auteur* qui paraît devant lui, ce n'est pas la femme, et s'il a le droit de me juger comme écrivain, son droit s'arrête là. Or, la rédaction de *Femina* semble lui en attribuer un autre, en intitulant l'article: *Impressions d'une jeune maman.* Il y a là une nuance, et un peu plus qu'une nuance. Vous êtes trop fin, cher ami, pour ne pas l'avoir aperçue.

Croyez-moi bien sincèrement vôtre.

Colette]

Colette's rage at being misrepresented and misunderstood—*méconnue:* taken for someone else, which is to say, confused with herself—is clear. What is somewhat murkier is Colette's own role in obscuring the distinction between fiction and autobiography in the text of "Maternité," which begins with a confirmation of pregnancy given by "a doctor whom I know, to a woman who is a patient of his, and whom I know even better" ["un médecin que je connais à une de ses clients que je connais mieux encore"].[91] We are familiar with this kind of double entendre from the pages of *La Naissance du jour:* as an artificer of autobiography, Colette presents a "me" who is not quite me.[92]

---

[91] Colette, "Maternité," 13:316.

[92] Philippe Lejeune in fact excludes Colette from the French autobiographical canon because she doesn't adhere to conventions of authorial sincerity (*L'Autobiographie en France* [Paris: Armand Colin, 1971], 72–73). Nancy Miller remarks that "to read Colette is not...to read a woman's autobiography...[but] to read the inscription of a *female self*...: the body of her writing and not the writing of her body" ("Women's Autobiography in France: For a Dialectics of Identification," in *Women and Language in Literature and Society,* ed. Sally McConnell-Ginet, Ruth Borker, and Nelly Furman [New York: Praeger, 1980], 271). Valérie Lastinger observes that the play of real and textual identities in the text is "another way to disintegrate, to put into pieces, the identity of the narrating self" ["une autre façon de morceler, de désintégrer le moi du je-narrateur"], and suggests that *Naissance* may be "an exercise in style" ["une sorte d'exercice de style"]

Colette elaborates on the autobiographical conundrum by describing her writing as a kind of *constructed* autobiography (implicitly a fictional subgenre): "what I know about myself, what I've tried to hide, what I've invented and what I've guessed" (62) ["ce que je sais de moi, ce que j'essaie d'en cacher, ce que j'en invente et ce que j'en devine" (315)]. Women's writing, she suggests, is in fact false autobiography, a cunning proffering of amorous confidences and half-truths that serve to hide deeper, less "sexy" truths: "By divulging these, she manages to hide other important and obscure secrets which she herself does not understand very well. The spotlight, the shameless eye which she obligingly operates, always explores the same sector of a woman's life, that sector tortured by bliss and discord round which the shades are thickest. But it is not in the illuminated zone that the darkest plots are woven" (62–63) ["En les divulguant, elle sauve de la publicité des secrets confus et considérables, qu'elle-même ne connaît pas très bien. Le gros projecteur, l'œil sans vergogne qu'elle manœuvre avec complaisance, fouille toujours le même secteur féminin, ravagé de félicité et de discorde, autour duquel l'ombre s'épaissit. Ce n'est pas dans la zone illuminée que se trame le pire" (315–16)]. Colette is suggesting that there is an entire (novelistic) world to explore outside of the love plot.

By suggesting that sexual and romantic revelations in her writing are not coextensive with truth, and in fact divulge no real secrets at all, Colette is combating not only dominant cultural assumptions about women and writing but also a philosophical tradition that equates sex and truth (a truth generally taken to be more accessible through women, held to emblematize sexuality). Janet Malcolm points to the triviality of sexual and other documented "truths" in her essay on Chekhov:

> As if the documentary proof of sexual escapades or of incidents of impotence disclosed anything about him, anything that crosses the boundary between his inner and outer life. Chekhov's privacy is safe from the biographer's attempts upon it—as, indeed, are all privacies, even those of the most apparently open and even

(Valérie C. Lastinger, "*La Naissance du jour:* La Désintégration du 'moi' dans un roman de Colette," *French Review* 61, no. 4 (March 1988): 550–51.

exhibitionistic natures. The letters and journals we leave behind and the impressions we have made on our contemporaries are the mere husk of the kernel of our essential life. When we die, the kernel is buried with us. This is the horror and pity of death and the reason for the inescapable triviality of biography.[93]

Moving from the aleatory status of sexuality in biography to the triviality of biography itself, Malcolm comes close to Colette's proclamation of the banality of love, and the triviality of the (auto)biographical genre construed in codependency with it. But Malcolm's words about the imposition of Chekhov's life on his art must be intensified in regard to Colette by the gender factor which is crucial to her (auto)biographical protest. What is at stake in Colette's text is *woman's art,* or the right to the artfulness of art when its maker happens to be a woman.

Colette's narrator/character Colette complains bitterly, as she distances herself from the attentions of Vial, of his attempts to know her through her books: "We're not concerned with my books here, Vial" (100) ["Nous n'avons que faire de mes livres ici, Vial" (341)]. I certainly do not want to be another Vial, confusing Colette with Colette. I'm reminded of Proust's insistence that when we think of an author, it is the books, and not the life, that matter, that "a book is the product of an other self."[94] This is perhaps what Colette had in mind as well when she wrote the initial epigraph (later discarded in favor of self-citation) to *La Naissance,* which she adapted from Proust: "this 'I' who is me and who is perhaps not me" ["ce 'je' qui est moi et qui n'est peut-être pas moi"].[95]

---

[93] Janet Malcolm, *Reading Chekhov: A Critical Journey* (New York: Random House, 2001), 35.

[94] "A book is the product of a self other than that which we display in our habits, in company, in our vices. If we want to try and understand this self, it is deep inside ourself, by trying to recreate it within us, that we may succeed" ["Un livre est le produit d'un autre moi que celui que nous manifestons dans nos habitudes, dans la société, dans nos vices. Ce moi-là, si nous voulons essayer de le comprendre, c'est au fond de nous-même, en essayant de le recréer en nous que nous pouvons y parvenir"]. Marcel Proust, *Contre Sainte-Beuve,* ed. Pierre Clarac (Paris: Gallimard [Pléiade], 1971), 221–22; the translation, with my modification, is from Marcel Proust, *Against Sainte-Beuve,* in *Against Sainte-Beuve and Other Essays,* trans. John Sturrock (London: Penguin, 1988), 12.

[95] Her source was a note preceding the publication of *Du Côté de chez Swann.* See Pichois's commentary in Colette, *La Naissance du jour,* 275n1.

Yet in the case of *La Naissance du jour,* the narrative thickens even as the plot thins. Speaking elsewhere in the text of her renunciation of love, Colette (the narrator/character) mentions her earlier works and how she has moved away from their focus on love: "In them I called myself Renée Néré or else, prophetically, I introduced a Léa. So it came about that both legally and familiarly, as well as in my books, I now have only one name, which is my own" (19) ["Je m'y nommais Renée Néré, ou bien, prémonitoire, j'agençais une Léa. Voilà que, légalement, littérairement et familièrement, je n'ai plus qu'un nom, qui est le mien" (286)]. My impulse, I repeat, is to read *La Naissance* as Colette calls it (as a text to be dissociated from her life), and above all, to keep author and narrator distinct. How, then, shall I read Colette's proclaimed disinvestments from her novelistic protagonists and her newly declared writing identity: "I now have only one name, which is my own" (19) ["Je n'ai plus qu'un nom, qui est le mien" (286)]? It is hard to avoid hearing this declaration as an invitation to an autobiographical pact.[96] This, then, is the other side of Colette's fatally autobiographical writing: a writing that produces what I earlier called autobiographically trapped criticism, but that might alternatively be considered, from the perspective of ensnared critics, to be autobiographically *entrapped* criticism. The slip from one to the other is slyly registered in Colette's words: "I couldn't hide from him the jealous discouragement, the unjust hostility that seizes me when I realize that people expect to find me true to life in the pages of my novels. 'You must allow me the right to hide myself in them, even if it's in the manner of *The Purloined Letter*'" (100) ["Je ne pus lui dissimuler le découragement jaloux, l'injuste hostilité qui s'emparent de moi quand je comprends qu'on me cherche toute vive entre les pages de mes romans. 'Laisse-moi le droit de m'y cacher, fût-ce à la manière de *La Lettre volée*'" (341)]. This is a very loaded— and certainly not innocent—plea.

"Let me hide in my books, if only in the manner of *The Purloined Letter*," Colette implores, bluntly protesting the confusion of literature with life—though the language is a bit cagey. What she literally

---

[96] See Philippe Lejeune, *Le Pacte autobiographique* (Paris: Seuil, 1975). As I noted earlier, however, Lejeune specifically excludes Colette from the autobiographical canon because he finds her deficient in sincerity.

requests is *the right* to hide, *"le droit* de m'y cacher," which she will presumably then choose to use or to decline. And who is the "me" envisaging a hiding place in the novel? Is it me, the author? Me, the woman? Me, the character? The ambiguous identity of "me" may well be the best concealer of all. Speaking to Vial less as her would-be lover than as her worst-case reader, Colette asks to be read like the purloined letter. As remedy for misreading, Colette hands her readers, through the interpolated first and worst one, Vial, this key to interpretation. It opens a labyrinth.

In responding to the editorial sleight of hand that had presented "Maternité" to the public as her autobiographical text, Colette, we recall, indignantly emphasized the need for absolute distinctions between art and life, author and woman: "I give the reader a work that I hope is literary; it's *the author* who appears before him, and not the woman" ["Je lui donne une œuvre que je souhaite littéraire, c'est *l'auteur* qui paraît devant [le lecteur], ce n'est pas la femme"]. In countering Vial's similar autobiographical assumption in the pages of *Naissance,* her response, worked through an intertext, is more literary and less absolute. By analogy with Poe's flagrantly hidden letter, Colette (whomever we may take this name to represent) asserts the right to hide by displaying herself, by nonchalantly presenting herself in her text—ostensibly undisguised because under no cover. Yet when we return to "The Purloined Letter," we are reminded that it is a text all about guile and cunning. From the Queen, whom the Minister observes hiding a compromising letter from the eyes of the King, to the Minister, who in turn is seen by the Queen stealing the letter with which better to manipulate her in the use of his own power, to the Prefect of Police, who stealthily but unsuccessfully searches the premises of the Minister's apartment for the letter and then attempts to inveigle free advice from Dupin, to Dupin, who, while feigning boredom, covers his eyes with dark glasses, shrewdly identifies the letter in the Minister's apartment and duplicitously leaves a facsimile in its place, to the lines from Crébillon's *Atrée* which close the text and echo the notes of trickery and betrayal we have heard throughout,[97] to the general narrator, who, as Ross Chambers has

---

[97] See Barbara Johnson, "The Frame of Reference: Poe, Lacan, Derrida," 133.

shown,[98] takes ironic distance from the stratagems of the textual players, to the critics who are positioned to outwit the author,[99] there is wiliness and calculation and at least potential deceit on every level of the narrative. Putting aside the directness of Colette's declaration, there is nothing simple about wanting to be read like a purloined letter, whose manifest presence depends on false recognitions and crafty manipulations of identity.

Poe's tale about identity and identification, artifice, cunning, and ruse reverberates in Colette's text. Though I said earlier that Colette, like Poe's letter on view in the Minister's card rack, exhibits herself "undisguised because under no cover," this is only literally true. The letter, unhidden in any traditional sense, exposed to all eyes, is, however, masked by a fold. Its presence is manifest, but its identity is obscured. Let me recall a few details from Dupin's explanation of his discovery:

> In scrutinizing the edges of the paper, I observed them to be more *chafed* than seemed necessary. They presented the *broken* appearance which is manifested when a stiff paper, having been once folded and pressed with a folder, is refolded in a reversed direction, in the same creases or edges which had formed the original fold....It was clear to me that the letter had been turned, as a glove, inside out, re-directed, and re-sealed.[100]

The mask is at once the fold and the change of address that it effects, not unlike the Möbius fold that imperceptibly turns the sense of "Colette" from the writer, to the character, to the woman, and back. As Poe's critics have remarked in various contexts, the Queen's letter contains a message whose specific content, never revealed, is unimportant. What matters in the tale is the form and trajectory of this letter: its circulation and address.[101] As the address changes, so does

[98]   Ross Chambers, "Narratorial Authority and 'The Purloined Letter,'" in *The Purloined Poe: Lacan, Derrida, and Psychoanalytic Reading*, ed. John P. Muller and William J. Richardson (Baltimore: Johns Hopkins University Press, 1988), 299–304. See also the other essays in the collection.

[99]   Ibid., 304.

[100]   Edgar Allan Poe, "The Purloined Letter," ibid., 22.

[101]   See essays ibid.

the identity of the letter: identity is revealed to be not a static matter but a fluid notion, a question of destination and circulation. So, as Lacan suggests, the letter is not so much "stolen," as the French translation of Poe's tale has it ("La Lettre volée"), but, following the etymology of "purloined," *put aside:* "We are quite simply dealing with a letter which has been diverted from its path, one whose course has been *prolonged;* or, to revert to the language of the post office, *a letter in sufferance.*"[102] If purloinment was, as I proposed in chapter 3, a reading strategy implicitly suggested by George Sand's text, which invites us to read laterally for reverberations, recollections, and modulations, rather than to seek reconstructions, it is deliberate in Colette, put forth as a writing strategy of deflection, modification, and circulation.

For Colette, the question of address was crucial. Isn't this part of what she meant when she asked to be read like a purloined letter? Her daughter's comments on the role of writing in her mother's life are revealing:

> She knew how to be alone, even with a man at her side.
> Writing is an escape for that kind of solitude.
> "A happy person doesn't make a good writer, alas!" she wrote in a letter.
> *What, in fact, does one do when one writes—and publishes? One goes off in search of the ideal interlocutor.* That is what she did.

> [Elle a su être seule, même avec un homme à ses côtés.
> Ecrire, c'est échapper à cette espèce-là de solitude.
> "Un être content ne fait pas un bon écrivain, hélas!", a-t-elle écrit dans une lettre. *Or, que fait-on lorsqu'on écrit—et qu'on publie? On part à la recherche de l'interlocuteur idéal.* Ainsi a-t-elle fait.][103]

---

[102] Jacques Lacan, "Seminar on 'The Purloined Letter,'" ibid., 43.
[103] Colette de Jouvenel, *Colette* (Paris: Société des amis de Colette, 1982), 21–22; emphasis added. For an extended reflection on the importance of structures of address (in the fields of desire and power), see Shoshana Felman, *What Does a Woman Want? Reading and Structural Difference* (Baltimore: Johns Hopkins University Press, 1993).

If writing, for Colette, may be defined, as her daughter suggests, as a quest for the ideal interlocutor, it is then a course in sufferance, an eternal circulation, a constant process of readdressing. *La Naissance du jour* of course contains quite a few epistles: letters to Colette which she appropriates from Sido and which might themselves be considered *lettres volées*. (All the more interesting, in this light, to read Colette's pronouncements to Robert de Montesquiou-Fezensac on recirculating letters: "A letter is a sacred object that should not be profaned by sale: it's scandalous and intolerable to throw to the winds the thoughts and impressions shared privately by two people" ["Une lettre est un objet sacré qu'aucune vente ne doit profaner: c'est un scandale intolérable que de dispenser aux quatre vents des pensées, des impressions, connues seulement de deux personnes"]).[104] Beyond Sido's reworked letters, however, Colette's larger text prominently stages questions of address. While taking a base-point third-person voice which assumes an anonymous reader, the narrator also frequently speaks in the first person to address each of two interlocutors: her (dead) mother and her would-be lover, Vial. The narrative is punctuated by extended dialogues which have a tendency to become meditative monologues, since in the first case the interlocutor is dead, represented by a letter or a memory or a ghost, and in the second is a mere figurehead, an ordinary man often incapable of following her gist and certainly unable to respond in kind. But it is in these passages addressed to a split "tu" that the most pensive, provocative interludes occur, or at least begin. So I would like to claim somewhat broadly that this is a text *addressed to* the (diegetic) lover and mother: the mother as lover (originally and by imprint forever after) and the lover as mother (insofar as he holds her in his gaze and mirrors the person she is supposed to be—though significantly, he fails here).

But this is simultaneously a text about *getting over* lovers and mothers—at first glance, within the fiction. I am thinking here of the plot, split between mourning the mother, whose ghost reappears intermittently until it is released at the end, and renouncing the lover, and with that, moving beyond a reliance on men. More significantly,

---

[104]   In Colette, *Lettres à sa fille*, 7.

however, this text is an inquiry into how a novel might move beyond the mirroring structure of mothers and lovers to find another aesthetic, another master plot, another theory of being that does not rely on reflection and mimesis. In what remains, I explore Colette's experimental forays into a novelistic world beyond mothers, lovers, and the mirrors they conventionally imply: the outer bounds of novelistic banality.

Beyond Banality

Le tout est de changer.
COLETTE

Colette had emphatic thoughts about the need to dislocate women's truth from its perceived lairs—as she makes plain in *La Naissance du jour:* "At no time has the catastrophe of love, in all its phases and consequences, formed a part of the true intimate life of a woman" (62) ["La catastrophe amoureuse, ses suites, ses phases, n'ont jamais, en aucun temps, fait partie de la réelle intimité de la femme" (315)]. But in fact she had flirted with such ideas before, and so this novel marks less an innovation of thought than one of action: she dares to push thought to act by constructing a meta-novel. In *Mes Apprentissages,* she describes one of her earlier efforts to escape the love plot: "I had become vaguely aware of a duty towards myself, which was to write something other than the *Claudines.* And so, drop by drop, I squeezed out the *Dialogues de bêtes.* In it I enjoyed the moderate but honourable satisfaction of not talking about love" ["Je m'éveillais vaguement à un devoir envers moi-même, celui d'écrire autre chose que les *Claudine.* Et, goutte à goutte, j'exsudais les *Dialogues de bêtes,* où je me donnai le plaisir, non point vif, mais honorable, de ne pas parler de l'amour"].[105] In *La Vagabonde* (1910), the title of the protagonist Renée Néré's second book is given as *À Côté de l'amour,*

---

[105] Colette, *Mes Apprentissages,* in *Œuvres,* 3:1041. Colette published the first four *Dialogues de bêtes* in 1904, and continued to add to and revise them until the 1930 edition of *Douze Dialogues de bêtes* (Paris: Mercure de France). The translation is from Colette, *My Apprenticeships,* trans. Helen Beauclerck, in *Uniform Edition of Works by Colette,* vol. 9 (London: Secker and Warburg, 1957), 85.

and we are told that the paltry commercial appeal of this book was counterbalanced by its literary value. The narrator explains: "In giving birth to it, I had savoured the voluptuous pleasure of writing, the patient struggling with a phrase until it becomes supple and finally settles down, curled up like a tamed animal, the motionless lying in wait that finally *charms* the word. My second volume sold very little" ["J'avais savouré, en mettant celui-là au monde, la volupté d'écrire, la lutte patiente contre la phrase qui s'assouplit, s'assoit en rond comme une bête apprivoisé, l'attente immobile, l'affût qui finit par *charmer* le mot. Mon second volume se vendit peu"].[106] Colette might well have taken her character's fictive title, *À Côté de l'amour*, as subtitle for *La Naissance du jour*, where she persistently asserts that women's truth does not reside in the hackneyed plots in which it is traditionally expected to nest.[107] She would continue to echo this decentering of love in her later works, as for example in the eloquent opening of *Bella-Vista* (1937):

> It is absurd to suppose that periods empty of love are blank pages in a woman's life. The truth is just the reverse. What remains to be said about a passionate love affair? It can be told in three lines. *He* loved me, I loved *Him*. His presence obliterated all other presences. We were happy. Then *He* stopped loving me and I suffered. Frankly, the rest is eloquence or mere verbiage. When a love affair is over, there comes a lull during which one is once more aware of friends and passers-by, of things constantly happening as they do in a vivid, crowded dream. Once again, one is conscious of normal feelings such as fear, gaiety, and boredom; once again time exists and one registers its flight. When I was younger, I did not realize the importance of these "blank pages." The anecdotes with which they furnished me— those impassioned, misguided, simple, or inscrutable human beings who plucked me by the sleeve, made me their witness for a moment, and then let me go—provided more "romantic"

---

[106]   Colette, *The Vagabond*, 23; *La Vagabonde*, 1:1084.

[107]   The phrase "à côté de l'amour," translated by McLeod as "next door to love," in fact is overdetermined; *à côté de* means not only next to, on the side of, next door to, beside, but also beside the point of, missing the point of.

subjects than my private personal drama. I shall not finish my
task as a writer without attempting, as I want to do here, to
draw them out of the shadow to which the shameless necessity
of speaking of love in my own name has consigned them.

[C'est folie de croire que les périodes vides d'amour sont les
"blancs" d'une existence de femme. Bien au contraire. Que
demeure-t-il, à le raconter, d'un attachement passionné? L'amour
parfait se raconte en trois lignes: *"Il* m'aima, je *L'*aimai, *Sa* présence supprima toutes les autres présences; nous fûmes heureux,
puis *Il* cessa de m'aimer et je souffris..." Honnêtement, le reste
est éloquence, ou verbiage. L'amour parti, vient une bonace qui
ressuscite des amis, des passants, autant d'épisodes qu'en com-
porte un songe bien peuplé, des sentiments normaux comme la
peur, la gaieté, l'ennui, la conscience du temps et de sa fuite. Ces
"blancs" qui se chargèrent de me fournir l'anecdote, les personnages émus, égarés, illisibles ou simples qui me saisissaient par
la manche, me prenaient à témoin puis me laissaient aller, je ne
savais pas, autrefois, que j'aurais dû justement les compter pour
intermèdes plus romanesques que le drame intime. Je ne finirai
pas ma tâche d'écrivain sans essayer, comme je le veux faire ici,
de les tirer d'une ombre où les relégua l'impudique devoir de
parler de l'amour en mon nom personnel.][108]

On the threshold of *La Naissance du jour,* Colette has one of her
ex-husbands broach to her the possibility she is on the brink of exploring
in the pages that follow: "But is it impossible for you to write a book
that isn't about love?" ["Mais tu ne peux donc pas écrire un livre qui
ne soit d'amour?"]. And she adds: "He might perhaps have taught me
what may legitimately take the place of love, in a novel or out of it"
(18–19) ["Il m'aurait peut-être enseigné ce qui a licence de tenir, dans
un roman et hors du roman, la place de l'amour" (285–86)]. The possibility of discovering "what may legitimately take the place of love

[108]   Colette, *Bella-Vista,* in *Œuvres,* 3:1097; translation from *Bella-Vista,* trans.
Antonia White, in *The Collected Stories of Colette,* ed. Robert Phelps (New York:
Farrar Straus & Giroux, 1983), 559.

in a novel" opens up nothing less than the reinvention of the genre.[109]
Colette does not completely abandon the love plot in *Naissance,* but
what she does instead is almost as radical. She offers a very thin romantic intrigue as a kind of sugar coating to get her reading public to
swallow the experimental pill. On a thematic level, the experiment
involves a character/narrator called Colette who strikes out on her
own, begins again, in middle age, carves new worlds at dawn, carves
a new dawn in midlife. But for the middle-aged *author* Colette, the
experiment is a formal one played out as a meditative narrative situated on the far side of plot, finding its place somewhere between
Flaubert's "book about nothing" ["livre sur rien"] and the nouveau
roman. Alongside the mother's ghost and the lover's shadow, *purloined,* set aside (*à côté de l'amour,* as the fictive title of Renée Néré's
novel puts it), exposed but enfolded in plot, is the letter of her text:
"the need to transform everything into literature."[110]

Another way to say this is that Colette needs literature in order
to transform everything: writing is a "metamorphic" form for her, to
borrow Julia Kristeva's term.[111] In my own appropriation of the term
in specific reference to *La Naissance du jour,* I have in mind a broad
textual aesthetic, which I want to approach first through some tangible elements before moving on to abstractions. Transformation figures thematically (and of course metaphorically) in obvious ways:
daughter is turned into mother, and mother into daughter; men are
turned into cacti, to mention a few examples. Formally, Colette alters Sido's letters, and autobiography is fictionalized while fiction
absorbs autobiographical and historical referentiality. Stylistically,
sentences change focus in mid-course, metaphors succeed one another, metamorphosing to create a mercurial prose that flows asso-
ciatively along visual, auditory, semantic, and mnemic pathways. As
metaphors morph, they metamorphose the text, diverting its narrative path to inaugurate a genre Kristeva refers to as a "mixture of el-
liptical narration and prose poetry" ["mélange de narration élliptique
et de poèmes en prose"].[112]

---

[109]   Since the 1980s, of course, the question has been theorized by Carolyn Heilbrun
and others; see Heilbrun, *Writing a Woman's Life* (New York: Norton, 1988).
[110]   I borrow these words from Renaud de Jouvenel's characterization of his step-
mother, cited earlier.
[111]   Kristeva, *Le Génie féminin,* especially 132–39.
[112]   Ibid., 138.

Change is intimately bound up with the process of writing for Colette; that is, writing gains power and significance as an agent of mobility and change. A brief detour through *La Vagabonde* (which can be read as a youthful rehearsal of *La Naissance du jour* in its grappling with problems of recognition and identity in writing) frames writing as it will remain in Colette: a mode of living in time, in spite of time—a mode that bestows on Renée Néré the greatest gift of all, "forgetting the hour" (12) ["l'oubli de l'heure" (1074)].[113] From the earliest pages of the novel, writing is associated with mobility: "a brand-new book with that smell of printers' ink and paper fresh from the press that makes you think of coal and trains and departures! (10) ["oh! Le livre nouveau, le livre tout frais dont le parfum d'encre humide et de papier neuf évoque celui de la houille, des locomotives, des departs!" (1072)]. In the novel's last pages, the other faces of mobility are unveiled as aging, mortality, change: "In his blindness he will not admit that I must change and grow old, although every second, added to the second that is fleeting, is already snatching me away from him" (165) ["son aveuglement me refuse le droit de changer, de vieillir, alors que tout instant, ajouté à l'instant écoulé, me dérobe à lui" (1211)]. Renée's return to writing is her answer to the inevitability of living in time, her response to a lover who wants to stop time and photographically freeze the moment. She turns to writing because, like time, it is a mobile process that cannot be fixed, a way to compete with time on the same terms. Writing comes to take on and subvert the reflecting role earlier played by the mirror for Renée, as it does more subtly for the Colette character in *La Naissance du jour*: "Raising my head, I look at myself... in the inclined mirror; then I turn to my writing again" (62) ["En levant la tête je me regarde... dans le miroir penché, puis je me remets à écrire" (*Naissance*, 315)]. There is, in *La Vagabonde*, a recurring relay from mirror to blank page until the page gradually prevails, giving writing the mobile force formerly attributed to her face reflected in the glass or in her lover's gaze: "To write, to write, to cover white pages with the rapid, uneven writing which he says is

---

[113] Anne Callahan persuasively argues that Colette "links [the narrator of *Naissance*] linguistically to Renée Néré when she describes her behavior with Vial [using the verb *vagabonder*]: 'Je vagabonde cette nuit autour de Vial'" ("The Vagabond: A Modern Heroine," in *Writing the Voice of Pleasure* [New York: Palgrave, 2001], 176): "I am capering around Vial tonight" (*The Vagabond*, 64; *La Vagabonde*, 317).

like my mobile face" (169) ["Écrire, écrire, lancer à travers des pages blanches l'écriture rapide, inégale, qu'il compare à mon visage mobile" (1214)]. Renée's writing epitomizes a tension between the clear and the diffuse, challenging commitment with possibility, legibility with blurriness, statement with suggestion, permanence with the ephemeral, and exact copy with alteration and even fragmentation. Mobility, as assumed in the writing process, takes the protean shape and the cinematic quality of succession: a refusal to freeze and to fix, an openness to metaphorize and to metamorphose. Her writing, like "Renée Néré"—her "go-nowhere name," to quote Ross Chambers— is alinear and intransitive, made in the image of Colette's best later works.[114]

The quality of mobility that inhabits Renée's (and Colette's) writing takes root in its most material aspects before taking flight in abstraction, as Renée describes in the opening pages of *La Vagabonde:* "To write, to be able to write, what does it mean? It means...letting your pen play round a blot of ink and nibble at a half-formed word, scratching it, making it bristle with darts and adorning it with antennae and paws until it loses all resemblance to a legible word and turns into a fantastic insect, a fluttering fairy-butterfly" (12) ["Écrire! Pouvoir écrire! cela signifie...les jeux de la plume qui tourne en rond autour d'une tache d'encre, qui mordille le mot imparfait, le griffe, le hérisse de fléchettes, l'orne d'antennes, de pattes, jusqu'à ce qu'il perde sa figure lisible de mot, mué en insecte fantastique, envolé en papillon-fée" (1074)]. This fantastic writing, both material and transcendent, closely resembles the final letter Colette attributes to Sido in *La Naissance du jour:* "arrows...strokes, swallow-like interweavings, plant-like convolutions—all messages from a hand that was trying to transmit to me a new alphabet" (142) ["des flèches...des traits, des entrelacs d'hirondelle, des volutes végétales, parmi les messages d'une main qui tentait de me transmettre un alphabet nouveau" (371)]. Before returning to this closing letter, I want to explore transformation as a textual aesthetic intimately related to the extra-banal mother: a process of perception everywhere present in, and nowhere inextricable

---

[114] I borrow the phrase "go-nowhere name" from Ross Chambers's excellent pages on *La Vagabonde* in *Loiterature* (Lincoln: University of Nebraska Press, 1999), 57.

from, the writing and reading of the text.[115] My reading of Colette's New Mother is influenced by Christopher Bollas's work on maternal aesthetics and the transformational object, which I framed in chapter 3.[116]

Bollas maintains that the "first human aesthetic" instilled in the infant by the mother's shaping of the environment "informs the development of personal character ... and will predispose all future aesthetic experiences that place the person in subjective rapport with an object" (33). The quest for an aesthetic object in adult life is, in fact, Bollas proposes, the pursuit of a self-altering medium: a quest driven less by the object itself than by its role as a signifier of metamorphoses of the self. Such a transformational object is sought for its promise of "an experience where self-fragmentations will be integrated through a processing form" (33).

Reflections of Lacan's mirror stage reverberate in this promise of illusory self-integration through the mother's organizing perceptions, and the mirror image in turn usefully carries us back to Colette's text. In its opening pages, we recall, Colette's literal glance in the looking glass (the projected mirror of Sido's gaze?) leads into a hypothesized mirror scene in which Sido would return from the grave, initially misrecognize her daughter, but then know and acknowledge her through a series of identificatory transformations that turn her daughter into herself and her daughter's lover into a flowering cactus. I take Sido's gazing ghost to be a concretization (if that can be the right term for a ghost) of a more diffused presence spectrally symbolized here: the "existential memory" of a primal transformative holding otherwise infused in the text as its own ubiquitous processes of transformation.

I want to argue that Colette's "metamorphic writing" is an aesthetic derivative of the transformational holding environment Bollas calls the "first human aesthetic." In other words, Colette's stylistic

---

[115] See Barbara Johnson's "Mallarmé as Mother" (in *A World of Difference* [Baltimore: Johns Hopkins University Press, 1987], 137–43) for a concept of mother as function or structure. Although my notion of mother corresponds to a textual aesthetic, Johnson's brilliant exposition helped me to think through and to clarify my own argument.

[116] Christopher Bollas, *The Shadow of the Object: Psychoanalysis of the Unthought Known* (New York: Columbia University Press, 1987); references are provided in the text.

template is the "lifestyle" she attributes to Sido: "Confined to her village...she had the power of conjuring up everywhere pinnacles, burgeonings, metamorphoses, exploding miracles" (24) ["Confinée dans son village...elle rencontrait partout, imprévus, suscités pour elle, par elle, des apogées, des éclosions, des métamorphoses, des explosions de miracles" (290)].[117] In analogizing Colette's writing style and Sido's lifestyle, however, I want to question, and attempt to modify, the trace of a classic mirror model (and the mimetic mode it implies) implicit in Bollas's theory, to have it correspond more faithfully to Colette's experimental aesthetic. If there is truth in Joan Hinde Stewart's claim that "the *Naissance* themes are resemblance, imitation, and identity; [that] this is a text structured by mimesis and mimetic desire,"[118] it is crucial to add that the structure of mimesis and mimetic desire is there only as a starting point to be played with and to be challenged. If *La Naissance du jour* initially stages mirror images and mimetic structures, it does so to put them in question and to go in search of an alternative, much as it lets itself be nominally structured by maternal instinct and erotic love, but is driven by the possibility of moving beyond them. The relay between the mirror and the page that culminates in the triumph of writing, in *La Vagabonde*, as I sketched earlier, is played out in *Naissance* in the idiom of recognition, and specifically in a persistent questioning of what it means to recognize and to be recognized.

I want to argue that recognition takes on the prominent role it plays in the novel because it offers a logical aesthetic and ethical alternative to mimesis. Three contemporary bodies of thought operating in very different contexts (Terence Cave's literary-aesthetic theory, Jessica Benjamin's object relations theory, and Kaja Silverman's psychoanalytically based film theory) independently appose mimesis to three very different forms of recognition.[119] Together, Cave's work on anagnorisis, or narrative recognition (as an element of plot),

---

[117]   Kristeva argues that Sido is style, and states that for Colette, "the transmutation of love into style would be carried out throughout her life" ["la transmutation de l'amour en style sera réalisée, tout au long de sa vie"] (*Le Génie féminin,* 29).

[118]   Joan Hinde Stewart, *Colette* (New York: Twayne, 1996), 58.

[119]   Terence Cave, *Recognitions: A Study in Poetics* (London: Oxford University Press, 1988); Jessica Benjamin, *Like Subjects, Love Objects: Essays on Recognition and Sexual Difference* (New Haven: Yale University Press, 1995); Kaja Silverman,

Benjamin's work on intersubjective recognition (as a developmental process), and Silverman's work on epistemological recognition (my term for the self-conscious form of image production she proposes) help me to understand the theoretical groundwork Colette's writing implicitly prepares for a broad ethical and aesthetic shift that has yet to come.

Both Benjamin and Silverman construct their theories of recognition in response to Lacanian-inspired mirror models of identification and image formation which bestow on the mother the terrifying power of identity construction. For Benjamin, however, there is an important distinction to be made between identification, which depends on incorporation or assimilation, and recognition, which she, unlike many others, understands as an intersubjective process dependent on each subject perceiving and acknowledging the other as "like subject" (8), which is to say, as different.[120] She refutes the idea of a good mother as one who "creates the illusion of perfect oneness," even for an infant, arguing that "more than midrange responsiveness usually constitutes not harmony but control" (87). Benjamin's good mother neither perfectly imitates nor flawlessly reflects her child's mood or intent or action, but rather, affirms it by "*translating* [it] into a different modality" (87; emphasis added). Benjamin explicitly replaces the mirror paradigm by a dynamic model dependent on more complicated processes of mutual recognition: "The metaphor of the mirror is...not appropriate to early mothering: mirror imitation is less satisfying than complex interaction. What *feels* perfect never *is* perfect" (87).

Silverman approaches "an ethics of the field of vision, and a psychoanalytic politics of visual representation" (2) through the mirror stage; but she reinterprets the ideal image as one situated "at a distance from the self," and in fact produced, or at least self-consciously *reproduced*, at such a distance, in order to facilitate an authentic relationship to the other and to otherness (44). Building on the work of

---

The Threshold of the Visible World (New York: Routledge, 1996). References to these works are provided in the text.

[120]   This is notably different from the Hegelian concept of recognition operating according to a master-slave model, as developed in *The Phenomenology of Spirit*. See too Kelly Oliver's presentation in *Witnessing: Beyond Recognition* (Minneapolis: University of Minnesota Press, 2001).

Paul Schilder, she suggests that the fantasy of bodily disintegration through which the subject apprehends the impossibility of sustaining an ideal image may in fact be "beneficent rather than tragic; *it is the precondition for change,* what must transpire if the ego is to form anew" (21; emphasis added). In gesturing beyond the paradigm of reflection, she is aiming not only toward a certain practice of relating creatively to the other ("the active gift of love") outside of culturally sanctioned ideals, but also, correlatively, toward an aesthetic practice capable of "assisting us in the difficult task of *living at a distance from the mirror*" (173; emphasis added). Although Silverman uses the term "recognition" less routinely than does Benjamin, it is everywhere implied in her writing through the central notion of acknowledging and idealizing the other *as* other, consciously and deliberately, away from an aesthetics and a politics of reflexivity.[121]

Cave is the only one of the three who explicitly addresses recognition as it operates within the field of poetics, similarly to and differently from mimesis. His work, juxtaposed with Benjamin's focus on mother-child dynamics and Silverman's on crafting images outside the mirror, completes a triple-pronged approach responsive to Colette's intertwined reworking of maternal aesthetics, ethics, and poetics in *La Naissance du jour*. Recognition, for Cave, "works against mimesis" (24); it is unstable where mimesis is reassuring (22, 489). Where mimesis presents itself as "an instance of...poise" within which "each moment of time is apprehended...discretely and calmly, in its own right" (22), recognition works retrospectively, as "the vehicle of nostalgia" (497). Its emblem, the scar, "is a mark of treacherously concealed narrative waiting to break the surface and create a scandal; it is a sign that the story, like the wound, may always be reopened" (24). Contrary to classical mimesis, which effects a reassuring fullness, recognition "claim[s] to resolve, conjoin and make whole...[while] busily bring[ing] to the surface all the possibilities that threaten wholeness." Whatever fullness it articulates is, then, "as radically unstable as a mirage" (489). Cave is fond of using

---

[121]   The term figures explicitly only sporadically, as when she urges "a constant conscious reworking of the terms under which we unconsciously look at objects...[and especially] the struggle...*to recognize* involuntary acts of incorporation and repudiation, and our implicit affirmation of the dominant elements of the screen, and then, to see again, differently" (184; emphasis added).

such infelicitous mirror imagery to explain recognition, which he describes at another point as "an activity taking place in a hall of mirrors where the only person present is a simulacrum" (21). The twist in his opposition of recognition to mimesis, however, is that finally they are, in his representation, less polarized antagonists than illusionary opponents: "ghostly double[s]" (5), or unstable reflections of each other. Mimesis is forever vulnerable to the wound of recognition, and mirroring is always potentially a visual trick.

Although Cave, Silverman, and Benjamin theorize three differing forms of recognition, I think it is not taking excessive license to read broadly across them some common themes: a preoccupation with mirrors; a quest for wholeness, harmony, and fullness of life; a fall into fragmentation, disruption, kaleidoscopic changes, and death. Rereading Colette, we might juxtapose the three discrete theories to make ends meet: to connect mothers with mimesis and to construct a way out of this bind.

Recognizing Mothers

Colette had a tortuous relationship to mirroring and mimesis that could be traced through much of her writing, including her correspondence as well as her fiction.[122] One might in fact see the history of her writing as a history of attempts to escape the mirror structure and aesthetic, and of subsequent slides back within it. It is not my purpose to chronicle such a history, but I can offer a few examples (beyond those I have discussed from *La Vagabonde* and *La Naissance du jour*) to indicate metonymically the parameters of the problem.

As Michel Del Castillo and Nicole Ferrier-Caverivière have each suggested, Colette's struggle for autonomy had incessantly to confront the expectation that she be her mother's reflection, a constraint succinctly articulated in Sido's correspondence with her daughter as "I am you" ["Moi, c'est toi"].[123] In the dynamics of her relationship

---

[122]   On mirrors in Colette, see Laurie Corbin, *The Mother Mirror: Self-Representation and the Mother-Daughter Relation in Colette, Simone de Beauvoir, and Marguerite Duras* (New York: Peter Lang, 1996).
[123]   Cited from Sido, *Lettres à sa fille*, by Michel Del Castillo, in *Colette, une certaine France*, 97.

with her own daughter, Colette would alternate between a similar mirroring expectation (as my opening anecdote began to suggest) and a recognition of her otherness. So, for example, she would write to Bel-Gazou words that echo, to a startling degree, her mother's claim on her: "I would like to see you fall into place before me as a little mirror of myself" ["J'aimerais te voir te classer devant moi comme un petit miroir de moi-même"].[124] Yet elsewhere she would very deliberately remind herself to step back from encroaching on her daughter's individuality: "When I was at Lelong's I saw such pretty, stylish sweaters that I left a credit so that you may choose one....There was a blue Shetland one with white collar and sleeves, so appealing that I almost bought it for you, but let's not forget that parents should never make plans for their children—even concerning Shetland!" ["J'ai vu chez Lelong...de si jolis petits sweaters "jeunes" que je t'ouvre un credit pour en choisir un....Il y en a un bleu avec manches et col rond blancs en Shetland, tellement aimable que j'ai faille (sic) te le prendre, mais!...n'oublions pas que les parents ne doivent jamais construire pour les enfants—même en Shetland!"].[125]

In her public writing (fictions and public relations correspondence), Colette more routinely proclaimed a politics and an aesthetics of determined distance and nonreflectivity. To her character Vial (in *La Naissance du jour*) as to her editor Pierre Lafitte (who published "Maternité" in *Femina*), Colette, we have seen, adamantly made clear that her text was not mimetic and was not to be read as a reflection of her life. Much earlier, in a short text significantly called "Le Miroir" (written in 1908 and later published in the collection *Les Vrilles de la vigne*), Colette had already constructed a parable of literary mirroring and its dangers (or, to borrow the terms she would later use in *La Naissance*, a parable of fatally autobiographical writing) in which she arranged a meeting between herself and her character, Claudine, and protested to her (though with questionable effect), "I am not your double" ["Je ne suis pas votre Sosie"].[126] Meanwhile, of course, Colette was dressed like Claudine, coiffed like Claudine, confused with Claudine (though the degree of her willful participation is unclear);

---

[124] Letter from the end of November 1926, in Colette, *Lettres à sa fille*, 113.
[125] Letter from the beginning of March 1932, ibid., 235.
[126] Colette, "Le Miroir," in *Les Vrilles de la vigne*, in *Œuvres*, 1:1030.

she would later borrow Claudine's name for her autobiographical house of fiction; and she would socialize, in her own name, with her character Vial in the pages of *La Naissance du jour*.

Like "Le Miroir," *La Naissance du jour* is a work at least partly about the inaccessibility of life to art, but a work that nevertheless inextricably entangles life's tentacles in art, and so risks confusing and reordering—and symbolically dismantling—the mimetic hierarchy. And the question of literature's responsibility to life is doubled by the problem I raised earlier of criticism's responsibility to literature—a problem of reflection and identification that might be likened to a secondary mimesis, if we see criticism and literature as analogous in the sense of their impossible accountability (to art and to life, respectively). Phyllis Rose well describes the dual dilemma: "A translation, a reduction, a condensation, an approximation, a metaphor is the best that can be achieved in art, no matter how inclusive, as an account of life, and the same is true for criticism as an account of art."[127] Once we accept the analogous relationship of criticism to art, and art to life, it goes without saying that a threat to literary mimesis contains an implicit threat to traditional ways of conceptualizing criticism's relationship to literature.

If *La Naissance* begins by framing a mirror, it ends by jumping the frame. The narrator, we recall, rhetorically bids her dismissed lover to leap through the window: "Saute la fenêtre" (369). Would it be too great a leap of reading to infer that he is meant both to clear the frame and to shatter the glass? At first glance, Colette's text seems to move from recognition to disintegration: from an opening mirror scene to a concluding scene of compounded fragmentation, thus reproducing the vicious circle of the Lacanian mirror model, in which aspirations toward wholeness are inevitably bound up with fantasies of the body in pieces. Yet textual nuances belie facile schematic identifications with this model.

We might begin to end by juxtaposing details of the contrasting opening and closing mirror themes in order to theorize about the alternative structures and strategies they suggest for reading and criticism. We recall that the novel opens with the narrator's ambivalent

---

[127] Phyllis Rose, *The Year of Reading Proust: A Memoir in Real Time* (Washington, D.C.: Counterpoint, 1997), 30.

self-identification with her mother. After the quadruply fabricated statement "I am the daughter of a woman who..." (5–6) ["Je suis la fille d'une femme qui..." (277–78)] which I examined earlier, she continues the specious identification by affirming her mirror resemblance to her mother, yet she paradoxically describes the image in the mirror as one of decomposition and failed recognition: "Now that little by little I am beginning to age, and little by little taking on her likeness in the mirror, I wonder whether, if she were to return, she would recognize me for her daughter, in spite of the resemblance of our features" (6) ["Maintenant que je me défais peu à peu et que dans le miroir peu à peu je lui ressemble, je doute que, revenant, elle me reconnaisse pour sa fille, malgré la resemblance de nos traits" (278)]. Colette's words suggest not only a vain maternal ghost disclaiming resemblance with an aging daughter, but also the author-daughter's disclaimer of the mirror, or in other words, her exposure of its illusory power. The image of coherence masks the truth of decomposition; recognition in the mirror is always misrecognition; and any authentic self-recognition must be based on recognition of the other *as other*, as the ensuing evocation of the cactus-lover makes clear: "I doubt that, if she were to return, she would recognize me....Unless she came back as day was breaking, and found me...half-naked...and shielding...the shadow of a man" (6–7) ["Je doute que, revenant, elle me reconnaisse....À moins qu'elle ne revienne quand le jour point à peine, et qu'elle ne me surprenne...demi-nue...et protégeant...une ombre d'homme" (278)].[128]

What *would* constitute the grounds for recognition is a more subtle *resemblance-in-difference:* a trace of the daughter's erotic passion, witnessed and quickly converted, in the daughter's imagination of the mother's eye, to an anticipated cactus bloom. I recall this scene once more because it illustrates a particular way of thinking about recognition that involves a shift from identity to difference, from integration to decomposition and then recomposition, from mirroring to metamorphosing—and, in summary, from mimetic resemblance and mirror ideology to something I will call differential recognition,

---

[128] I am echoing the Lacanian axiom that mirror recognition is based in misrecognition, but departing from it in proposing that another kind of recognition (outside the mirror) is possible.

or recognition beyond the mirror. The principle on which this revi-
sionary recognition is based is metaphor rather than mimesis. Like
all good metaphors, Colette's work by opposition, by putting into
relation two terms we do not usually think together. Recognition in
Colette works very much like the process of metaphor in her writing: it holds two apparently opposing entities together in a relationship that is based neither in unity nor in antagonism but rather, in
change.[129]

Just as the opening scene of recognition doesn't present quite the
totalizing face expected, the ending scene of fragmentation doesn't
bring about the anticipated destruction, so that the classic mirror
cycle of imagined wholeness and fantasized disintegration is revised.
Let's turn to the closing scene. Colette's citation of what she represents as Sido's last letter contains a parody along with a threat.[130] It
is, first, a parodic synopsis of Colette's own metamorphics, whose
extreme form is precisely this "new alphabet" where signs without
syntax are superimposed: "Signs that looked joyful, arrows emerging
from an etched word, little rays, two words, 'yes, yes' and the words
'she danced,' very clear... strokes, swallow-like interweavings, plant-
like convolutions—all messages from a hand that was trying to transmit to me a new alphabet" (142) ["Des signes qui semblent joyeux,
des flèches partant d'un mot esquissé, de petits rayons, deux 'oui, oui'
et un 'elle a dansé' très net... des traits, des entrelacs d'hirondelle,
des volutes végétales, parmi les messages d'une main qui tentait de
me transmettre un alphabet nouveau" (371)]. But as is often the case,
the parody veils a threat. There is first the possibility—proposed but
rapidly denied—of contemplating the mother's text as "un confus
délire": a succession of metamorphosing signs that fall outside

---

[129] The structure of metaphorics, argues Lacan ("L'Instance de la letter dans
l'inconscient ou la raison depuis Freud," in *Écrits I* [Paris: Seuil (Points), 1966],
249–89], is Oedipal: one term annihilates and replaces its predecessor. Kristeva,
by contrast, characterizes Colette's metaphorics in a way that sounds almost
like a pre-Oedipal merging process, using Colette's eponymous metaphor from
Les Vrilles de la vigne to describe perceptions that subtly whirl or curl into one
another—like tendrils of a vine; she refers to "'the inexpressible relationship' that
couples objects, twists perceptions together" ["la 'mise en rapport indicible' qui
accouple les objets, vrille les perceptions les unes aux autres" (Kristeva, *Le Génie
féminin*, 137)]. I am arguing for something in between the two.
[130] Sido's last letter, currently in an anonymous private collection, is to my
knowledge not reproduced in any publication.

language. An alternative epistolary interpretation explicitly replaces delirium with a playful picture, but implies a much more sinister state of affairs: "Instead of a confused delirium, I see in that letter one of those haunted landscapes where we find, playfully *hidden,* a face among the leaves, an arm in the fork of a tree, a torso under a cluster of rocks" (142) ["Au lieu de la contempler comme un confus délire, j'y lis un de ces paysages hantés où par jeu l'on *cacha* un visage dans les feuilles, un bras entre deux branches, un torse sous des nœuds de rochers" (371; emphasis added)]. This reading, contrary to the rejected "dereading" of delirium, is full of meaning: it speaks of dismemberment and hidden limbs scattered in a haunted landscape. It harks back to the beginning of the same paragraph, where Colette explains that she received the letter after her mother's death, and goes on to exclaim: "Ah! Let's *hide* under that last letter the image that I don't want to see: a head half vanquished, turning its dry neck impatiently from side to side on the pillow, like a poor goat tethered too short" (142) ["Ah! *Cachons* sous la dernière lettre l'image que je ne veux pas voir: une tête à demi vaincue qui tournait de côté et d'autre, sur l'oreiller, son col sec et son impatience de pauvre chèvre attachée court" (371; emphasis added)]. Colette's proposed reading of Sido's dying letter as a body in pieces, "playfully" *hidden* from the reader in a *haunted landscape,* corresponds by displacement to her earlier expressed desire to *hide* the *haunting* image of her mother's agony, or, in other words, to convert this ending into a breaking dawn announced by "messages from a hand that was trying to transmit to me a new alphabet, *or the sketch of some site envisaged at dawn under rays that would never attain the sad zenith*" (142) ["les messages d'une main qui tentait de me transmettre un alphabet nouveau, *ou le croquis d'un site entrevu à l'aurore sous des rais qui n'atteindraient jamais le morne zenith*" (371; emphasis added)]. Death dawns, and the signs of delirium become an original alphabet. In place of decomposition we are given concealment and camouflage, which is to say, change writ large.

So Colette's system of metamorphics—vitally linked to the dying mother as a kind of cover-up—somehow ends up binding birth and death. The postulation of Sido's dying dawn glimpses of a transcendent alphabet of body fragments makes way for the moment when the breaking dawn enters her daughter's bedroom, filling her with a hunger to (re)write that she describes as "the deep hunger for the moment which gives birth to the day" (143) ["la faim profonde du moment qui enfante le jour" (371)]. This birth of day, this moment of "giving birth" to day, presented as temporally continuous with the breaking dawn of Sido's death, shows birth coming from death, or more precisely, the newly born day as reborn, in writing, from a death that is at once literal and a figure for the already lived. The metaphor of birth that announces this text (lost in translation as *Break of Day*) and returns periodically in its pages is a second coming, reappearing as well in a recurrent meditation on surviving love's demise. It is an implicit renaissance in writing that is at one point triply articulated as "to shed one's skin, to reconstruct, to be born again" (112) ["faire peau neuve, reconstruire, renaître" (349)]—a series of terms that begins to evoke resurrection with the metaphor of that graphic illustration of change, molting, metamorphosis.

Although change may easily be associated with mobility, flux, disorder, disintegration, decay, and death, in patterns that Sander Gilman has expertly explored, we might reverse the coin to argue that decomposition and death may also, more positively, be seen as harbingers or even variants of change.[131] In order to do so, it is helpful to compare Colette's reading of Sido's dying letter with her contiguous rewriting of her dismissed lover, and to understand them as part of the same project.

Directly preceding her transmission of Sido's last letter, Colette begins her exorcism of Vial with the program of metamorphosis we glimpsed earlier: "Flee, my favorite! Don't reappear until you have become unrecognizable. Jump through the window and as you touch the ground, change, blossom, fly, resound... slough off your skin. When you return to me I must be able to give you... your name of 'pink cactus' or some other flame-shaped flower that uncloses painfully, the name you will acquire when you have been exorcised" (140) ["Fuis, mon favori! Ne reparais que méconnaissable. Saute la fenêtre, et en touchant le sol change, fleuris, vole, résonne... rejette ta dépouille. Lorsque tu me reviendras, il faut que je puisse te donner... ton nom de 'Cactus rose' ou de je ne sais quelle autre fleur en forme de flamme,

---

[131] See Sander Gilman, *Difference and Pathology: Stereotypes of Sexuality, Race, and Madness* (Ithaca: Cornell University Press, 1985).

à éclosion pénible, ton nom futur de créature exorcisée" (369)]. This passage anticipates the twists and turns and multiple reformulations of Sido's letter, whose asyntactic, alinear ciphers we recall: "signs...arrows...little rays...strokes, swallow-like interweavings, plant-like convolutions" (142) ["des signes...des flèches...de petits rayons...des traits, des entrelacs d'hirondelle, des volutes végétales" (371)]. Sido's analphabetic letter then reverberates immediately in Colette's restated project for Vial's transformation, which respects the rules of grammar but violates mimetic syntax: "He will turn into a thicket, sea-spray, meteors, unbounded open book, cluster of grapes, ship, oasis..." (143) ["Le voici halliers, embruns, météores, livre sans bornes ouvert, grappe, navire, oasis..." (371)].

The text ends suspended on these words, which suggest that the banished lover will fly the coop of mimetic fiction, leaping into a world that is transformative rather than imitative. But as we follow more slowly at his heels, we note that Colette qualifies the end with a careful description of the means: "Not so fast! Not so fast! That deep hunger for the moment which gives birth to the day must learn patience: the ambiguous friend who leapt through the window is still wandering about. He did not put off his shape as he touched the ground. He has not had time enough to perfect himself. But I only have to help him and he will turn into a thicket, sea-spray, meteors, unbounded open book, cluster of grapes, ship, oasis..." (143) ["Pas si vite, pas si vite! Qu'elle prenne patience, la faim profonde du moment qui enfante le jour: l'ami ambigu qui sauta la fenêtre erre encore. Il n'a pas, en touchant le sol, abdiqué sa forme. Le temps lui a manqué pour se parfaire. Mais que je l'assiste seulement et le voici halliers, embruns, météores, livre sans bornes ouvert, grappe, navire, oasis..." (371)]. The ambiguity that attaches to her friend, "l'ami ambigu," synecdochically refers to the scene (in process) and the situation (unresolved), as the becoming-exorcised lover—like the maternal ghost with which the book opens—hovers, hesitates between forms and aesthetic principles. Colette makes clear that what is needed to effect the metamorphosis (to put change in the place of an economy of reflection and fragmentation) is the intervention of her writing, and she leaves this intervention hypothetical: *"But I only have to help him and..."* (143) [*"Mais que je l'assiste seulement et..."* (371; emphasis added)].

Born from her mother's death and her lover's expendability, or, more precisely, reborn from the rewriting of maternal absence as midlife self-sufficiency, Colette creates herself, in *La Naissance du jour*, through her re-creation of a mother-attributed aesthetic whose transformational characteristics—"pinnacles, burgeonings, metamorphoses, exploding miracles" ["apogées, éclosions, méta-morphoses, explosions de miracles"]—uncannily anticipate Bollas's theorization of a transformational maternal dynamics. Dispersed like Sido's epistolary body parts and thoroughly diffused—*transfused*—in the text, the mother in the writing, to use Flaubert's concept of the author, is, like God in the universe, present everywhere and visible nowhere. Colette's recollections of her mother's place relative to other (mostly animal) mothers in attendance during her childhood resonate with this notion of a hidden force: "Mothers, offspring, fer-tile in turn: all this was never far during the first twenty years of my life. Did I used to think less about my own mother than about all those mothers surrounding me? It's possible. *One doesn't think about the presence of air*" ["Des mères, des rejetons, féconds à leur tour: voilà qui ne m'a jamais manqué, pendant les vingt premières années de ma vie. Pensais-je moins à ma propre mère qu'à toutes ces mères qui m'entouraient? C'est possible. *On ne songe pas à la presence de l'air*"].[132] What earlier appeared to be a radical disper-sion of the maternal body ends looking more like a quiet diffusion, literally an etherealization: fragmentation is a prelude to the inces-sant background hum of change. Yet the introduction of a new aes-thetic feels tentative, even unstable. Colette leaves us suspended in that uncanny landscape where the maternally infused transforming surround (like the notion of the *Heimlich*, which intensifies until it turns into its opposite) might at any moment be confused with a reassuring sense of fusion, and then as quickly revert to a disquieting image of scattered maternal limbs.

---

[132] Colette, "Des Mères, des enfants," in *En Pays connu*, 417; emphasis added. Co-lette's description evokes another haunted landscape, scene of another—pagan—metamorphosis that I paraphrase from Ovid: Orpheus torn in pieces by the Maenads, his limbs scattered, his breath vanished in the wind, but his voice still audible in the echoes of his lyre and tongue carried off by the waters. Ovid, *Meta-morphoses*, trans. Mary M. Innes (Harmondsworth: Penguin, 1976), 11.1–105.

So it is in this context that I come to reevaluate the sense of being myself changed by reading Colette, recast as reader and critic. I now know that one doesn't read Colette to be held by the visions or embracing truths that warm us and fleetingly make us whole when reading Proust. Nor does one read her to pose as a reliable critical reflector. Reading Colette, anticipating resistance and resisting incoherence, one works to shape and hold meaning among the flickering nuances of her kaleidoscopic prose. But even as I affirm the futility of resurrecting the mother in Colette, and Colette as mother, I reread *La Naissance du jour* to be transformed by Colette's ungentle hand, as my own remakes her text.

EPILOGUE

Books and Children (New Mythologies)

In the mid-1950s Roland Barthes took *Elle* magazine to task for an article that played the double game of promulgating a conservative ethic of female procreativity in the guise of promoting women's creativity.[1] In the text of one of his better-known mythologies, "Novels and Children" ("Romans et enfants"), Barthes first recalls the feature photo of seventy women novelists—graphically assembled, he suggests, like a remarkable zoological species[2]—and he reviews a journalistic maneuver that consists of juxtaposing the miraculously double birthlines of these women of letters: "*Jacqueline Lenoir (two daughters, one novel); Marina Grey (one son, one novel); Nicole Dutreil (two sons, four novels), etc.*" (50). He goes on to articulate the message implicit in the *Elle* article, with typically pungent irony—an irony so keen that every time I teach this text to undergraduates, there are some who recoil in dismay and indignation at the misogynistic letter of his words: "Women, be therefore courageous, free;

---

[1] See Roland Barthes, "Romans et enfants," in *Mythologies* (Paris: Seuil [Points], 1957): 53–55. The article "70 Romancières, 300 romans: Les Femmes de lettres s'imposent" in *Elle*, by Roger Kemp, appeared in no. 467 (December 22, 1954): 62–65.

[2] The mythology begins: "If we are to believe the weekly *Elle*, which some time ago mustered seventy women novelists on one photograph, the woman of letters is a remarkable zoological species: she brings forth, pell-mell, novels and children." Roland Barthes, "Novels and Children," in *Mythologies*, trans. Annette Lavers (London: Jonathan Cape, 1972), 50; subsequent citations are from this translation and are provided in the text.

play at being men, write like them; but never get far from them; live under their gaze, compensate for your books by your children; enjoy a free rein [to dabble in your career] for a while, but quickly come back to your condition" (50).

Books and Children

Before continuing, I should clarify that Barthes is not my subject here; I take his prescient text as an opening onto some of the questions and problems raised by the persistent (if changing) calculus, in modern Western culture, of women's children and books. In fact some of the ostensibly less clairvoyant—from a contemporary perspective some might even say borderline benighted—postures and turns of his analysis provide enlightenment about current-day versions of the calculus; and let me emphasize that they do so by example and not by contrast.

The modernity I attribute (somewhat cynically) to Barthes's "Romans et enfants" is, then, less predicated on an undeniably progressive element of his text than on a certain lack of progress since. To be sure, certain notes of Barthes's discourse sound dated today, as for instance when he declares, "one novel, one child, a little feminism, a little connubiality" (50). It seems absurd in our time to equate women's novels with feminist statements (we have surely seen too many backlash counterexamples), and unenlightened to assume women's children to be conjugal acts. There is at least a fledgling precedent now for rejecting the motherhood myth and the motherhood imperative itself;[3] we no longer expect books always to be indemnified by babies. But if conditions have evolved, the underlying wager remains the same. The balance may shift, but the scales are a fixture, and the plates are clearly marked: books and children, children and books— *livres contre enfants, enfants contre livres,* as French would render it.[4]

---

[3]   See, for example, Adrienne Rich, *Of Woman Born: Motherhood as Experience and Institution* (New York: Norton, 1976); Jane Lazarre, *The Mother Knot* (Durham: Duke University Press, 1997); Sharon Hays, *The Cultural Contradictions of Motherhood* (New Haven: Yale University Press, 1996); Ann Crittenden, *The Price of Motherhood* (New York: Henry Holt, 2001).

[4]   Colette, we have seen, was oppressed by the social pressures that weighed her motherhood and daughterhood against each other.

Counterbalanced, each is weighed against the other, and the problem is not how accurately the measure is taken but that it is taken at all. In Alicia Ostriker's words, "That women should have babies rather than books is the considered opinion of Western civilization. That women should have books rather than babies is a variation on that theme."[5] Children and books have been binarized for women living and writing in the Occident. This opposition, this antagonism—or in Susan Suleiman's substantivization, "the either/or"—like all binaries, can be stood on its head, but offers no exit.[6]

Let me offer a second example of the pseudo-evolution of thinking since "Novels and Children." To begin, let's recall a certain unexamined authorial stance. Barthes's inevitable subject position—that of a man writing about perceptions of women writing and mothering—could not today pass without commentary. We would question the angle and direction of his gaze, and we would want to know more about other views: notably, the perspectives—and perhaps even the thoughts and the words—of the seventy photographed mothers of letters, whose assembled eyes look out from the photograph to meet our own, resisting objectification (unsuccessfully so, in the insert on the lower part of the page, which reproduces the photo but replaces the women's faces with numbers corresponding to a key listing their names and an enumeration of their children and books).[7] But the passage of more than half a century has not fully illuminated the cultural gaps inhabiting the darker corners of Barthes's discourse. Although feminist theory brought along a sharp focus on mothers, it has represented them much more often as objects than as subjects, and has tended, like Barthes, not to hear or read their texts.

Only in 2001, in Moyra Davey's *Mother Reader: Essential Writings on Motherhood*, do we find a compilation of the scattered texts by mothers writing motherhood and writing over the past half century; this anthology has few precedents.[8] The pragmatic reasons for

---

5   Alicia Ostriker, "A Wild Surmise: Motherhood and Poetry," in *Mother Reader: Essential Writings on Motherhood*, ed. Moyra Davey (New York: Seven Stories Press, 2001), 155.
6   Susan R. Suleiman, "Writing and Motherhood," in *Mother Reader*, 120.
7   See Kemp, "70 Romancières," 62–63.
8   Davey, *Mother Reader*. For a rare precursor to Davey's anthology, see Brenda O. Daly and Maureen T. Reddy, eds., *Narrating Mothers: Theorizing Maternal Subjectivities* (Knoxville: University of Tennessee Press, 1991), which is, however,

both the belatedness and the rarity of first-person mother-texts are manifest. As Davey reminds us in her introduction, "there is a dearth of such literature because mothers do not have the time to record their experience."[9] But the impediment is not merely practical. We know that practice is always shaped by culture, and as Suleiman argues, powerful ideological models (including psychoanalysis) decree that "*mothers don't write, they are written.*"[10] If, as Melanie Klein's theory of artistic creation proposed, the work of art is the mother's body continually destroyed and reimagined by the child/artist, and if, as Barthes suggested elsewhere, a writer is "someone who plays with the body of his [her?...] mother," then, Suleiman asks, "what about the writer who *is* the body of the mother?...Does the mother who writes, write exclusively as her own mother's child?"[11] Thinking through these questions in a post-binary world would mean a passage from reading Barthes speaking of *Elle*'s mother-writers to reading a body of writers who are also mothers and who themselves speak of writing as mothers: a passage that, relatively speaking, has only just begun. That is, once we expose the "either/or" as a *huis clos* predicament, there is no emergency exit; the solution, if not resignation, is a slow, collective working-through.[12]

I have in mind here a version of Shoshana Felman's "bond of reading," an exchange that "conjugat[es] literature, theory, and autobiography

---

a collection not of primary writings but of critical writing about mothers writing. The late blooming of anthologies of writing about motherhood by mothers is to be contrasted with the explosion of anthologies of critical writing about mothers, usually from a daughter's point of view, beginning in the 1980s. They are too numerous to list; see, for example, Shirley Nelson Garner, Claire Kahane, Madelon Sprengnether, eds., *The (M)other Tongue* (Ithaca: Cornell University Press, 1985)—in which, however, Suleiman's "Writing and Motherhood" was first anthologized; Donna Bassin, Margaret Honey, and Meryle Mahrer Kaplan, eds., *Representations of Motherhood* (New Haven: Yale University Press, 1994).

9   Davey, intro. to *Mother Reader*, xiv.
10   Suleiman, "Writing and Motherhood," 117.
11   Ibid., 117–18. Suleiman is referring to the work of Melanie Klein in *Love, Guilt, and Reparation,* and quoting Roland Barthes from *Le Plaisir du texte.*
12   See Suleiman's framing of the question: "Is there no alternative to the either/or?...Or is Kristeva right in insisting that 'while a certain feminism takes its pouting and its isolation for protest and perhaps even for dissidence, genuine feminine innovation...will not be possible until we have elucidated motherhood, feminine creation, and the relationship between them?'" Suleiman, "Writing and Motherhood," 120, citing Julia Kristeva, "Un Nouveau Type d'intellectual: Le Dissident," *Tel Quel,* no 74 (Winter 1977): 6–7.

together through the act of reading," with "reading" understood to mean a sharing of stories or, in Felman's words, "the *story of the Other* (the story read by other women, the story of other women, the story of women told by others)."[13] Felman's methodology, designed to create or give access to the missing genre of women's autobiography, can be invoked for the derivative of this genre, the story of the mother, a story whose absence stands in the missing history of women's autobiography as a phantom prehistory or pre-story. Such a reading bond, for maternal stories, by necessity means reading by juxtaposition more often than by retrospection: thinking laterally through and across the other(s) rather than thinking back. For as Alicia Ostriker has asked, evoking Virginia Woolf, "through whom can those who are themselves mothers, when they want to know what this endeavor in their lives means, do their thinking?"[14]

Disillusioned by contemporary uses and abuses of retrospective reading, I was intrigued to come across a reference to Colette reflecting on George Sand's propagation of novels and children, in a study of Sand's *Histoire de ma vie*. In a passage in her *George Sand and Autobiography*, Janet Hiddleston contrasts the frequent presence of Sand's children in her letters with their rare appearances in her autobiography, concluding that the autobiography conforms with the emotionally muted male tradition within which she was living and writing. Hiddleston emphasizes Sand's unusual position in a world in which "most women writers at least before the twentieth century were childless, and writing and motherhood are often seen as parallel but incompatible.... Sand is one of the few to have achieved both, being at the same time mother and writer."[15] Here Hiddleston goes on to confirm Sand's double fecundity through the eyes of Colette: "Colette marvels at how she managed to do it all: 'Comment diable s'arrangeait George Sand?'" [How the devil did George Sand manage?] (26). Knowing that Colette was another mother who "managed

---

[13] Shoshana Felman, *What Does a Woman Want? Reading and Sexual Difference* (Baltimore: Johns Hopkins University Press, 1993), 14.

[14] Ostriker, "A Wild Surmise," 159. On the "cultural silencing of mothers' voices," see Sara Ruddick, "Talking about 'Mothers,'" in Davey, *Mother Reader*, 195 (excerpted from Ruddick, *Maternal Thinking: Toward a Politics of Peace* [Boston: Beacon Press, 1989].)

[15] Janet Hiddleston, *George Sand and Autobiography* (Oxford: Legenda, 1999), 26; subsequent references are provided in the text.

to do it all"—more or less, and for better or for worse—I found both puzzling and provocative the reference to her wonderment before a juggling act presumably not so very different from her own difficult game, all the more so because my understanding was that Sand's relationships with her children, not unlike Colette's with her daughter, were less than awe-inspiring.

A return to the correspondence and to biographical accounts corroborated my memory. To the question "How the devil *did* George Sand manage?" many of her biographers in effect answer "not all that well." (In fact Francine Mallet quite bluntly states, "George did not succeed at all with her daughter.")[16] The image so envied by Flaubert of the older George Sand buoyed up in her work by the hearty din of familial joy, surrounded by a bevy of pets, guests, and grandchildren, leaves out her complex relations with the previous generation. Also not represented in this picture is her unusually close lifelong embrace of her son Maurice (subject of a memoir called *Le Plus Grand Amour de George Sand* [George Sand's Greatest Love])[17] and the early distancing and eventual estrangement of her daughter Solange. While it is true that Sand functioned as writer and mother, it is also true that she depended on servants and boarding schools (like many others of her day and class) to do so, and still struggled enormously for time. The Sand who was made legend as "la bonne dame de Nohant" was without doubt a less ambivalent figure than that of the mother stretched between her work and her children—not to mention her lovers, her friends, and the upkeep of her property. The correspondence bears a record of the strain. Here, for instance, is an excerpt of a reply to her half-brother Hippolyte Chatiron in 1841, following his intervention in her dealings with Solange (he had prevailed upon Sand to heed the pleas of Solange, then twelve, who wanted to spend the summer at Nohant rather than continuing *en pension* in Paris): "She would not allow me to work for a minute at Nohant. And also she is beginning to be no longer completely a small child, though she still is one, and she needs to be watched in a way that is not possible for me unless I give up my

---

[16]   Francine Mallet, *George Sand* (Paris: Grasset, 1976), 77.
[17]   Maurice Toesca, *Le Plus Grand Amour de George Sand* (Paris: Albin Michel, 1980).

work."[18] In her *George Sand et Solange*, Isabelle Chovelon shows the evolution of a daughter: first a tiny child playing on the carpet beside her mother's writing table; then a young girl silently and resentfully watching her mother, chronically "overwhelmed by work" as she writes (331); and later, become sullen and difficult, a young woman reproaching her mother for the time given to extrafamilial concerns (349), notably writing. Juxtaposed to Sand's fraught relations with her daughter, there is her intense emotional investment in a series of surrogate daughter figures including Augustine Brault, Pauline Viardot, Lina Calamatta (Maurice's wife), and Maurice and Lina's daughters (Sand's granddaughters).

"Comment diable s'arrangeait George Sand?" asked Colette, in Hiddleston's text. "What the devil was *Colette* thinking?" I asked myself after revisiting Sand's often painful life as a writing mother. When I turned back to *L'Étoile vesper*, the source Hiddleston gives for Colette's musing on Sand, I found the citation, identical to the line reproduced by Hiddleston—but rather different in its original context, which I reproduce as follows:

> It's taken me a long time to scribble some forty volumes. So many hours stolen from traveling, idleness, reading, even from healthy feminine flirtatiousness! How the devil did George Sand manage? That sturdy woman of letters found it possible to finish one novel and start another in the same hour. And in the process, she lost neither a lover nor a puff of the narghile, not to mention a *Story of My Life* in twenty volumes, and I am overcome with astonishment.[19]

---

[18]   Letter of May 1841, from Isabelle Chovelon, citing Sand's *Correspondance*, in *George Sand et Solange: Mère et fille* (Paris: Christian Pirot, 1994), 176; subsequent references are provided in the text.

[19]   "Il m'a fallu beaucoup de temps pour noircir une quarantaine de volumes. Que d'heures dérobées au voyage, à la flânerie, à la lecture, voire à une féminine et saine coquetterie. Comment diable s'arrangeait George Sand? Cette robuste ouvrière de lettres trouvait moyen de finir un roman, d'en commencer un autre dans la même heure. Elle n'en perdait ni un amant, ni une bouffée de narghilé, sans préjudice d'une *Histoire de ma vie* en vingt volumes, et j'en tombe d'étonnement." Colette, *L'Étoile vesper*, in *Œuvres*, vol. 4, ed. Claude Pichois and Alain Brunet (Paris: Gallimard [Pléiade], 2001), 878; the translation is my modification of *The Evening Star*, in Colette, *Recollections*, trans. David Le Vay (New York, Macmillan, 1986), 284–85; all references are to these editions.

In fact Colette is not using the very same balance system at stake in the texts we have been considering; she is reckoning books and lovers, books and leisure, books and opium, books and makeup, books and clothes—and so on—but she makes not even an allusion to books and children.

This is not a shaggy dog story, even though Colette's concerns in the original passage turn out to be so very much beside the point of Sand's (and Hiddleston's) writing/child dilemma. But my point *depends* on the apparent pointlessness of reading Sand as mother when in fact Colette meant to be reading her as hedonist. My larger point, more accurately a *point d'intérrogation*, or question mark, has to do with the phenomenon of retrospective reading and writing, and the projections or retrojections we carry with us in this enterprise.

We have been looking at a reading chain (I say a chain and not a bond of reading, because it extends backward in time and is for the most part neither dynamic nor interactive): Sand is read by Colette who is read by Hiddleston who is read by me, and I, by implication, in turn am read by you. At each point there is a play of identification: a transference, as it were. Let me begin to explain the links at the near end of this chain by disclosing an affiliation with Janet Hiddleston. Although I never had the opportunity to meet Hiddleston before her sudden and untimely death in 2000, I did get to know her daughter, Suzanne Raitt, a few years earlier, when we were fellows together at the National Humanities Institute. Through the daughters' friendship Hiddleston generously offered to let me read her manuscript at that time, prior to publication, when I was working on *Histoire de ma vie*. I won't venture into detail about my identifications and disidentifications with this other, older Janet, also a scholar and teacher of French, a writer, a daughters' mother (she had four), and implicitly one of the very rare foremothers I've been privileged to encounter. Yet I want to emphasize that a psychic investment exists, and inevitably influences the way I read (and no doubt misread) Hiddleston's work on Sand through Colette. In turn I would suggest that her identifications with Sand (and Colette) as mother and foremother orient her readings; Hiddleston's choices, her decisions about how to weight the scales of her own life, repeat or conflict with Sand's (and Colette's) solutions in ways that help to determine how and why she reads their texts.

I think it is important that we hold together in an uncertain knot these three mismatched threads: Hiddleston's picture, mistakenly attributed to Colette, of a George Sand "having it all," Colette's image of a George Sand having a fine old time, and the portrait I etched of a George Sand struggling to make family lines and work deadlines meet.[20] The contradictory strands, far from invalidating one another, together mark the tangled space of writing what I have been calling salvation biography: the project of saving the mother's (often virtual) text by creating a foremothers' lineage that reflects one's own disappointments and desires. Such a project is epitomized by myths of matriarchal prehistory,[21] or on a more modest scale, by the Laffont series of biographies of women by women that I discussed earlier, which aims to project the illustrious images of contemporary women onto their unwritten ancestors. Let me recall that the proclamation on the cover of the "Elle était une fois" series proclaims it to be "a collection of encounters between a woman of today and a woman of the days of old...a collection of mirror biographies, where two women reflect each other, echo each other, respond to each other."

Hiddleston's Sand meets Colette's, and my own, and they lead heroically right into this house of mirrors, limning the temptations and dangers that await us when we seek to resurrect or reconstruct stories that are technically inaccessible but emotionally familiar or alluring. The call of such stories, far away within us in a floating, wordless state, suggests an *Unheimlich* turned inside out, so close as to be alien, so intimate that the territory looms unknown.[22]

I no longer believe, as I once did, that we need to leave maternal resurrection biography untouched, rejected for its sins against authenticity and aesthetics. But if much is at stake in these untold mother stories, the question of how they might be told, otherwise, without doing excessive violence to truth, and beauty, and personal

---

[20] See Chovelon, *George Sand et Solange.*

[21] See, for example, Cynthia Eller, *The Myth of Matriarchal Prehistory: Why an Invented Past Won't Give Women a Future* (Boston: Beacon Press, 2000).

[22] As my metaphors suggest, there is work to be done here on feminine nostalgia: on the links between maternal salvation stories and a longing for home. It is time to confront the quest for maternal biography with the considerable body of nostalgia theory. See, for example, the work of Jean Starobinski, Michael Roth, Svetlana Boym, Susan Stewart, and Sigmund Freud (whose collected works present the grandest theory of nostalgia ever).

agency, remains. I want, in closing, to review some of the recurring preoccupations of the preceding essays, and to use them to speculate on some new avenues of approach.

Looking Back

In the beginning were the reconstructed stories: women's stories written as daughters' stories, stories of mothers' lives, would-be histories and sometime fantasies that establish or attempt retroactively to instate a lineage, a legacy, a heritage of women's intellectual and aesthetic achievement, and a matrix of influence. The practical problems are manifest: missing or unrecorded information,[23] buried elements that emerge in fragments through archival work, to be reconstituted as a whole, totalized, or interpreted in the reflected light of current-day concerns.

There followed the emergence of more elusive and more problematic ethical-ideological-philosophical presuppositions inherent in the salvation mission, regardless of its material fruitfulness or shortfall in any individual case. The ethical problems feminists confront in the struggle to give voice to unrecorded women's lives were first raised for me in my encounter with the paradigmatic silent woman—the hysteric—and were prolonged by my frustrated efforts to retell her story without replacing it.[24] Now, years later, and in this other context, I am not convinced that contemporary feminist efforts to fill in lost stories of women's lives, however sincerely intentioned, can any more successfully or nonviolently retrieve these lives than the endeavors of the medical men of the nineteenth century who spoke, in their own voice, for—*in the place of*—the archetypal silent woman: the hysteric. The analogy suggests a kind of fetishistic logic inherent in the retrieval mission, as allegorized in the case of the quest for Kuchuk Hanem through the eyes of Louise Colet: in the very attempt to save women's

---

[23]   See my comments on Sand's autobiography in chapter 3; Linda Nochlin, "Why Have There Been No Great Woman Artists?" in *Women, Art, Power, and Other Essays* (London: Thames & Hudson, 1991), chap. 7; Christine Planté, *La Petite Soeur de Balzac* (Paris: Seuil, 1984).
[24]   See Janet Beizer, *Ventriloquized Bodies: Nineteenth-Century Narratives of Hysteria in France* (Ithaca: Cornell University Press, 1994).

lives in the interest of telling a different story about them, feminism appropriates the same old methodological models, and so mimes patriarchy's work of violation and suppression of difference.

The salvation mission, like the related venture to recuperate hysteria by women seeking retrospectively to give it a voice, involves not only a voice-over that, ironically, replicates what we hear in nineteenth-century medical presentations of hysteria's case, but a historical switch as well. In simplest terms, the lives that salvation narratives yearn to express are sought by *looking back* at a shadowy past. The cultural stakes of this retrospection lie deep and strong. One rarely looks back without having some sense of what one hopes to find. What is being sought? What is lost, and what urgency compels its rediscovery? Christa Wolf's words about the popularity of goddess myths bear repeating: "This harking back to an irretrievable ancient past reveal[s] more clearly than anything else the desperate plight in which women see themselves today."[25]

What are the means and myths by which the salvation quest is structured? Janice Haaken turns to biblical legend for a myth that might play opposite Oedipus to represent women's vision in apposition to men's, and finds the story of Lot's wife: "But if men suffer from guilt over what they cannot bear to see in their unconscious desires and, like Oedipus, gouge out their own eyes, women have faced an opposing dilemma. For Lot's wife, the story ends before we know what she has seen.... Like Lot's wife, women have their experiences entombed in men's accounts of the past. Unraveling entombed memories is...both a creative and a revelatory project."[26] Although the act of looking back may seem to be, as Haaken suggests, "creative and...revelatory" for women, in fact "transgressive, even sinful,"[27] it isn't necessarily working to blaze new visionary pathways or to invent new ways of looking. I am alluding first to the phantasmatic element attached to the processes of mirroring and idealizing that we have seen exemplified, respectively, by the "Elle était une fois" series of

[25] Christa Wolf, *Cassandra*, trans. Jan von Heurck (London: Virago, 1984), 195.
[26] Janice Haaken, *Pillar of Salt: Gender, Memory, and the Perils of Looking Back* (New Brunswick, N.J.: Rutgers University Press, 1998), 5. Although Haaken's specific subject is recollections of childhood sexual abuse, her study opens onto the larger realm of women's memory.
[27] Ibid., 1.

biographies and by Eunice Lipton's quest, in which desire retrojected produces memory, shapes recollection and reconstruction. Such processes may revise but do not dismantle or radically reconfigure the Freudian Family Romance scenario according to which the (presumably male) child navigates the Oedipal complex by staging fantasies that reinvent his family. For women, in particular, raised in a culture that holds mothers to the impossible and contradictory standards of omnipotence and subservience, ideality and insignificance, such fantasies can only cast the inverted shadow of doomed presents and unattainable futures onto imaginary pasts.[28] The experiences of Lot's wife may be so deeply "entombed" in men's accounts of the past, or, in other terms, so tightly bound up and wound around them, as to be inextricable, inoperable, not independently viable.

Looking back, I've been suggesting, is not an ideologically autonomous activity. At play in the resurrection of illustrious maternal precursors are not only proto-feminist voices such as that of Virginia Woolf, but also the Fathers' voices: among them we hear echoes of Freud's Family Romance model, and Harold Bloom's paradigm of strong precursor fathers. The Fathers' voices reverberate as well in the African American search for roots, which intersects the mother quest in interesting ways. A glance at how the mother rescue mission is symbolically situated in this greater cultural geography will be enlightening.

The Morals of Genealogy

1855: George Sand begins *Histoire de ma vie* with hundreds of pages about her father and her paternal legacy, tracing her father's family through the Maréchal de Saxe and back to Auguste II, king of Poland. She gives her maternal antecedents short shrift, though emphatically

---

[28] See Jessica Benjamin, "The Omnipotent Mother," in *Like Subjects, Love Objects: Essays on Recognition and Sexual Difference* (New Haven: Yale University Press, 1995), 81–113; Lynn Davidson, *Motherloss* (Berkeley: University of California Press, 2000); and Dorothy Dinnerstein's superb classic analysis of the fatal consequences of women's powerful child-rearing roles, *The Mermaid and the Minotaur: Sexual Arrangements and Human Malaise* (New York: Harper & Row, 1976).

not by choice: "One is not only the offspring of one's father, one is also a little, I believe, that of one's mother—*maybe even more so.*"[29] Sand goes on, however, to attribute the obscurity of her maternal line to economic rather than gender factors: "The genealogies of ordinary people cannot compete with those of the rich and powerful in this world. No title, no escutcheon, no painting preserves the memory of these obscure generations who spend time on this earth without leaving a trace. The poor die entirely."[30] Unable to trace her mother's line in history, she tracks it in myth, replacing traditional genealogy with an intriguing ornithological totem.[31] Family tree is supplanted by family nest.

1923: Virginia Woolf famously analyzes the difficulties history has imposed on women writing, after the practical impediments of children and money, education, space and time: "But whatever effect discouragement and criticism had upon their writing...that was unimportant compared with the other difficulty which faced them...*that is that they had no tradition behind them....For we think back through our mothers if we are women.*"[32] What is often overlooked in the adaptation of this sentence to a myriad of heritage-seeking feminist purposes is what follows it in Woolf's text. For at this point of stating the futility of thinking backward when there is no available tradition to draw on, "no common sentence ready for her use,"[33] Woolf changes the direction of her thoughts, begins to think *ahead* from her present standpoint of reflection on nineteenth and early twentieth-century women's writing, implies a need to invent rather than to retrieve. Musing on the affinity of the woman writer for the form of the novel, "young enough to be soft in her hands," she

[29] George Sand, *Story of My Life: The Autobiography of George Sand*, trans. Thelma Jurgrau et. al. (Albany: SUNY Press, 1991), 77; Sand, *Histoire de ma vie*, in *Œuvres autobiographiques*, vol. 1, ed. Georges Lubin (Paris: Gallimard [Pléiade], 1970–71), 15, emphasis added.

[30] Sand, *Story of My Life*, 114; Sand, *Histoire de ma vie*, 1:71. Despite Sand's analysis, gender factors are always at work in occult ways; it is unlikely that a rich woman from a prominent family would have taken a poor proletarian man as her lover.

[31] See chapter 3 for details.

[32] Virginia Woolf, *A Room of One's Own* (London: Harcourt Brace Jovanovich, 1929), 79, emphasis added.

[33] Ibid.

wonders about pliability, reshaping, change: "Yet who shall say that even now 'the novel' (I give it inverted commas to mark my sense of the words' inadequacy), who shall say that even this most pliable of all forms is rightly shaped for her use? No doubt we shall find her knocking that into shape for herself when she has the free use of her limbs; and providing some new vehicle.... But these are difficult questions which lie in the twilight of the future."[34]

1976–1980: A special workshop session at the Midwest Modern Language Association on mothers and daughters in literature turns into a volume of essays titled *The Lost Tradition: Mothers and Daughters in Literature.* In their preface and introduction Cathy N. Davidson and E. M. Broner describe the essays, collectively or individually, as "a looking back in order to look forward," "a mourning for the mother-daughter relationship in contemporary fiction," a process of "restoring the blurred image of our mothers," and "a lineage not traced in any genealogy."[35]

1987–1993: Under the direction of Marie-Josèphe Guers, the publishing house of Robert Laffont issues a series of twenty-two "mirror biographies" of women "of old" by illustrious contemporary women, which appear under the rubric "Elle était une fois."

The specific entries on this timeline are arbitrary, culled from among many others addressed in the preceding pages of this book, and from many others left unmentioned, but they are emblematic of the attempt to rehabilitate (literal and metaphorical) genealogy for women. The enterprise becomes more fraught, however, when juxtaposed with a parallel timetable whose entries should be collated with the first for a more comprehensive picture.

1909: Freud publishes his influential "Family Romances," theorizing on how a child distances himself from his parents by creating

---

[34]   Ibid., 80.
[35]   Cathy N. Davidson and E. M. Broner, eds., *The Lost Tradition: Mothers and Daughters in Literature* (New York: Frederick Ungar, 1980), foreword, xi–xii; intro., 2.

fantasies of illegitimacy or adoption through which a more illustrious lineage may emerge.

1954: Robert Kemp writes an article in *Elle* magazine that probably would be forgotten had it not inspired Barthes's "Romans et enfants." After the annotated group photo about which Barthes writes his mythology comes the lesser-known accompanying text, headed "Since Colette, no more 'bluestockings': instead, writers"[36]—a heading that gives a reasonably good indication of the author's patronizing tone and perspective relative to the burgeoning numbers of his female colleagues. Kemp goes on to emphasize the isolation of women writers in history and culture, and their relative obscurity (just a few over the vast course of history are known, and those only to "very scholarly men," who, despite their great cultivation and knowledge, seem aware of these women writers less for their literary success than for their *succès de scandale*). Not surprisingly, those who escaped the shadows to which they were consigned by their sex in order to become known to the male intellectual elite do not seem to have done so by the power of their letters. They include George Sand, "whose cigars and multiple love affairs were horrifying to families"; Louise Colet, "whose fits of anger were more famous than wine"; Colette, "all the more influential because she was censured"; and Simone de Beauvoir, "faithful lieutenant of the great captain of existentialism." The opening remark in Kemp's commentary gives a good summary sense of the whole: "They used to be called 'bluestockings,' for unclear reasons, and this was not meant to be flattering. Someone unkindly declared one day: 'A witty woman? Let's run in the other direction.' They constituted a tiny group in society, one *almost without genealogy.*"[37]

1973: Harold Bloom revises Freud's "Family Romances" as a theory of intrapoetic relationships in *The Anxiety of Influence,* arguing that "strong poets...wrestle with their strong precursors, even to the death[,]...denying obligation as the hungry generations go on

---

[36] "Depuis Colette, plus de 'bas bleus': des écrivains." Kemp, "70 Romancières," 64–65.
[37] Ibid., emphasis added.

treading one another down."[38] Bloom's paradigm of strong precursor fathers whose textual precedents instill an anxiety of influence in a line of literary sons doesn't disparage women's poetic genealogy, as Kemp's narrative does, but simply omits all thought of it.

1976–1977: Alex Haley's *Roots,* the book, advertised as a "genealogical novel," followed by *Roots,* the television miniseries, take the world by storm, not only, according to the thirtieth-anniversary edition, "tap[ping] deeply into the black American hunger for an African ancestral home" but also, as *Kirkus Reviews* points out, "setting off a wave of interest in books about America's many pasts."[39] The order of influence between the pandemic American obsession with genealogy and the more specific African American quest is, of course, a chicken-egg question, but the two are no doubt imbricated, as is the contemporary hunger for a feminine poetic lineage.

2006–2007: Henry Louis Gates hosts a PBS documentary series, *African-American Lives,* that presents the use of genealogy and DNA to trace the roots of eight prominent African Americans back through American history to Africa. In conjunction with this program he publishes *Finding Oprah's Roots: Finding Your Own,* drawing his material from the episode featuring the genealogical/genetic research for constructing Oprah Winfrey's family tree.[40] The publicity release on the PBS Web site explains the motivation for the series, which engaged a team of researchers, genealogists, and forensic DNA analysts to "reconstruct the family trees" of four entertainers, an astronaut, a neurosurgeon, a pastor, and a sociologist: "By spotlighting African-American role models, the series hopes to inspire millions to consider their own heritage, and underscore for all Americans the importance of knowing their past, in order to unlock the future." This goal is immediately confirmed by a quotation from Gates: "I hope that this

---

[38] Harold Bloom, *The Anxiety of Influence: A Theory of Poetry* (New York: Oxford University Press, 1973), 5–6.

[39] Michael Eric Dyson, intro. to Alex Haley, *Roots: The Saga of an American Family,* Thirtieth-Anniversary Edition (New York: Vanguard Books, 2007), ix; Gregory McNamee, in *Kirkus Reviews,* June 1, 2007, 515.

[40] Henry Louis Gates Jr., *Finding Oprah's Roots: Finding Your Own* (New York: Crown, 2007). The PBS documentary *Oprah's Roots* first aired in January 2007.

project will encourage...all Americans, especially those of African descent—to explore their roots."[41]

The question of origins evoked by Gates and the PBS African American genealogy project, as by the *Roots* novel and miniseries thirty years earlier, is poignantly reiterated in the *African-American Lives* publicity release on the PBS Web site: "For some Americans, the essential question 'Where do I come from?' cannot be answered; their history has been lost or stolen."[42] In *Finding Oprah's Roots*, Gates rephrases the question in an arresting way:

> Have you ever been to Ellis Island?...For millions of immigrants, it was the gateway not only to the New World, but to a veritable new world of identity....People come to Ellis Island every day...hoping to find a connection to history by uncovering or reexperiencing their ancestors' past....Unfortunately, there is no Ellis Island for those of us who are descendants of survivors of the African slave trade. Our ancestors...were stripped of their history, their family ties, and their cultural and linguistic identities.[43]

This same year, Michael Dyson looks back and assesses the change wrought thirty years earlier by Haley's *Roots:* "No longer were we *genealogical nomads* with little hope of learning the names and identities of the people from whose loins and culture we sprang."[44] Dyson's language is marked by a metaphorical shift from the arboreal to the human, but its tenor of deracination is unchanged.

The uprooting that has until recently so absolutely cut off the African record for most African Americans is a searing version of the genealogical severance that Robert Kemp and Virginia Woolf

---

[41] PBS News, "African-American Lives, a four-hour documentary series tracing black history through genealogy and DNA science, to premiere February 2006 on PBS," 1, http://www.pbs.org/aboutpbs/news/20050713_africanamerican lives.html.

[42] Ibid.

[43] Gates, *Finding Oprah's Roots*, 21.

[44] Dyson, intro., ix, emphasis added.

addressed, the first with disdain and the second with empathy, in terms of writing women, and that Davidson and Broner evoke with nostalgic determination: "We are looking for a lineage not traced in any genealogy. We are tracking our roots back to ancient mothers whose origins are the earth itself but whose traces are as dust."[45] I'd like to begin to question the way the ancestral void is culturally represented by quoting from an article in the *Philadelphia Daily News* previewing the same PBS series I've been discussing. The author of this article injects a minor note of skepticism into the genealogical-genetic quest for Gates's eight celebrity subjects: "At the very least, we know that these people are famous and successful not for who their distant ancestors were but for who they themselves are, and in some cases despite who their parents were."[46]

By displacing the focus away from the vertical axis associated with looking back, searching for one's identity through a line of ancestors, and tracing teleological pathways from origins to ends, this note of caution broaches the possibility of recentering the lives of the disinherited in a temporally present, spatially horizontal mode. It begins to suggest that the enterprise of looking back through the forebears should not be naturalized. To put it another way, it leads to wondering whether the contemporary fascination with genealogical knowledge, and the devastation occasioned by its lack, might be culturally induced, and complicit with Western institutions.[47] My intent is not to minimize the suffering that genealogical erasure can inflict, but rather to inquire into its causes and to consider its ideological bases.

---

[45] Davidson and Broner, *The Lost Tradition*, 2. I mean to insist on the difference between this nostalgic proclamation and Virginia Woolf's observation—despite the fact that it has been appropriated to found women's postmodern genealogical thinking—that one can't think with an absent tradition.

[46] "Henry Louis Gates Delves into Celebs' Genealogy on PBS," *Philadelphia Daily News*, February 1, 2006.

[47] The fact that genealogy is already prominent in the Bible supports my point about cultural institutionalization. The genealogy obsession in America has begun to foment journalistic commentary. Among the numerous articles speculating on its causes and forms, see John Seabrook's *New Yorker* article "The Tree of Me" (March 26, 2001, 58–71), discussed in chapter 5; and Steven Pinker's essay "Strangled by Roots: The Genealogy Craze in America," which appeared as I was finishing these pages, in *The New Republic*, August 6, 2007, 32–35.

The idea of genealogy in Western societies is patrilineal. The idea of lost lineage, uprooted family trees, unanchored psyches—graphically rendered by Dyson's figure of the "genealogical nomad"—is patrilineal as well. It strikes me, then, that there is something profoundly conservative in the enterprise of looking back in order to place oneself and define one's identity relative to others. Women and other groups that have not had the privilege of influence cannot know its anxiety—though they may, as I earlier suggested, be subject to a secondary anxiety about its lack. Although I understand why it is tempting for the culturally disenfranchised (notably women and African Americans) to claim the accoutrements of the enfranchised, I'm not sure that an appropriation of dominant ideological means well serves the purpose of distinguishing and legitimizing the identity of culturally subjugated others. Such a stance reveals a derivative and conservative approach to the question of imagining the past.[48]

What I have been calling genealogical thinking, as I suggested in earlier chapters, encompasses not only the idea of tracing ancestors and defining oneself by taking the measure of one's legacy (variously understood as the transmission of bloodlines, genes, ethnicity, money, property, religion, social or economic status, and so on), but linear thought more generally: teleology, the logic of the endpoint, of narratives that tie beginnings to ends, and mimesis, the logic of the mirror, of faith in the reproducibility of model and copy, including a secondary critical mimesis that believes in the possibility of accounting for literature. What are the alternatives to thinking genealogically? What are alternative metaphors and models, potential new ways of saying and doing? How can women begin to reimagine lost time, lost lives, outside of modes that would plant us in the dirt alongside a river, condemned, like Narcissus, to see our own eyes mirrored back to us for generations past and future; or encrust us in the salt of our nostalgic tears, like Lot's wife, frozen for all time in a narrative not of our making; or fix us in trees, hung from ancestral limbs, forever cured of our nomadic genealogy? Such a cure will not necessarily improve our condition.

---

[48]   A reviewer of a grant proposal I submitted for this book expressed surprise that I invoked Bloom's conservative and outmoded *Anxiety of Influence*. I can only respond, belatedly, that this is precisely the point.

Thinking outside the Mirror: Fracturing, Uprooting, Listening, Responding

Gilles Deleuze and Félix Guattari place a higher value on metaphoric nomads—so much so that they name the kind of thinking they call for in *Anti-Oedipus* and practice in *A Thousand Plateaus* "nomad thought." It is defined in opposition to "state philosophy," which is representational, analogous, and based on principles of self-resemblance, fixity, and identity. This official kind of thinking, termed "phallogocentric" by postmodern deconstructive feminists, is named "arborescent" by Deleuze and Guattari—a metaphor that continues in the conceptual mode I have been referring to as "genealogical thinking," whose preferred metaphor is the family tree, whose aesthetic principle is mimesis, and whose operational image is the mirror. Nomad thought, on the contrary, works outside institutionally based conceptual systems, is mobile, fluid, antihistorical, and immersed in change.[49] It is correlated with a different model of knowledge, which they name "rhizomatic," to challenge the established "arborescent" or "root" model.

What does it mean to substitute rhizomes for trees?[50] Vastly different from a tree or a root, which "plots a point, fixes an order" (7), and follows a binary logic of "tracing and reproduction" (12), a rhizome "connects any point to any other point" (21), and is associated with the logic of "a map that is always detachable, connectable, reversible, modifiable, and has multiple entryways and exits" (21). It has "no beginning or end; it is always in the middle, between things, interbeing, *intermezzo*... another way of traveling and moving: proceeding from the middle, coming and going rather than starting and finishing"

[49] On "nomad thought," see Gilles Deleuze and Félix Guattari, *Anti-Oedipus: Capitalism and Schizophrenia*, trans. Robert Hurley, Mark Seem, and Helen R. Lane (Minneapolis: University of Minnesota Press, 1983); Deleuze and Guattari, *A Thousand Plateaus: Capitalism and Schizophrenia*, trans. Brian Massumi (1987; reprint, New York: Continuum, 2003); Deleuze, "Nomad Thought," in *The New Nietzsche*, ed. David B. Allison (New York: Dell, 1977), 142–49. See too Massumi's introduction to his translation of *A Thousand Plateaus*, x–xv, for an excellent concise summary.

[50] See Deleuze and Guattari, *A Thousand Plateaus*, chap. 1, "Introduction: Rhizome," for the most detailed development of this model; subsequent references are provided in the text.

(25). Rhizomatic thinking works laterally through the conjunction "and...and...and" (25), in opposition to the operation of arborescent thinking, which is rooted in history and filiation.

Deleuze and Guattari signal the socioeconomic inflections of genealogy, well over a century after George Sand made similar observations about what she called "the genealogies of ordinary people." Here again is George Sand: "No title, no escutcheon...preserves the memory of the obscure generations who spend time on this earth without leaving a trace";[51] and then Deleuze and Guattari: "There is always something genealogical about a tree. It is not a method for the people" (8). In contrast, "the rhizome is an antigenealogy" (11, 21). They pursue the opposition: "The tree is filiation, but the rhizome is alliance, uniquely alliance" (25). Their words and my own, which I retrieve now from my discussion of biological and adoptive motherhood (chapter 5), resonate deeply: "A cultural hierarchization of [different forms of] family connectedness...places genealogy before affiliation." The echoing may serve to support a leap from the particularities of adoption to a more overarching kind of thinking: abstracted, adoption is an element of a larger epistemological model that offers an alternative to the familiar biological-genealogical one.

When we consider the discursive reaches of family trees and roots, it is clear that the metaphors we live by are not "just rhetoric"— random words, arbitrary images—but models for knowing and apprehending experience. Deleuze and Guattari comment that "it is certainly odd how the tree has dominated Western reality and all of Western thought, from botany to biology and anatomy, but also gnosiology, theology, ontology, all of philosophy...the root-foundation, *Grund, racine, fondement*" (18). We must add to this list what is already implied: that the tree has also dominated Western narrative and is central to the traditional Western novel. Zola's *Rougon-Macquart* cycle is the emblem of the arborescent novel: this archetype of mimesis, doubly structured by the family tree (*l'arbre généalogique*) and its pathological double, the "tree of nervosity" (*l'arbre de la nervosité*), current in scientific circles of the period, displays the degenerative reflections of inherited pathology over the course of five generations.

---

[51] Sand, *Story of My Life,* 114; Sand, *Histoire de ma vie,* 1:71.

The everyday stories we tell about our individual lives tend to obey the same logic of generational reflection (purged of the pathological, which, however, remains symbolically focal), still, today. A feature article in *New York Magazine* called "The Nuclear Family, Exploded," talks about how the cultural anxiety level is raised as the traditional idea of family is being challenged by new structures (stepparents, gay parents, interracial parents, the blending of biological and adopted children) even in the face of the genealogy mania, "a cultural obsession with the heritability of just about everything."[52] One parent interviewed tells of what she has learned from parenting an adopted child after a newborn birth child with whom she noticed "the unnerving attention paid to any reflection of my husband and myself" (92). She muses: "Yet each of us [knows]...how much of growing up is about choosing a story, one that explains what made us who we are. This is a culture that increasingly fetishizes one shard of that story, the blood connection" (92). But there are other stories, not about "the primacy of our origins" but about "the daily work of parenting," in the interviewee's words (92)—and also about the unfolding of self and the surprises of becoming.

Inheritance is not the only model, genealogy not the only rhetoric, mimesis not the sole aesthetic for narrative. Ross Chambers introduced the metaphor of "fostering" in his essay on Binjamin Wilkomirski's purported authorship of *Fragments.*[53] An initial reception of

---

[52] Emily Nussbaum, "The Nuclear Family, Exploded," *New York Magazine*, August 20, 2007, 26; subsequent references are provided in the text. One informant responds, with evident relish about breaking the chain of inheritance, "I'm glad my children are not genetically related to me. There are many of us in that camp. There are things in me, physically, biologically, psychologically, that shouldn't be inherited" (91).

[53] Ross Chambers, "Orphaned Memories, Foster-Writing, Phantom Pain: The *Fragments* Affair," in *Extremities: Trauma, Testimony, and Community,"* ed. Nancy K. Miller and Jason Tougaw (Urbana: University of Illinois Press, 2002), 92–111. The essay is included in revised form, retitled as "Orphaned Memories, Phantom Pain: Toward a Hauntology of Discourse" in Chambers's *Untimely Interventions: Aids Writing, Testimonial, and the Rhetoric of Haunting* (Ann Arbor: University of Michigan Press, 2004), 189–243; subsequent references are provided in the text. I quote from the earlier version because its emphases better suit my purposes. The Wilkomirski affair tends to provoke heated debate and hot passions about both the ethics of appropriating memories (especially those assumed to belong to individual survivors of the Holocaust, or to have been lost to its victims) and the ethics of authorship. Let me make clear before continuing that neither Chambers's argument nor my own, which devolves from his, denies the

Fragments as a powerful and moving Holocaust memoir was followed by public outrage when the memoir was discovered to have
been written by Bruno Dössekker, who was not in fact a Holocaust
survivor, at least not in the sense he attributed to his ostensible
autobiographical narrator-author Wilkomirski, who writes of his
childhood internment in Majdanek and Auschwitz-Birkenau before
arriving at a Swiss orphanage at the end of the war, and later being
adopted by foster parents.[54] Writing beyond the scandal caused by
the revelation of Dössekker's delusion or fraud, which he reinterprets as "cultural symptom" (symptom of the impossible status of
testimonial truth about the extermination [99]), Chambers argues
for the existence of "Wilkomirskis, or orphaned memories, who haunt
the collective consciousness but *need a Dössekker*—a 'host'—if they
are to achieve . . . some degree of discursive status within culture" (98).
Chambers suggests that the uncanny status of *Fragments* (a memoir
that is literally ghostwritten) corresponds to its unlikely transmission of eyewitness testimonies—those of the "silenced voices of
those who died" (99)—the necessarily limited survivor testimony
of children. Clearly "those who did not survive cannot give survivor testimony"—except through the fostering capacity of language.

---

seriousness of these discussions. His intent, however, is to "reframe the discussion and ask what it means for a culture to be haunted by a collective memory"
(92); my own is, in turn, to reframe *his* discussion in order to think about alternatives to genealogical rhetoric. As I proceed in this series of deflections, I refer
readers who may want to know more about the complexities of the Wilkomirski
affair, which is not my subject here, to two sources as a point of departure for further research. Susan Rubin Suleiman, "Do Facts Matter in Holocaust Memoirs?"
in *Crises of Memory and the Second World War* (Cambridge: Harvard University
Press, 2006), 159–77, provides an excellent introduction to the fraught issues of
literary ethics and categories and how they matter for understandings of the Holocaust. Stefan Maechler, *The Wilkomirski Affair: A Study in Biographical Truth*,
trans. John E. Woods (New York: Schocken Books, 2001), is a detailed account by a
historian engaged by Wilkomirski's literary agent to investigate the author's claim
to the authenticity of his memoir; it includes the text of *Fragments.*
[54] "The confusion about what it meant that Wilkomirski was Dössekker who is
not Wilkomirski was compounded by the difficulties that now emerged concerning the book's actual genre. *Fragments* claimed to be memoir, but it could not
now be regarded as autobiographical, since the memories are not Dössekker's but
Wilkomirski's, who however apparently never existed and can't therefore be the
book's author." Chambers, "Orphaned Memories," 94. To complicate matters,
Dössekker changed his name with his identity to Binjamin Wilkomirski when he
became persuaded that he was a child survivor of the Holocaust, so he both *is not*
and *is* the person he is impersonating.

Through his identification with Wilkomirski's pain, Dössekker, himself an orphan, grafts his own childhood story, transformed, onto "the set of orphaned memories named Wilkomirski, in the form of a phantom pain experienced by readers." The survival of these memories is the work of writing that Chambers calls "a fostering of the orphaned." He explains: "Foster writing...fosters in the double sense of that word. It's a surrogate, offering a form of hospitality or pseudo-home to that which is culturally homeless and agencing a phantom cultural existence for it. But thus it fosters, that is, encourages, the entry of the culturally homeless into culture, albeit in the uncanny form it owes to the highly mediated act of its presencing" (101).

Chambers's thesis about Dössekker's surrogate Holocaust memoir has nothing to do with the subject of retrieving mothers' lives, but it has everything to do with formal (rhetorical, generic, aesthetic) questions about how this might be done. The metaphor of "fostering," as it switches rhetorical gears, taking us out of the biological, also shapes the concept of a narrative that crosses genres (it is neither autobiography nor historical fiction nor any other genre clearly identifiable by traditional categories),[55] and introduces an aesthetic that has much more to do with deflected than with reflected truths.

I have been suggesting that the unrepresented stories of women (and, tangentially, of other groups as well) are ill served by master tropes and master narratives—ironically, the very means that have operated as forces of their own repression. Genealogical metaphors, generational narratives, discourses of inheritance are unresponsive to our age and not equipped to write our future in inventive ways. We need new modes whose goals are no longer to reflect and to complete and to impose transcendent truths. We need truths that are relative, fresh stories that are fragmentary and whose transmission can only be oblique, partial, mosaic. We need a new vocabulary and a new rhetoric.[56] Chambers's "fostering" is a pioneering example of a rhetoric that opens wide new vistas of thought.

---

[55] See Chambers, "Orphaned Memories," 94–55, for an indication of the generic quandary.

[56] At times we can catch rhetorical and lexical systems in the act of metamorphosing, as, for example, John Seabrook's observation in "The Tree of Me," cited in chapter 5, that "the controlling structure for the family seems to be evolving from a tree into something more like a root system, hairy with adoptive parents,

The discourses of fostering, and of adoption as I sketched it in chapter 5, begin to challenge biological-genealogical ways of imagining not only the family but also narrative, aesthetics, ethics, and epistemology. As this book unfolded, it encountered other strategies that reject or deflect or replace genealogical thinking. I'll review several, briefly. In chapter 3, George Sand puts in the place of her missing maternal genealogical knowledge a myth both personal and creative: Corambé and the scene of birds winds everywhere from the autobiography through the rampant undergrowth of her novels. In chapter 4, Huguette Bouchardeau coolly refuses nostalgic retrospection with her dismissal of literal and metaphoric lineage in one fell swoop: "George Sand is not at all a model for me. Neither is my mother, by the way."[57] The coincidence of Bouchardeau's distinctive voice and the engaging genre of the interview provokes a reconfiguration of critical senses and stances, privileging critical listening before critical vision and opening critical subjectivity to dialogic modes. In chapter 5, when I address cultural associations of genealogy with property and ownership, the lexical ramifications of the verb "to own" begin to suggest that genealogy has implications, too, for storytelling: not only for

---

two-mommy families, sperm-bank daddies, and other kinds of family appendages that don't fit onto trunks and branches" (58); or Salman Rushdie's musing to the effect that he is not rootless but rather, "multiple-rooted…: I feel not that I've uprooted from everywhere, but that I've rooted in too many places," and he reinterprets roots in an untraditional way (his roots are poly-urban rather than national): "I find myself belonging more to cities than to nations.… [T]hese things seem to be where I put my roots down, you know, the idea of the city rather than the idea of the nation" (interview with John Ashbrook, NPR, *On Point*, September 27, 2005). In both cases the writer is using the word "root" in a qualified and approximate way, as if groping for a concept not exactly covered by the word—a concept perhaps not unlike the one to which Deleuze and Guattari assign the word "rhizome." As I was finishing the notes to this chapter, I came across a book to which I would have liked to give more than the marginal attention I am limited to now. François Noudelmann writes a cultural critique in which he asks questions close to my own, in *Hors de moi* (Paris: Éditions Léo Scheer, 2006), 11: "It is impossible today to escape this pursuit of identity: the father's name, the mother's womb, the ancestral earth.… How did the structures of kinship, so relative in fact, become a dogmatic and normative reference for our mental representations?" Noudelmann's book has the great merit of developing an important distinction between anthropological approaches to genealogy, which examine genealogical conventions as cultural constructions in their very relativity, and normative ("dogmatic") genealogy, which assumes acquired patterns to be driven by natural laws or cultural necessity. (I paraphrase from *Hors de moi*, 11.)

[57] See my interview with Bouchardeau in chapter 5.

the kind of stories we tell but for how we tell them. "Owning," or "owning up," in the sense of confessing, implies narrative authority and entitlement—a presumption of audience and interest that reflects the presumptive centrality of the self, and centralizes the idea of reflection—as opposed to possibilities of dialogue, responsiveness, responsibility. In chapter 6, Colette's experimental forays beyond the mirror model of mother-daughter relations and novelistic form imply bold new modes of critical and ethical thinking. Read conjointly with the work of Jessica Benjamin, Terence Cave, and Kaja Silverman on recognitions, and rethought through my exchange with Bouchardeau, Colette's *Naissance* suggests that recognition, in poetics and criticism as well as human relations, need not be predicated on identification, projection, and domination, but may depend instead on difference, deference, and mutual respect.

Kelly Oliver's work in *Witnessing: Beyond Recognition*, which I hadn't yet read when I wrote the preceding chapters, provides a provocative footnote to my thoughts on recognition.[58] Working from Emmanuel Levinas's perspective on grounding subjectivity in our obligation to the Other, Oliver, like Jessica Benjamin, draws on psychological and neuroscientific research which shows that the behavior of an infant, even newborn, is responsive (13). She proposes a notion of subjectivity based not on domination but on the ability to address the Other—a position she explains as the "ethical obligation to respond and to enable response-ability" (15). She builds the concept of "witnessing" on this two-hinged obligation to be responsive to and to foster responsiveness, giving it an interesting supplementary twist. Witnessing, for Oliver, includes both eyewitness testimony and the possibility of bearing witness to what is potentially beyond what one can oneself see or experience. This is why she calls witnessing "beyond recognition," although she concedes that there are different varieties and interpretations of recognition: "If recognition is necessary to subjectivity, it isn't the kind of recognition... through which we recognize others only when we have understood them and passed judgment on them.... [T]o recognize others requires acknowledging that their experiences are

---

[58]   Kelly Oliver, *Witnessing: Beyond Recognition* (Minneapolis: University of Minnesota Press, 2001); subsequent references are provided in the text.

real even though they may be incomprehensible to us" (106). This begins to sound very much like the phenomenon I called "recognition-in-difference" when it emerged in Colette's *Naissance:* contemplating her mother's ghostly return, Colette imagined that this mother-ghost would initially misrecognize her middle-aged daughter, then recognize her *through* change and alterity, *as other.* Oliver doesn't call for a shift from looking to listening, as I do, but she does disqualify the presumption of vision as "an objectifying gaze," and she specifies that "the problem...is not with vision per se but with the particular notion of vision presupposed in theories of recognition or misrecognition" (11). Oliver further observes that vision could connect rather than separate, that it need not act as a distancing agent, and that it is coordinated with the operation of the other senses. And finally, she rejects "mirroring operations," suggesting that "self-reflection is not a turn inward but a turn toward otherness. It is not a return but a detour" (219).[59]

To the proclaimed goal of the "Elle était une fois" authors to produce "a collection of mirror biographies," I would counter with an analogous detour or deflection. Let me turn to Salman Rushdie's model of the exile's fractured mirror as an opening model. I propose that feminist salvation biographers, like expatriates, are exiles: they are exiles in culture, displacing the experience of geographic or national exile back into time, seeking to reconstruct the past with a broken glass. Cracked mirrors, Rushdie says, necessarily—and even valuably—reflect partial memories, broken objects, *remains.* He explains, "Human beings do not perceive things whole; we are not gods but wounded creatures, cracked lenses, capable only of fractured perceptions."[60] Similarly, Henri Raczymow bases an ethic and an aesthetic on absence and fragmentation: "In my work,...a void is created by the empty memory I spoke of, which propels my writing

---

[59]   The articulation of these various a-genealogical theories and metaphors and strategies is the matter for another book—or better yet, an ongoing conversation. My purpose here is to indicate an escape route from the tired metaphors and models we have lived and thought with, and to suggest that it is time for a stereophonic approach that would let us hear ethics and aesthetics as strains of the same overture, perceiving silence and blanks with respect for their being, and attention to their meaning.

[60]   Salman Rushdie, "Imaginary Homelands," in *Imaginary Homelands: Essays and Criticism, 1981–1991* (London: Granta, 1991), 12.

forward. My books do not attempt to fill in empty memory. They are not simply part of the struggle against forgetfulness. Rather, I try to present memory *as* empty. I try to restore a non-memory, which by definition cannot be filled in or recovered."[61] Shoshana Felman insists on the need to discover one's autobiography *as missing,* and Colette muses at length on *une manque,* a dropped stitch that she wants not to pick up, and which is, *as missing,* integrated within and contributing to the pattern of meaning.[62] Loss is a constituent part of the life story.

What I am gesturing toward, in the place of imaginary biography, would mean sacrificing a dream of transparency in order to assume the story of a life always already lost, and forever irretrievable. Assuming this loss would mean adopting a version of the stance Alain Corbin takes in his reconstructed life of an unknown nineteenth-century clog maker: "to conjure up an image in the round from the shape of the mold, from what the very silence...reveals."[63] Corbin, however, avows a certain disinvestment in and distance from the object of his resurrection: "a man to whom I have no emotional ties, with whom I share no *a priori* faith or mission or commitment."[64] Maternal resurrection quests quite differently obey a connective force more like Marianne Hirsch's notion of "postmemory": a memory whose "connection to its object or source is mediated not through recollection but through an imaginative investment and creation" (420). Assuming the loss with generosity and restraint would mean

---

[61] "Dans mon travail, ...un vide est rendu possible par cette mémoire absente dont je parlais. Elle est chez moi le moteur de l'écriture. Et mes livres ne cherchent pas à compler cette mémoire absente—je n'écris pas, banalement, pour lutter contre l'oubli—mais à la présenter, justement, comme absente. Je tente de restituer une non-mémoire, par définition irrattrapable, incomblable." Henri Raczymow, "La Mémoire troué," *Pardès* 3 (1986), 181; in English, "Memory Shot Through with Holes," trans. Alan Astro, *Yale French Studies* 85 (1994), 104.

[62] Felman, *What Does a Woman Want?* 14–19, 142–51; Colette, *La Vagabonde,* in *Œuvres,* vol. 1, ed. Claude Pichois (Paris: Gallimard [Pléiade], 1984), 1225.

[63] "Pratiquer une histoire en creux, de ce qui est révélé par le silence même." Alain Corbin, *Le Monde retrouvé de Louis-François Pinagot: sur les traces d'un inconnu* (Paris: Flammarion, 1998), 13; in English, *The Life of an Unknown: The Rediscovered World of a Clog Maker in Nineteenth-Century France,* trans. Arthur Goldhammer (New York: Columbia University Press, 2001), xii.

[64] "Un être...avec lequel je ne partage, *à priori,* aucune croyance, aucune mission, aucun engagement." Corbin, *Le Monde retrouvé,* 8; *Life of an Unknown,* viii).

also taking a position somewhere between Corbin and Hirsch: that is, not only facing the empty spaces and the blanks but *fostering* the hollows and the holes while resisting the temptation to fill them; taking on absence, opacity, and lack, refusing silence our voice, but giving it our beating heart, and our ear.

SELECT BIBLIOGRAPHY

Adorno, Theodor. "The Essay as Form." Translated by Bob Hullot-Kentor and Frederic Will. *New German Critique* 32 (Spring–Summer 1984): 151–71.

"African-American Lives." PBS News documentary. http://www.pbs.org/aboutpbs/news/20050713_africanamericanlives.html (accessed January 15, 2007).

Apter, Emily. *Feminizing the Fetish*. Ithaca: Cornell University Press, 1991.

Apter, Emily, and William Pietz, eds. *Fetishism as Cultural Discourse*. Ithaca: Cornell University Press, 1993.

Arendt, Hannah. *Eichmann in Jerusalem: A Report on the Banality of Evil*. New York: Penguin, 1964.

Ascher, Carol, Louise DeSalvo, and Sara Ruddick, eds. *Between Women: Biographers, Novelists, Critics, Teachers, and Artists Write about Their Work on Women*. Boston: Beacon Press, 1984.

Auriant, Émile. *Koutchouk-Hanem, L'Almée de Flaubert*. Paris: Mercure de France, 1943.

Backscheider, Paula R. *Reflections on Biography*. Oxford: Oxford University Press, 2001.

Baker, Nicholson. *U and I: A True Story*. New York: Vintage, 1992.

Balzac, Honoré. *La Maison Nucingen*. 313–92. In *La Comédie humaine*. Vol. 6, edited by Pierre-Georges Castex. Paris: Gallimard [Pléiade], 1976–81.

——. *Théorie de la démarche*. 259–302. In *La Comédie humaine*. Vol. 12, edited by Pierre-Georges Castex. Paris: Gallimard [Pléiade], 1976–1981.

Barnes, Julian. *Flaubert's Parrot*. New York: Knopf, 1985.

Barthes, Roland. "Écoute." 217–30. In *L'Obvie et l'obtus*. Paris: Seuil, 1982; in English, "Listening." 245–60. In *The Responsibility of Forms*, translated by Richard Howard. New York: Farrar, Straus and Giroux, 1985.

——. "La Mort de l'auteur." *Mantéia* 5 (1968): 12–17; in English, "The Death of the Author." 142–48. In *Image-Music-Text*, edited and translated by Stephen Heath. London: Fontana/Collins, 1977.

——. *Mythologies.* Paris: Seuil [Points], 1957; in English, *Mythologies,* translated by Annette Lavers. London: Jonathan Cape, 1972.

——. "On échoue toujours à parler de ce qu'on aime." 333–42. In *Le Bruissement de la langue.* Paris: Seuil, 1984.

——. *Le Plaisir du texte.* Paris: Seuil, 1973.

——. *S/Z.* Paris: Seuil, 1970.

Bartholet, Elizabeth. *Family Bonds: Adoption and the Politics of Parenting.* Boston: Houghton Mifflin, 1993.

Bassin, Donna, Margaret Honey, and Meryle Mahrer Kaplan, eds. *Representations of Motherhood.* New Haven: Yale University Press, 1994.

Baumsla, Naomi, and Dia L. Michels. *Milk, Money, and Madness: The Culture and Politics of Breastfeeding.* Westport, Conn.: Bergin & Garvey, 1995.

Beauvoir, Simone de. *Une Mort très douce.* Paris: Gallimard, 1972.

Behar, Ruth. *The Vulnerable Observer: Anthropology That Breaks Your Heart.* Boston: Beacon Press, 1996.

Behdad, Ali. *Belated Travelers: Orientalism in the Age of Colonial Dissolution.* Durham: Duke University Press, 1994.

Beizer, Janet. *Ventriloquized Bodies: Narratives of Hysteria in Nineteenth-Century France.* Ithaca: Cornell University Press, 1994.

Benjamin, Jessica. *Like Subjects, Love Objects: Essays on Recognition and Sexual Difference.* New Haven: Yale University Press, 1995.

Benjamin, Walter. "The Storyteller: Reflections on the Works of Nikolai Leskov." 83–109. In *Illuminations,* edited by Hannah Arendt and translated by Harry Zohn. New York: Schocken, 1969.

Bernheimer, Charles. "'Castration' as Fetish." *Paragraph* 14, no. 1 (March 1991): 3.

——. *Figures of Ill Repute.* Cambridge: Harvard University Press, 1989.

Bersani, Leo. "Mallarmé in Mourning." Review of *A Tomb for Anatole* by Stéphane Mallarmé, translated by Paul Auster. *New York Times Book Review,* January 15, 1984, 10.

Berthier, Philippe. "Corambé: Interprétation d'un mythe." 7–20. In *George Sand,* edited by Simone Vierne. Paris: Sedes, 1983.

Berthu-Courtivron, Marie-Françoise. *Espace, demeure, écriture: La Maison natale dans l'oeuvre de Colette.* Paris: Nizet, 1992.

——. *Mère et fille: L'Enjeu du pouvoir. Essai sur les écrits autobiographiques de Colette.* Geneva: Droz, 1993.

Bidney, Martin. "Parrots, Pictures, Rays, Perfumes: Epiphanies in George Sand and Flaubert." *Studies in Short Fiction* 22 (Spring 1985): 209–17.

Birkerts, Sven. "Biography and the Dissolving Self." *Harper's Magazine* (March 1995): 24–26.

Biskopik, Joan. "High Court's Justice with a Cause." *Washington Post*, April 17, 1995.

Blackburn, Julia. *Daisy Bates in the Desert: A Woman's Life among the Aborigines*. New York: Vintage, 1995.

Bloom, Harold. *The Anxiety of Influence: A Theory of Poetry*. New York: Oxford University Press, 1973.

Bollas, Christopher. *The Shadow of the Object: Psychoanalysis of the Unthought Known*. New York: Columbia University Press, 1987.

Bonnefis, Philippe. "Exposition d'un perroquet." *Revue des sciences humaines* 181 (January–March 1981): 59–78.

Booth, Alison. *How to Make It as a Woman: Collective Biographical History from Victoria to the Present*. Chicago: University of Chicago Press, 2004.

Borges, Jorge Luis. *Dreamtigers*, translated by Mildred Boyer and Harold Marland. Austin: University of Texas Press, 1964.

Bouchardeau, Huguette. *George Sand: La Lune et les sabots*. Paris: Laffont, 1990.

——. Interview with Janet Beizer. Tape recording, July 27, 1999. Paris.

——. *Les Roches rouges: Portrait d'un père*. Paris: Écriture, 1996.

——. *Rose Nöel*. Paris: Seghers, 1990.

Boym, Svetlana. *The Future of Nostalgia*. New York: Basic Books, 2001.

Bozon-Scalzetti, Yvette. "Vérité de la fiction et fiction de la vérité dans *Histoire de ma vie*: Le Projet autobiographique de George Sand." *Nineteenth-Century French Studies* 12–13 (Summer–Fall 1984): 95–118.

Breslin, James E. B. *Mark Rothko: A Biography*. Chicago: University of Chicago Press, 1993.

——. "Terminating Mark Rothko: Biography Is Mourning in Reverse." *New York Times Book Review*, July 24, 1994, 19–20.

Bulletin of the International String Figure Association. Pasadena: ISFA Press, 1994–.

Bulletin of String Figures Association. Tokyo: Nippon Ayatori Kyokai, 1978–93.

Burge, Kathleen. "SJC Quandary: What Determines Motherhood." *Boston Globe*, August 29, 2001.

Butler, Judith. *Gender Trouble: Feminism and the Subversion of Identity*. New York: Routledge, 1999.

Les Cahiers du GRIF. "Le Genre de l'histoire," no. 37/38 (Spring 1988).

Callahan, Ann. "The Vagabond: A Modern Heroine." Chap. 5. In *Writing the Voice of Pleasure: Heterosexuality without Women*. New York: Palgrave, 2001.

Calvino, Italo. "Lightness." Chap. 1. In *Six Memos for the Next Millennium*. New York: Vintage, 1988.

Cardinal, Marie. *Les Mots pour le dire*. Paris: Grasset, 1975.

Carroll, Raymonde. *Cultural Misunderstandings: The French-American Experience*. Translated by Carol Volk. Chicago: University of Chicago Press, 1988.

Cave, Terence. *Recognitions: A Study in Poetics*. London: Oxford University Press, 1988.

Chambers, Ross. "An Invitation to Love: Simplicity of Heart and Textual Duplicity in 'Un Cœur simple.'" 123–50. In *Story and Situation: Narrative Seduction and the Power of Fiction*. Minneapolis: University of Minnesota Press, 1984.

——. *Loiterature*. Lincoln: University of Nebraska Press, 1999.

——."Orphaned Memories, Foster-Writing, Phantom Pain: The *Fragments* Affair." 92–111. In *Extremities: Trauma, Testimony, and Community*, edited by Nancy K. Miller and Jason Tougaw. Urbana: University of Illinois Press, 2002.

——. *Untimely Interventions: AIDS Writing, Testimonial, and the Rhetoric of Haunting*. Ann Arbor: University of Michigan Press, 2004.

Charcot, Jean Martin. *L'Hystérie*, edited by E. Trillat. Toulouse: Privat, 1971.

Chateaubriand, François-René de. *René*. 97–130. In *Atala-René*, edited by Gérard Gengembre. Paris: Pocket, 1996.

Cheever, Susan. *A Woman's Life: The Story of an Ordinary American and Her Extraordinary Generation*. New York: William Morrow, 1994.

Chodorow, Nancy. *The Reproduction of Mothering: Psychoanalysis and the Sociology of Gender*. Berkeley: University of California Press, 1978.

Chovelon, Isabelle. *George Sand et Solange: Mère et fille*. Paris: Christian Pirot, 1994.

Cixous, Hélène. "Sorties." 115–20. In *La Jeune Née* by Hélène Cixous and Catherine Clément. Paris: 10/18, 1975.

Clément, Catherine. *Adrienne Lecouvreur ou le cœur transporté*. Paris: Laffont, 1991.

Cohn, Dorrit. "Fictional *versus* Historical Lives: Borderlines and Borderline Cases." *Journal of Narrative Technique* 19, no. 1 (Fall 1989): 3–24.

Colet, Louise. *Les Pays lumineux*. Paris: E. Dentu, 1879.

——. *Les Pays lumineux: Voyage d'une femme de lettres en Haute Égypte*, edited by Muriel Augry. Paris: Cosmopole, 2001.

Colette. *Bella-Vista*. 558–600. In *The Collected Stories of Colette*, edited by Robert Phelps and translated by Antonia White. New York: Farrar Straus and Giroux, 1983.

——. *Break of Day*, translated by Enid McLeod. New York: Farrar, Straus and Giroux, 1961.

——. *Claudine in Paris*. 189–326. In *The Claudine Novels*, translated by Antonia White. London: Penguin, 1963.

——. *Colette, Sido: Lettres*, edited by Bertrand de Jouvenel, Jeannie Malige, and Michèle Sarde. Paris: des femmes, 1984.

——. *Douze Dialogues de bêtes*. Paris: Mercure de France, 1930.

——. *The Evening Star*. 149–288. In *Recollections*, translated by David Le Vay. New York: Macmillan 1972.

——. *Lettres à sa fille, 1916–1953*, edited by Anne de Jouvenel. Paris: Gallimard, 2003.

——. *My Apprenticeships*. 1–133. In *Uniform Edition of Works by Colette*, translated by Helen Beauclerk. Vol. 9. London: Secker and Warburg, 1957.

——. *My Mother's House and Sido*, translated by Una Vicenzo Troubridge and Enid McLeod. New York: Farrar, Straus and Giroux, 1995.

——. *Œuvres*, edited by Claude Pichois. 4 vols. Paris: Gallimard [Pléiade], 1984–2001.

——. *Œuvres complètes*, edited by Claude Pichois. 16 vols. Paris: Club de l'Honnête Homme, 1973–1976.

——. *Sido*, translated by Enid McLeod. New York: Farrar, Straus and Giroux, 1975.

——. *The Vagabond*, translated by Enid McLeod. London: Penguin, 1954.

Corbin, Alain. *Le Monde retrouvé de Louis-François Pinagot: Sur Les Traces d'un inconnu*. Paris: Flammarion, 1998; in English, *The Life of an Unknown: The Rediscovered World of a Clog Maker in Nineteenth-Century France*, translated by Arthur Goldhammer. New York: Columbia University Press, 2001.

Corbin, Laurie. *The Mother Mirror: Self-Representation and the Mother-Daughter Relation in Colette, Simone de Beauvoir, and Marguerite Duras*. New York: Peter Lang, 1996.

Cottrell, Robert D. *Colette*. New York: Frederick Ungar, 1974.

Crittenden, Ann. *The Price of Motherhood*. New York: Henry Holt, 2001.

Daly, Brenda O., and Maureen T. Reddy, eds. *Narrating Mothers: Theorizing Maternal Subjectivities*. Knoxville: University of Tennessee Press, 1991.

Damrosch, Leo. *Jean-Jacques Rousseau: Restless Genius*. New York: Houghton Mifflin, 2005.

Davey, Moyra, ed. *Mother Reader: Essential Writings on Motherhood*. New York: Seven Stories Press, 2001.

Davidson, Cathy N., and E. M. Broner, eds. *The Lost Tradition: Mothers and Daughters in Literature*. New York: Frederick Ungar, 1980.

Davidson, Lynn. *Motherloss*. Berkeley: University of California Press, 2000.

Delbée, Anne. *Une Femme*. Paris: Presses de la Renaissance, 1982.

Del Castillo, Michel. *Colette, une certaine France*. Paris: Stock, 1999.

Deleuze, Gilles. "Nomad Thought." 142–49. In *The New Nietzsche*, edited by David B. Allison. New York: Dell, 1977.

Deleuze, Gilles, and Félix Guattari. *Anti-Oedipus: Capitalism and Schizophrenia*, translated by Robert Hurley, Mark Seem, and Helen R. Lane. Minneapolis: University of Minnesota Press, 1983.

——. A Thousand Plateaus: Capitalism and Schizophrenia, translated by Brian Massumi. 1987. Reprint, New York: Continuum, 2003.

Deleuze, Gilles, and Claire Parnet. *Dialogues*, translated by Hugh Tomlinson and Barbara Habberjam. New York: Columbia University Press, 1987.

Derrida, Jacques. *Of Grammatology*, translated by Gayatri Chakravorty Spivak. Baltimore: Johns Hopkins University Press, 1974.

Detambel, Régine. *Colette: Comme Une Flore comme un zoo*. Paris: Stock, 1997.

Didier, Béatrice. "Femme/identité/écriture: À Propos De L'*Histoire de ma vie* de George Sand." *Revue des Sciences Humaines* 42 (October–December 1977): 561–76.

Dinnerstein, Dorothy. *The Mermaid and the Minotaur: Sexual Arrangements and Human Malaise*. New York: Harper & Row, 1976.

Du Camp, Maxime. *Un Voyageur en Égypte vers 1850: "Le Nil"* de *Maxime du Camp*, edited by Michel Dewachter and Daniel Oster. Paris: Sand/Conti, 1987.

Dudley, Geoffrey A. "A Rare Case of Female Fetishism." *International Journal of Sexology* 8, no. 1 (August 1954): 32–34.

DuPlessis, Rachel Blau. *The Pink Guitar*. New York: Vintage, 1990.

Dyson, Michael Eric. Introduction to *Roots: The Saga of an American Family* by Alex Haley. ix–xi. Thirtieth Anniversary Edition. New York: Vanguard Books, 2007.

Edelman, Hope. *Motherless Daughters: The Legacy of Loss*. New York: Delta, 1995.

Eisinger, Erica Mendelson, and Mari Ward McCarty, eds. *Colette: The Woman, The Writer*. University Park: Pennsylvania State University Press, 1981.

Eller, Cynthia. *The Myth of Matriarchal Prehistory: Why an Invented Past Won't Give Women a Future*. Boston: Beacon Press, 2000.

Ender, Evelyne. *Sexing the Mind*. Ithaca: Cornell University Press, 1995.

——. "A Writer's Birthpains: Virginia Woolf and the Mother's Share." 257–72. In *Families*, edited by Werner Senn. Tübingen: Gunter Narr Verlag, 1996.

Epstein, William H., ed. *Contesting the Subject: Essays in the Postmodern Theory and Practice of Biography and Biographical Criticism.* West Lafayette, Ind.: Purdue University Press, 1991.

Ernaux, Annie. *Une Femme.* Paris: Gallimard, 1987.

Fahey, Diane. *Metamorphoses.* Sydney: Dangaroo Press, 1988.

Fay-Sallois, Fanny. *Les Nourrices à Paris au XIX siècle.* Paris: Payot, 1980.

Feldman, Jessica R. *Gender on the Divide: The Dandy in Modernist Literature.* Ithaca: Cornell University Press, 1993.

Felman, Shoshana. *What Does a Woman Want? Reading and Sexual Difference.* Baltimore: Johns Hopkins University Press, 1993.

Flaubert, Gustave. *Correspondance*, edited by Jean Bruneau. 6 vols. Paris: Gallimard, 1973–2007.

——. *L'Éducation sentimentale.* 7–163. In *Œuvres complètes*, edited by Jean Bruneau and Bernard Masson. Vol. 2. Paris: Seuil, 1964.

——. *Madame Bovary.* Paris: Flammarion, 1986; in English, *Madame Bovary*, translated by Francis Steegmuller. New York: Random House, 1957.

——. *Trois Contes*, edited by Pierre-Marc de Biasi. Paris: Seuil, 1993.

——. *Trois Contes*, edited by Peter Michael Wetherill. Paris: Garnier, 1988.

——. *Voyage en Égypte*, edited by Pierre-Marc de Biasi. Paris: Grasset, 1991.

Flaubert, Gustave, and George Sand. *Gustave Flaubert–George Sand: Correspondance*, edited by Alphonse Jacobs. Paris: Flammarion, 1981; in English, *Flaubert–Sand: The Correspondence*, translated by Francis Steegmuller and Barbara Bray. London: HarperCollins, 1993.

Flieger, Jerry Aline. *Colette and the Phantom Subject of Autobiography.* Ithaca: Cornell University Press, 1992.

Foucault, Michel. Introduction to *Herculine Barbin: Being the Recently Discovered Memoirs of a Nineteenth-Century French Hermaphrodite*, translated by Richard McDougall. vii–xvii. New York: Pantheon, 1980.

——. "Le 'Non' du père." *Critique* 18, no. 178 (March 1962): 195–209.

Francis, Claude, and Fernande Gontier. *Colette.* Paris: Perrin, 1997.

Frappier-Mazur, Lucienne. "Nostalgie, dédoublement et écriture dans *Histoire de ma vie.*" *Nineteenth-Century French Studies* 17 (Spring–Summer 1989): 265–75.

Freud, Sigmund. "Family Romances." 235–41. In *The Standard Edition of the Complete Psychological Works of Sigmund Freud*, edited by James Strachey et al. Vol. 9. London: Hogarth Press, 1959.

——. "Fetishism." 214–19. In *Sexuality and the Psychology of Love*, edited and translated by Philip Rieff. New York: Collier Books, 1963.

——. "Mourning and Melancholia." 237–58. In *The Standard Edition of the Complete Psychological Works of Sigmund Freud*, edited by James Strachey et al. Vol. 14. London: Hogarth Press, 1957.

——. "The 'Uncanny.'" 122–61. In *On Creativity and the Unconscious*, edited and translated by Benjamin Nelson. New York: Harper and Row, 1958.

Freud, Sigmund, and Josef Breuer. *Studies on Hysteria*. In *The Standard Edition of the Complete Works of Sigmund Freud*, edited by James Strachey et al. Vol. 2. London: Hogarth Press, 1955.

Fuss, Diana. *Identification Papers*. New York: Routledge, 1995.

Gallop, Jane. "The Other Woman." 160–78. In *Thinking through the Body*. New York: Columbia University Press, 1988.

——. "Precursor Critics and the Anxiety of Influence." 105–9. In *Profession*, edited by Rosemary G. Feal. New York: MLA of America, 2003.

Garner, Shirley Nelson, Claire Kahane, and Madelon Sprengnether, eds. *The (M)other Tongue: Essays in Feminist Psychoanalytic Interpretation*. Ithaca: Cornell University Press, 1985.

Gates, Henry Louis Jr. *Finding Oprah's Roots: Finding Your Own*. New York: Crown, 2007.

Gilbert, Sandra, and Susan Gubar. *The Madwoman in the Attic*. New Haven: Yale University Press, 1979.

Gilman, Sander. *Difference and Pathology: Stereotypes of Sexuality, Race, and Madness*. Ithaca: Cornell University Press, 1985.

Giorgio, Adalgisa, ed. *Writing Mothers and Daughters: Renegotiating the Mother in Western European Narratives by Women*. New York: Berghahn Books, 2002.

Goodman, Ellen. "What We Discover as We Get to Know Our Children." *Boston Globe*, August 29, 1993.

Gray, Francine du Plessix. *Rage and Fire: A Life of Louise Colet*. New York: Simon and Schuster, 1994.

Grevisse, Maurice. *Le Bon Usage*. Gembloux, Belgium: Duculot, 1975.

Haaken, Janice. *Pillar of Salt: Gender, Memory, and the Perils of Looking Back*. New Brunswick, N.J.: Rutgers University Press, 1998.

Haddon, Kathleen. *String Games for Beginners*. Cambridge: W. Heffer & Sons, 1958.

Hamilton, Nigel. *Biography: A Brief History*. Cambridge: Harvard University Press, 2007.

Hays, Sharon. *The Cultural Contradictions of Motherhood*. New Haven: Yale University Press, 1996.

Hegel, George Wilhelm Friedrich. *The Phenomenology of Spirit*. Translated by A. V. Miller. Oxford: Clarendon Press, 1977.

Heilbrun, Carolyn. "What Was Penelope Unweaving?" Chap. 8. In *Hamlet's Mother and Other Women*. New York: Columbia University Press, 1990.

——. *Writing a Woman's Life*. New York: Columbia University Press, 1988.

Hewlett, Sylvia Ann. *Creating a Life*. New York: Miramax, 2003.

Hiddleston, Janet. *George Sand and Autobiography: A Reading of Histoire de ma vie*. Oxford: Legenda [European Humanities Research Center], 1999.

Hillman, James. *The Soul's Code: In Search of Character and Calling*. New York: Random House, 1996.

Hirsch, Marianne. "Mothers and Daughters." *Signs* 7, no. 1 (Autumn 1981): 200–222.

——. "Past Lives: Postmemories in Exile." 418–46. In *Exile and Creativity*, edited by Susan Rubin Suleiman. Durham: Duke University Press, 1998.

Holmes, Richard. *Dr. Johnson and Mr. Savage*. New York: Vintage, 1993.

——. *Footsteps: Adventures of a Romantic Biographer*. London: Penguin, 1985.

Hornstein, Gail. "The Ethics of Ambiguity: Feminists Writing Women's Lives." 51–68. In *Women Creating Lives: Identities, Resilience, and Resistance*, edited by Carol E. Franz and Abigail J. Stewart. Boulder: Westview Press, 1994.

Huffer, Lynne. *Another Colette: The Question of Gendered Writing*. Ann Arbor: University of Michigan Press, 1992.

——. *Maternal Pasts, Feminist Futures: Nostalgia, Ethics, and the Question of Difference*. Stanford: Stanford University Press, 1998.

Jacobus, Mary. *First Things: The Maternal Imaginary in Literature, Art, and Psychoanalysis*. New York: Routledge, 1995.

James, Henry. "George Sand." 708–34. In *Literary Criticism: French Writers*. New York: Library of America, 1984.

Joeres, Ruth-Ellen Boetcher, and Elizabeth Mittman, eds. *The Politics of the Essay: Feminist Perspectives*. Bloomington: Indiana University Press, 1993.

Johnson, Barbara. *The Critical Difference: Essays in the Contemporary Rhetoric of Reading*. Baltimore: Johns Hopkins University Press, 1980.

——. *A World of Difference*. Baltimore: Johns Hopkins University Press, 1987.

Jong, Erica. *The Devil at Large: Erica Jong on Henry Miller*. New York: Turtle Bay Books, 1993.

Jouvenel, Bernard de. *Un Voyageur dans le siècle*. Paris: Laffont, 1979.

Jouvenel, Colette de. *Colette*. Paris: Société des amis de Colette, 1982.

Jouvenel, Renaud de. "Mon Enfance à l'ombre de Colette: Lettres de Colette à Renaud de Jouvenel." *La Revue de Paris* (December 1966): 3–19.

Kakutani, Michiko. "Rituals for Grieving Extend Past Tradition into Public Displays." *New York Times*, September 18, 2001.

Kemp, Roger. "70 Romancières, 300 romans: Les Femmes de lettres s'imposent." *Elle* no. 467, December 22, 1954, 62–65.

Klein, Melanie. "Mourning and Its Relation to Manic-Depressive States." 344–69. In *Love, Guilt, and Reparation and Other Works, 1921–1945*. London: Virago, 1988.

——. "Some Theoretical Conclusions Regarding the Emotional Life of the Infant." 198–236. In *Developments in Psychoanalysis*, edited by Melanie Klein et al. London: Hogarth Press, 1989.

Knibiehler, Yvonne, and Catherine Fouquet. *L'Histoire des mères du moyen âge à nos jours*. Paris: Montalba, 1980.

Kofman, Sarah. "Ça cloche." 89–116. In *Les Fins de l'homme: À Partir Du Travail de Jacques Derrida*, edited by Philippe Lacoue-Labarthe and Jean-Luc Nancy. Paris: Galilée, 1981.

Kristeva, Julia. *Le Génie féminin: Colette*. Paris: Fayard, 2002.

——. "Un Nouveau Type d'intellectuel: Le Dissident." *Tel Quel*, no. 74 (Winter 1977): 6–7.

Lacan, Jacques. "L'Instance de la lettre dans l'inconscient ou la raison depuis Freud." 249–289. In *Écrits I*. Paris: Seuil (Points), 1966.

Ladenson, Elisabeth. "Colette for Export Only." *Yale French Studies* 90 (1996): 25–46.

Laforgue, Pierre. *Corambé: Identité et fiction de soi chez George Sand*. Paris: Klincksieck, 2003.

Lastinger, Valérie C. "*La Naissance du jour*: La Désintégration du 'moi' dans un roman de Colette." *French Review* 61, no. 4 (March 1988): 542–51.

Lazarre, Jane. *The Mother Knot*. New York: McGraw-Hill, 1976.

Leclerc, Annie. "La Lettre d'amour." 117–40. In *La Venue à l'écriture* by Hélène Cixous, Madeleine Gagnon, and Annie Leclerc. Paris: Union générale d'éditions, 1977.

Lejeune, Philippe. *L'Autobiographie en France*. Paris: Armand Colin, 1971.

——. *Le Pacte autobiographique*. Paris: Seuil, 1975.

Lessana, Marie-Magdeleine. *Entre Mère et fille: Un Ravage*. Paris: Pauvert, 2000.

Levy, Robert I. "Tahitian Adoption as a Psychological Message." 71–87. In *Adoption in Eastern Oceania*, edited by Vern Carroll. Honolulu: University of Hawaii Press, 1970.

Lifton, Betty Jean. *Journey of the Adopted Self: A Quest for Wholeness*. New York: Basic Books, 1994.

Lipton, Eunice. *Alias Olympia: A Woman's Search for Manet's Notorious Model and Her Own Desire*. New York: Scribners, 1992.

——. "Tracking Manet's *Olympia*: An Art Historian's Trip Out of Art History." Lecture delivered at the University of Virginia, Charlottesville, November 11, 1993.

Lourie, Margaret A., Domna C. Stanton, and Martha Vicinus, eds. "Women and Memory." *Michigan Quarterly Review: Special Issue* 26, no. 1 (Winter 1987).

Lukacher, Maryline. "Fictions biographiques: Flaubert et *Le Voyage en Égypte*." *Revue des sciences humaines* 263 (July–September 2001): 183–93.

Lutwack, Leonard. *Birds in Literature*. Gainesville: University Press of Florida, 1994.

Maechler, Stefan. *The Wilkomirski Affair: A Study in Biographical Truth*, translated by John E. Woods. New York: Schocken Books, 2001.

Magazine littéraire. "Les Écritures du moi: De L'Autobiographie à l'autofiction," no. 409 (May 2002).

Mahuzier, Brigitte. "Colette's 'Écriture gourmande.'" 99–113. In *French Food*, edited by Lawrence R. Schehr and Allen S. Weiss. New York: Routledge, 2001.

Malcolm, Janet. *Reading Chekhov: A Critical Journey*. New York: Random House, 2001.

——. *The Silent Woman: Sylvia Plath and Ted Hughes*. New York: Knopf, 1994.

——. *Two Lives: Gertrude and Alice*. New Haven: Yale University Press, 2007.

Mallet, Francine. *George Sand*. Paris: Grasset, 1976.

Mallet-Joris, Françoise. *La Double Confidence*. Paris: Plon, 2000.

Mannoni, Octave. "Je sais bien, mais quand même...." 9–33. In *Clefs pour l'imaginaire ou l'autre scène*. Paris: Seuil, 1969.

Margadant, Jo Burr. *The New Biography: Performing Femininity in Nineteenth-Century France*. Berkeley: University of California Press, 2000.

Marks, Elaine. *Colette*. New Brunswick, N.J.: Rutgers University Press, 1960.

Martin, Emily. "The Egg and the Sperm: How Science Has Constructed a Romance Based on Stereotypical Male-Female Roles." *Signs* 16, no. 3 (1991): 485–501.

——. *The Woman in the Body: A Cultural Analysis of Reproduction*. Boston: Beacon Press, 1987.

Maury, Alfred. *Croyances et légendes du moyen âge*. Paris: Champion, 1896.

May, Georges. *L'Autobiographie*. Paris: Presses universitaires de France, 1979.

McNamee, Gregory. "Anniversaries: Roots at 30." Review of *Roots: The Saga of an American Family; 30th Anniversary Edition* by Alex Haley. *Kirkus Reviews*, June 1, 2007, 456.

Melchior-Bonnet, Sabine. *The Mirror: A History*, translated by Katharine H. Jewett. New York: Routledge, 2001.

Merwin, W. S. "'Where Late the Sweet Birds Sang.'" Review of *Birds in Literature* by Leonard Lutwack. *New York Review of Books*, August 11, 1994, 40.

Miller, Nancy K. "Arachnologies: The Woman, the Text, and the Critic." 270–95. In *The Poetics of Gender*, edited by Nancy K. Miller. New York: Columbia University Press, 1986.

——. *Bequest and Betrayal: Memoirs of a Parent's Death*. New York: Oxford University Press, 1996.

——. *But Enough about Me: Why We Read Other People's Lives*. New York: Columbia University Press, 2002.

——. "The Entangled Self: Genre Bondage in the Age of the Memoir." *PMLA* 122, no. 2 (March 2007): 537–48.

——. "Women's Autobiography in France: For a Dialectics of Identification." 258–73. In *Women and Language in Literature and Society*, edited by Sally McConnell-Ginet, Ruth Borker, and Nelly Furman. New York: Praeger, 1980.

Modell, Judith S. *Kinship with Strangers: Adoption and Interpretations of Kinship in American Culture*. Berkeley: University of California Press, 1994.

Montaigne, Michel. *The Complete Essays*, translated by Donald Frame. Stanford: Stanford University Press, 1957.

Morris, Sarah P. *Daidalos and the Origins of Greek Art*. Princeton: Princeton University Press, 1992.

Muller, John P., and William J. Richardson, eds. *The Purloined Poe: Lacan, Derrida, and Psychoanalytic Reading*. Baltimore: Johns Hopkins University Press, 1988.

Nabokov, Vladimir. *The Real Life of Sebastian Knight*. New York: Vintage, 1992.

Naginski, Isabelle Hoog. *George Sand mythographe*. Clermont-Ferrand: Presses Universitaires Blaise Pascal, 2007.

——. *George Sand: Writing for Her Life*. New Brunswick, N.J.: Rutgers University Press, 1991.

Nietzsche, Friedrich. *Beyond Good and Evil*, translated by R. J. Hollingdale. Harmondsworth: Penguin, 1973.

Nochlin, Linda. "Why Have There Been No Great Woman Artists?" Chap. 7. In *Women, Art, Power, and Other Essays*. London: Thames & Hudson, 1991.

Noudelmann, François. *Hors de moi*. Paris: Éditions Léo Scheer, 2006.

Nussbaum, Emily. "The Nuclear Family, Exploded." *New York Magazine*, August 20, 2007, 20–27 and 91–92.

Oliver, Kelly. *Witnessing: Beyond Recognition*. Minneapolis: University of Minnesota Press, 2001.

"Oprah's Roots." PBS documentary. Aired January 2007.

Ovid. *Metamorphoses*, translated by Mary M. Innes. Harmondsworth: Penguin, 1976.

Palmer, Gabrielle. *The Politics of Breastfeeding*. London: Pandora, 1988.

Parinaud, André. *Colette, mes vérités: Entretiens avec André Parinaud*. Paris: Éditions Écriture, 1996.

Perrot, Michelle. *Les Femmes ou les silences de l'histoire*. Paris: Flammarion, 1998.

——, ed. *Une Histoire des femmes est-elle possible?* Paris: Rivage, 1984.

Perry, Ruth, and Martine Watson Brownley, eds. *Mothering the Mind*. New York: Homes & Meier, 1984.

Pertman, Adam. *Adoption Nation: How the Adoption Revolution Is Transforming America*. New York: Basic Books, 2000.

Philadelphia Daily News. "Henry Louis Gates Delves into Celebs' Genealogy on PBS," February 1, 2006.

Phillips, Adam. *On Flirtation*. Cambridge: Harvard University Press, 1994.

Pichois, Claude, and Alain Brunet. *Colette*. Paris: Éditions de Fallois, 1999.

Pinker, Steven. "Strangled by Roots: The Genealogy Craze in America." *New Republic*, August 6, 2007, 32–35.

Planté, Christine. *La Petite Sœur de Balzac*. Paris: Seuil, 1984.

Pommier, Chantal. *George Sand et Colette: Concordances et destinée*. Paris: Royer, 2004.

Proust, Marcel. *Contre Sainte-Beuve*, edited by Pierre Clarac. Paris: Gallimard [Pléiade], 1971; in English, *Against Sainte-Beuve*. 1–102. In *Against Sainte-Beuve and Other Essays*, translated by John Sturrick. London: Penguin, 1988.

Racine. *Phèdre*, edited by Boris Donné. Paris: Gallimard [Flammarion], 2000; in English, *Phèdre*, translated by Margaret Rawlings. New York: Dutton, 1962.

Raczymow, Henri. "La Mémoire trouée." *Pardès* 3 (1986): 177–82; in English, "Memory Shot Through with Holes," translated by Alan Astro. *Yale French Studies* 85 (1994): 98–105.

Ramsay, Raylene. *French Women in Politics: Writing Power, Paternal Legitimization, and Maternal Legacies*. New York: Berghahn Books, 2003.

Reid, Martine. "Flaubert et Sand en correspondance." *Poétique* 85 (February 1991): 53–68.

——. *Signer Sand*. Paris: Belin, 2003.

Rhiel, Mary, and David Suchoff, eds. *The Seductions of Biography*. New York: Routledge, 1996.

Rich, Adrienne. *Of Woman Born: Motherhood as Experience and Institution*. New York: Norton, 1976.

Rishbeth, Henry. "Kathleen Haddon." *Bulletin of the International String Figure Association* 6 (1999): 1–16.

Roberts, Cokie. *Founding Mothers: The Women Who Raised Our Nation*. New York: Harper Collins, 1994.

Rose, Phyllis, ed. *The Norton Book of Women's Lives*. New York: Norton, 1993.

——. *The Year of Reading Proust: A Memoir in Real Time*. Washington, D.C.: Counterpoint, 1997.

Roth, Michael S. "Dying of the Past: Medieval Studies of Nostalgia in Nineteenth-Century France." *History and Memory* 3, no. 1 (Spring 1991): 5–29.

Roth, Philip. *The Breast*. New York: Vintage, 1994.

Rousseau, Jean-Jacques. *Œuvres complètes*, edited by Bertrand Gagnebin and Marcel Raymond. Paris: Gallimard [Pléiade], 1959.

Ruddick, Sara. *Maternal Thinking: Toward a Politics of Peace*. Boston: Beacon Press, 1989.

Rushdie, Salman. "Imaginary Homelands." 9–21. In *Imaginary Homelands: Essays and Criticism, 1981–1991*. London: Granta, 1991.

——. Interview with John Ashbrook. *On Point*. National Public Radio, September 27, 2005.

Sagan, Françoise. *Sarah Bernhardt: Le Rire incassable*. Paris: Laffont, 1987.

Said, Edward. *Orientalism*. New York: Vintage, 1979.

Saint Phalle, Nathalie de. *Jane Fillion ou la belle d'un seigneur*. Paris: Laffont, 1988.

Sand, George. *Histoire de ma vie*. In *Œuvres autobiographiques*, edited by Georges Lubin. Vols. 1 and 2. Paris: Gallimard [Pléiade], 1970–71; in English, *Story of My Life: The Autobiography of George Sand*, translated by Thelma Jurgrau et al. Albany: SUNY Press, 1991.

Santner, Eric. *Stranded Objects: Mourning, Memory, and Film in Postwar Germany*. Ithaca: Cornell University Press, 1993.

Sarraute, Nathalie. *Enfance*. Paris: Gallimard, 1983.

Schor, Naomi. "Female Fetishism: The Case of George Sand." 363–72. In *The Female Body in Western Culture*, edited by Susan Rubin Suleiman. Cambridge: Harvard University Press, 1986.

——. *George Sand and Idealism*. New York: Columbia University Press, 1993.

——. "Il et elle: Nohant et Croisset." 269–82. In *George Sand: Une Correspondance*, edited by Nicole Mozet. Paris: Christian Pirot, 1994.

Seabrook, John. "The Tree of Me." *New Yorker*, March 26, 2001, 58–71.

Sheringham, Michael. *French Autobiography: Devices and Desires, Rousseau to Perec*. Oxford: Clarendon Press, 1993.

Showalter, Elaine. *A Literature of Their Own: British Women Novelists from Brontë to Lessing*. Princeton: Princeton University Press, 1977.

Silverman, Kaja. *The Threshold of the Visible World*. New York: Routledge, 1996.

Stallybrass, Peter, and Allon White. *The Politics and Poetics of Transgression*. Ithaca: Cornell University Press, 1986.

Starobinski, Jean. "The Idea of Nostalgia." *Diogènes* 54 (1966): 81–103.

Stewart, Joan Hinde. *Colette*. New York: Twayne, 1996.

Stewart, Susan. *On Longing: Narratives of the Miniature, the Gigantic, the Souvenir, the Collection*. Durham: Duke University Press, 1993.

Suleiman, Susan R. "Do Facts Matter in Holocaust Memoirs?" 159–77. In *Crises of Memory and the Second World War*. Cambridge: Harvard University Press, 2006.

——. "Writing and Motherhood." 113–37. In *Mother Reader: Essential Writings on Motherhood*, edited by Moyra Davey. New York: Seven Stories Press, 2001.

Thurman, Judith. *Secrets of the Flesh: A Life of Colette*. New York: Knopf, 1999.

Tinter, Sylvie. *Colette et le temps surmonté*. Geneva: Slatkine, 1980.

Toesca, Maurice. *Le Plus Grand Amour de George Sand*. Paris: Albin Michel, 1980.

Valéry, Paul. *Œuvres*, edited by Jean Hytier. Paris: Gallimard [Pléiade], 1987.

Vinton, Iris. *The Folkways Omnibus of Children's Games*. Harrisburg, Pa.: Stackpole Books, 1970.

Vonnegut, Kurt. *Cat's Cradle*. New York: Delacorte, 1963.

Waldman, Amy. "A Knock at the Door, with the Message of Death." *New York Times*, October 5, 2001.

Ward Jouve, Nicole. *Colette*. Bloomington: Indiana University Press, 1987.

Warner, Judith. *Perfect Madness: Motherhood in the Age of Anxiety*. New York: Riverhead, 2005.

Wing, Nathaniel. "Reading Simplicity: Flaubert's 'Un Cœur simple.'" *Nineteenth-Century French Studies* 21 (Fall–Winter 1992–93): 88–101.

Wolf, Christa. *Cassandra*, translated by Jan von Heurck. London: Virago, 1984.

Woolf, Virginia. *A Room of One's Own*. London: Harcourt Brace Jovanovich, 1929.

Yalom, Marilyn. *A History of the Breast*. New York: Knopf, 1997.

Zackheim, Michele. *Violette's Embrace*. New York: Riverhead, 1996.

INDEX